Infected Empires

Global Media and Race

Series Editor: Frederick Luis Aldama, The Ohio State University

Global Media and Race is a series focused on scholarly books that examine race and global media culture. Titles focus on constructions of race in media, including digital platforms, webisodes, multilingual media, mobile media, vlogs, and other social media, film, radio, and television. The series considers how race—and intersectional identities generally—is constructed in front of the camera and behind, attending to issues of representation and consumption as well as the making of racialized and antiracist media phenomena from script to production and policy.

Patricia Saldarriaga and Emy Manini, *Infected Empires: Decolonizing Zombies*
Bronwyn Carlson and Jeff Berglund, eds., *Indigenous Peoples Rise Up: The Global Ascendency of Social Media Activism*
Matthew David Goodwin, *The Latinx Files: Race, Migration, and Space Aliens*
Hyesu Park, ed., *Media Culture in Transnational Asia: Convergences and Divergences*
Melissa Castillo Planas, *A Mexican State of Mind: New York City and the New Borderlands of Culture*
Monica Hanna and Rebecca A. Sheehan, eds., *Border Cinema: Reimagining Identity through Aesthetics*

Infected Empires

Decolonizing Zombies

PATRICIA SALDARRIAGA AND EMY MANINI

Rutgers University Press

New Brunswick, Camden, and Newark, New Jersey, and London

Library of Congress Cataloging-in-Publication Data
Names: Saldarriaga, Patricia, author. | Manini, Emy, 1968– author.
Title: Infected empires : decolonizing zombies / Patricia Saldarriaga, Emy Manini.
Description: New Brunswick : Rutgers University Press, 2022. | Series: Global media and race | Includes bibliographical references and index.
Identifiers: LCCN 2021031066 | ISBN 9781978826786 (paperback) | ISBN 9781978826793 (cloth) | ISBN 9781978826809 (epub) | ISBN 9781978826816 (mobi) | ISBN 9781978826823 (pdf)
Subjects: LCSH: Zombies in motion pictures. | Zombies in popular culture. | Postcolonialism in motion pictures.
Classification: LCC PN1995.9.Z63 S35 2022 | DDC 791.43/675—dc23/eng/20211028
LC record available at https://lccn.loc.gov/2021031066

A British Cataloging-in-Publication record for this book is available from the British Library.

www.rutgersuniversitypress.org

Manufactured in the United States of America

For Clara, Paul, Rosa, and Miranda

Contents

Infected Empires

Introduction

In a hospital bed in an empty room, a coma patient slowly opens her eyes and then begins to take in her surroundings. First, she tries to remember the basics: where she is, when she is, her name. All through the year 2020, hospital patients recovering from COVID-19 were coming out of comas and learning how long they'd been out and what had happened in the interim. One of these people is Arizona state representative Lorenzo Sierra. In an interview on NPR, Sierra said that shortly after waking, he was asked if he could say his name. He thought, "Of course I can. And when it came time to actually verbalize it, I'm reaching for it. And it was absolutely horrifying because I couldn't remember my name in that moment."[1] Many COVID-19 patients continue to deal with serious aftereffects for months, and the full effects of the virus are still unknown. As Frank Cutitta, another survivor, told NPR, though he considers himself very lucky, "there are many, many people who would rather be dead than left with what they have after this."[2] Still, these survivors have escaped the death that has befallen more than 700,000 people in the United States at the time of this writing (and more than 5 million worldwide) and are preparing themselves to face the future post-COVID.

Now consider another scene: In a hospital bed in an empty room, a coma patient slowly opens his eyes and then begins to take in his surroundings. But in this case, no doctor comes to ask his name—no one comes at all. After a long while, he feels compelled to rise on his own and open the door to his room. What he finds is incomprehensible: the hospital is a disaster zone. Outside, the streets are empty. He walks along searching for signs of life, finding none. Finally, he sees a figure slowly coming toward him. But there's something wrong with the way it's moving. This patient has awoken to a dead world, in which he must learn to survive. Of course, this second scenario is an easily recognizable horror movie trope. The waking sleeper who finds himself in the middle of a zombie apocalypse appears in *The Walking Dead* series[3] and in the film *28 Days Later*[4]—two of the most popular and successful zombie productions of recent decades.[5] Why would we seek out entertainment that explores such dark territory when the real world is plenty dark? What does the pop culturally recognizable zombie narrative have to teach us about confronting life in the twenty-first century?

A study published in September 2020 found that horror movie fans and morbidly curious individuals were better equipped to deal with the COVID-19 pandemic than those that avoided such narratives and images. They concluded that "exposure to frightening fictions allow audiences to practice effective coping strategies that can be beneficial in real-world situations."[6] By imagining the worst-case scenario, not only do horror movie fans find the adrenaline thrill they seek but, as a side effect, they use their imaginations to speculate about what that experience would be like, what they might do to survive in those scenarios, and what effects such a catastrophe might have on society at large. Though zombies don't truly exist (*yet?*), the type of societal breakdown, chaos, and threat of bodily harm depicted in zombie films are analogous to potential consequences of real-world catastrophic events. Eva Horn explores narratives of catastrophe, and notes that often we look at the event that causes the sudden downturn in human fortunes from the perspective of the future. That is to say, just like our coma patient in the zombie scenario, "it is a gaze in the future perfect, a future that *will have been* . . . a gaze looking back on the future *as past*."[7] This allows the consumers of apocalyptic narratives to imagine the causes of the event and see how these imagined future-perfect events reveal something "*that already exists in the present*."[8] These moments of revelation expose the cause of our potential extinction. Our shell-shocked patient, who had been asleep to the reality of the world around him, wakes to find the veil has dropped, the scales have fallen from his eyes, and he is now awake to a toxic new reality.

The word "apocalypse" means "revelation" and is a reference to the biblical book from which it comes. John, the author of the Book of Revelation, claimed to have had a vision of the coming Judgment and Tribulation of the world, in which only the faithful would find glory. The book was meant to assure oppressed Christians that by enduring their difficult present, they would be rewarded for eternity while their Roman oppressors would suffer pain and pestilence as righteous punishment. Western culture has appropriated the term "apocalypse" to be any narrative about the end of the world. By now we are familiar with apocalyptic tropes: beyond the cataclysmic explosions, spreading disease, or massive technological dysfunction lies a wasteland—a dog-eat-dog future of terror and starvation where a sheltered few sometimes enjoy the last remaining resources, and the hordes (both zombie and human) fight over the scraps. The apocalyptic cultural productions that obsess over end times have increased every decade from the 1960s until today. The causes of the end are many—rampant disease, bioterrorism, nuclear annihilation, climate crisis, the rise of artificial intelligence, alien invasion—and each one can be interpreted to mirror a specific fear of modern existence. At the same time, apocalyptic rhetoric in politics has become mainstream in the last four decades. From Cold War fears of global annihilation, through the global warming crisis, religion-fueled terrorist attacks, and the threat of nuclear escalation, catastrophic imagery has become a mainstay of political speech. Often, these narratives are employed with biopolitical ends, in order to convince the citizenry to have faith in one prescribed narrative, in which the just will prevail and the evil will perish.[9] Horn observes a related phenomenon, noting a passivity in the face of catastrophic narratives. While we derive "a secret pleasure in watching the world go up in flames," she doesn't find that the revelation of the toxic structures that will be our downfall inspires any preventative action or political activism, or the move to hold ourselves responsible for the coming dystopia.[10] We hope that this might not be the case.

We propose that by using a decolonizing perspective we can examine zombie cinema to show how it questions accepted narratives of apocalypse. In this decolonizing project, how do we identify the "infected empires"? Following Michael Hardt and Antonio Negri, we acknowledge that although the European imperialist powers that spread their reach throughout the Americas, Africa, and Asia are no more, the concept of "Empire" survives in globalization. "The passage to Empire emerges from the twilight of modern sovereignty. In contrast to imperialism, Empire establishes no territorial center of power and does not rely on fixed boundaries or barriers. It is a *decentered* and *deterritorializing* apparatus of rule that progressively incorporates the entire global realm within its open, expanding frontiers. Empire manages hybrid identities, flexible hierarchies, and plural exchanges through modulation networks of command. The distinct national colors of the imperialist map of the world have merged and blended in the imperial global rainbow."[11] This description of a networked system of global power (including declining nation-states, supranational organizations, and multinational corporate entities) that "seeks to directly rule over human nature"[12] is in line with the concept of "coloniality."[13] Coloniality differs from colonialism because it "refers to long-standing patterns of power that emerged as a result of colonialism"[14] that continue to exist. Therefore, we take the "infected empires" to be the systems of power that perpetrate biopolitical control of populations through explicit or hidden narratives of nation, race, gender, disability, and human relation to the natural world. These systems are based in power relations rooted in the colonial past and Enlightenment humanist philosophies; they carry the disease of violent global exploitation (coloniality) and spread it through the powers referred to by Hardt and Negri as Empire. We begin with the concept of biopolitics following Foucault and proceed through Mbembe's necropolitics, because zombies are a perfect illustration of the way that bio- and necropolitics seek to regulate the terms of life and death. We concur with Ariadna Estévez's assertion that biopolitics and necropolitics are not mutually exclusive, but in fact are closely integrated concepts.[15]

Why "decolonizing zombies"? In the title of this book, we propose to use the verb both transitively and intransitively. We use it intransitively, as a descriptor, in that we see zombies as decolonizing imaginary entities, iconoclastic bringers of destruction upon the power relations that exist in our world. We use it transitively, in that we strive to offer a decolonizing reading of zombies. By analyzing how structures of oppression result in the liminal undead state, we show how these subjects can regain inclusion into the (post)humanist project. Zombies are usually perceived as soulless, mindless savages; terror-inducing cannibals. Cinema has made it easy for spectators to visualize intersecting characteristics of the racialized, objectified, and disabled zombie body. These characteristics coincide with the narratives that have been used to describe migrants, people of color, the disabled, the poor, and the marginalized in general. However, if zombies have been made to represent the undesirable Other, through their embodiment they are foregrounding issues of otherization. In this way, zombies are creating a discourse of resistance. They are slowly developing into creatures that evolve, think, and feel, and that can visualize a different future. In true apocalyptic fashion, the zombie's presence indicates the end of an old world and reveals possibilities for a transformed futurity. This zombie state, existing on the border of life and death, could also be framed using Gramsci's notion of the interregnum, in which moments of crisis show a transitional process that subjects may experience in which the expected change never arrives. The term "interregnum" traditionally refers to the space between the reign of one sovereign and the next and is a concept that helps us to understand the crisis that is developing within Empire as defined by Hardt and Negri. This space between an old order and a new one opens up possibilities for our decolonizing reading of zombie films, which we use to challenge critical texts and illustrate the theoretical work zombies can do.

Zombies are entrenched in the horror genre. They are bloodthirsty, monstrous, and grotesque. Yet they hold a fascination for us, between repulsion and attraction, exposing truths about humanity. They destroy all that we consider to be productive and good about ourselves as a species. They are perfect examples of body horror: they are what we are all slowly becoming, a figure of the inevitability and distasteful biological reality of death. Part of our fascination with them has to do with the nature of the horror film and the uniquely intimate effect it has on the spectator. The visceral response one has to watching horror is a by-product of the mirroring effect described by Noël Carroll.[16] Watching horror provokes bodily reactions in the viewer: we may cringe, hold our breath, scream, or tightly shut our eyes. To a certain degree, our actions run parallel to the characters we see on screen and are the result of physical sensations we may experience (perhaps nausea, increased heart rate, or a rush of adrenaline). The distorted, once-human figures of the zombies are also especially suggestive of the ways in which we are invited to feel their presence. The impossibility of their existence, dead and alive, their insides visible on the outside, is an example of what Carroll calls "fusion,"[17] and what Anna Powell refers to as the "transgression of those biological and cultural norms" that are representative of humans who become monsters.[18] She writes, "These entities refuse to remain the objects of our aesthetic contemplation and seek to incorporate us into the dynamic hybrid of their virtual assemblage. We also become with the monsters as mutant spectators."[19] The very liminal quality of the inexplicable walking corpse invites us in: we are repulsed but there is a terrible recognition in it. Ultimately, the extreme gore violence we see on the screen in a typical zombie film is a form of horrible intimacy. Marco Abel proposes the reading (or viewing) of violent texts as "masocriticism," which "requires a giving over of oneself to the Other, to becoming-other, to the process of being affected and effectuated by and from the future."[20] The visceral, thrilling reactions we feel toward the zombie—the revulsion and fascination—are based in what we see of ourselves in them or what we fear we will see in the near future. With these observations in mind, we explore the way zombies break us down in order to propose alternative narratives of the present and the post-catastrophe imaginary future.

Our book looks at the zombie as a transnational cinematic phenomenon, and we introduce a vision of a global zombie. As the zombie germinated in the Americas and spread to infect the entire world, each culture that contends with it puts its own spin on the monster. We begin with an in-depth study of the ontology of the zombie, especially trying to situate this creature at the intersection of being a person, a thing, and/or a body. In chapter 1, "What Is a Zombie?," we attempt to come to a definition of this ever-evolving ghoul, in particular from the perspective of the separation of the soul and body that is assumed in the undead. We study the ways in which the zombie rejects this duality, which involves a decolonization of the soul and raising Epicurus from the dead. In chapter 2, "Mutilate the State!," we trace the connections and implications between the zombie myth born in colonialism and the epistemic violence that enforces the continuation of coloniality of thought that has propped up the structure of the modern nation-state. By looking at the zombie in its current expressions of racial difference, immigration, and border culture, we expose the ways in which zombie narratives continue to challenge structures of power, in terms of agitation and resistance to the state violence that is the legacy of the colony. In chapter 3, "Devouring Capitalism," we consider the ways in which capital maintains coloniality over bodies and lives. Our reading decolonizes the value of humanity in labor, life, and even in death. We look at zombies as subjects of gore capitalism, dead bodies and commodities that resist their economic exploitation through necroactivism.

We look at other categories of identity, including queerness, disability, class, and gender considering the revolutionary ideas of crip futurity. Looking at history through a zombie lens of queer temporality, and rejecting chrononormativity, we can perceive a different way of understanding history and imagine an inclusive future. In chapter 4, "Bodies That Splatter," we look at the queering and cripping tendencies of zombies and their narratives. By offering a countervisuality in order to decolonize the gaze, and queer temporality to decolonize time, zombies resemanticize and decompose the identity categories of ableism, heteronormativity, and patriarchy. Next, in chapter 5, "Of Matter, Dust, and Earth," we expand on the notion of crip futurity by examining the zombie effect on the natural world, which decolonizes nature, freeing it from its identity as a use-value for humans and reconsidering our place within it.

In addition to our global approach and the broad geographical range of films we examine, we offer a more sustained focus on Latin America, and specifically its legacy of colonialism. The zombie would not exist outside of the bloodstained laboratory of colonialism and slavery that took place in the American continent and spread like an infection around the globe, including Africa and Asia. The range of theory that originates in the Global South informs our approach, especially in our criticism of classical theory, allowing us to make sense of the gore aspects in zombie cinema that reflect the violence of a neoliberalist system.

Zombie films illustrate the consequences of a host of oppressive societal systems including capitalism, globalization, and environmental, immigration, and health policies. Through the use of horror, these films emphasize the traces of affects in humanity and allow for visualization and understanding of historical trauma. The figure of the zombie functions, in a way, as a reflection of the ideologies we have imposed upon it. With this book, we provide a reading of zombie films that sheds light on how empires of the global order have been infected since their inception with the seeds of their own disease from colonialism through globalization. The stage is set for the figure of the zombie to work its decolonizing influence.

1

What Is a Zombie?

The zombie is a dangerous thing, a threat to human life. It is a creature that may be made useful as a scapegoat, as labor, or as an object to be abused and then destroyed and cast aside. As we will see throughout this book, the zombie hasn't always craved human flesh. When it first appeared in cinema, the zombie was a product of vodou magic that, with potions and rites, was brought back to life and forced to work as a slave. Bite by bite the zombie has changed, adapting itself to new cultural paradigms until, as we see it commonly now, it is infected with a virus that causes automatic resuscitation and ravenous hunger for uninfected flesh. Though the living can recognize the physical features of the person that the zombie once was, the classic zombie itself is incapable of recognizing anyone or anything and is exclusively guided by survival instincts. Thus, it satisfies its basic needs by indiscriminately devouring the living and existing within its horde of equals. The zombie is considered a disposable object, a thing, or often an empty signifier: the body of the zombie only represents but does not include the presence of the person it was before. And it is precisely this constitution of the zombie that cannot be defined as a *person* but only as a *body* and as a *thing* that forces us to question whether the zombie has undergone a radical excision between body and soul, as in the Cartesian model,[1] or whether, following the theories of Spinoza and Esposito regarding the relations between body/soul/thing,[2] the zombie is a creature that finds its definition precisely at this intersection.

The Soulless Epicurean Zombie

We begin with the separation of the body and the soul of a being that has become a zombie. William Seabrook's *The Magic Island*, published in 1929, introduced the figure of the zombie to the Western imaginary.[3] Seabrook's travel account described Haitian zombies in fearful terms. We can infer that his description is a response to his own fear of a Black population able to free itself from slavery and establish its own nation. This depiction, including images that produce horror and disgust, indeed a variety of affects, was used as a model for the first cinematic incarnation we know of: *White Zombie*, released only three years later.[4] According to Seabrook, "the zombie, they say, is a soulless human corpse, still dead, but taken from the grave and endowed by sorcery with a mechanical semblance of life—it is a dead body which is made to walk and act and move as if it were alive."[5] Even today, in the twenty-first century, this feature has not changed much. It is indeed common to hear that a zombie is a soulless body, resuscitated matter. And though frequently the soul is used simply as a metaphor for the brain, heart, or cognitive capacity, it is important to dig deeper into what is meant by "the soul" because this idea is, in fact, connected to coloniality.[6] For though the zombie is rooted in West African beliefs and the syncretic vodou religion in Haiti, it has been appropriated by writers and travelers like Seabrook and by Hollywood, and appears in popular culture around the world.

When the Europeans encountered indigenous Americans, they believed that they weren't people because they didn't have souls. The soul, according to Catholic teachings of the colonial era, was associated with belief in a Christian God. In the Valladolid debate, also known as the Las Casas–Sepúlveda controversy, which took place from 1550 to 1551, the matter of how to treat the indigenous peoples inhabiting the Americas was discussed. At issue was the question of whether indigenous people were actually rational beings, which was under debate due to suspicion that the native peoples of the colonies engaged in cannibalism, violent murder, and other crimes. The debaters determined that though inferior, the native people deserved to be taught and evangelized by the Spaniards, something that justified subsequent wars in the name of Christianity. This distinction and separation between the "civilized" man who had been blessed with a soul and the "savage" indigenous being who lacked one is explicitly linked to the definition of the native cultures of the New World. For Bonar L. Hernandez, it was precisely this Valladolid debate that created the polarized framework that separated the civilized Europeans from the barbaric Americans.[7] In this way, the forced labor that indigenous people were subjected to was justified, since they were limited in their ability to make their own decisions. This perception of soulless indigenous people was due, of course, to their lack of Catholic religiosity, and it normalized the theft of their free will under the imperialist system. This system also explains the treatment of the enslaved brought from Africa and Asia in later centuries. Seeing a zombie as a creature without a soul is therefore intimately linked to the colonialist perception of the non-Catholic as a nonperson and therefore an object to be colonized and evangelized. Seabrook's "soulless zombie" is the result of a colonial mentality shared with the conquerors of the Americas that conceived the Other as a dangerous savage.

In the seventeenth century, the theories of Renée Descartes confirmed this position that radically separates the body from the soul.[8] The French philosopher even used the concept of God as geometrically perfect in order to give invisible qualities to the soul. According to his arguments, the soul is an indivisible substance that is dependent only upon God and can exist in isolation, even when separated from the body. Although the body is divisible into different sections, organs and functions, the soul, like God, is a concept that cannot be broken down into parts.[9] Descartes's theories did not pass unquestioned, above all in reference to the possibility of independent movement of the body, absent the soul/mind. For writers such as Pierre Gassendi (1592–1655), an atomist who opposed Descartes in the seventeenth century, it is difficult to prove the independence of the soul and the body, provided that the body is dependent on cognitive ability (soul or rational mind) to move as desired.[10]

Regardless of how you approach it, in the cultural history of the soul, the issue of its independence has always been under debate. Though many of the great thinkers of antiquity, such as Plato (428–327 B.C.) or Aristotle (384–322 B.C.), had an abstract idea of the conception of the soul, later philosophers, especially Lucretius (99–55 B.C.) and Epicurus (341–270 B.C.) argued whether the soul might actually form part of bodily matter. For the Epicureans, who were rediscovered in the seventeenth century, the soul is simply the effect of the material of the body and, like the rest of the atoms that compose the human body, is part of the materialist vision of the universe. Therefore, death ends everything: no soul can exist apart from the body. And it is for this reason that Epicureanism proclaimed the necessity of eliminating fear from the mind (or the soul), even fear of natural catastrophic phenomena or the end of the world.[11] In fact, Epicureans promoted the enjoyment of life while it lasted, because in the moment that the body ceased to exist, human existence would end as well.

For Baruch Spinoza, human essence was inconceivable without the body, since the soul was a product of the body's ideas. Spinoza's concept of the soul constitutes a type of dialectic with respect to the body (the soul exists to the extent to which it is the idea of the body, and the body exists to the extent to which it is the idea of the soul). The body contains the idea of the soul and constitutes the representation of that soul.[12] There is a lot of debate as to whether Spinoza believed in the immortality of the soul. As stated by Steven Nadler, there is only one mention of it in his *Ethics*. However, the philosopher talks about the eternity of the mind. While eternity itself is not linked to any concept of time, the mind is eternal because it is part of God's nature.[13]

Roberto Esposito, on the other hand, refers us to the Roman judicial system in order to rethink what defines a person, a body, and a thing, and the relationships between them. According to Roman law, a person is defined as the possessor of things (of slaves, for example); the person distinguishes himself from the thing though he possesses it, even if it is a part of him and is located inside his person. The thing, on the other hand, has the right to be possessed and is considered a property, though with exceptions. Things that belonged to nobody were available to anyone who would make them their own. Anything that was extracted from nature or from other men became a property thanks to the *manu captum* law, according to which these things belonged unquestionably to their new owner. This way, captured slaves and individuals who were not owners of themselves (*alienis iuris*) were reduced to things possessed by those considered persons precisely due to these laws.

Esposito states that the body has been excluded from the completely human essence because it is usually understood as being controlled by instincts and passions.[14] The reduction of people to things was certainly motivated by the reduction of their bodies to property and the elimination of free will, as we have seen with slaves and indigenous populations. For this philosopher, the body has never had a well-defined legal role, being taken into consideration only at birth or death. There is no consensus when we talk about parts of the body either. What are they? Are they persons or things? Although it seems that human beings cannot and should not be reduced to their bodies, it looks like parts of their bodies can be isolated from the rest of the body (e.g., blood, organs, sperm, etc.).[15]

What happens, then, with body parts that zombies have bitten and taken from other bodies and have consumed? According to Roman law, these parts belong to them; they possess them, which would give them the status of people. Under this law, zombies are people. But the fact that the consumed body parts are now inside of the zombie body makes zombies a representation of a multitude. Although these new zombie bodies are composed of the consumption of many bodies within one, these new parts, while being added to the zombie through ingestion, actually maintain their own difference because they are not being digested and therefore are not integrated into the undead consumer.

Since antiquity and the Middle Ages, similar representation of composite subjects has been used to represent the order of the state employing symbols of coordinated entities, but those were conceived with different hierarchies in mind.[16] In a parable by Titus Livius, for example, the state was represented by different body parts, different entities that symbolized all citizens.[17] When the body parts got tired of working and went on strike, these members complained that the stomach was the only beneficiary of their work. They rejected their exploitation. Soon enough, these parts realized that none of them could survive without feeding the stomach. This bodily hierarchy changed over time: it was sometimes based on the head (Christianity); the stomach (Livius 64 B.C.–12 A.D.); and, as explained by Esposito, the soul (Hobbes 1588–1679), or even equally distributed (Rousseau 1712–1778). If we compare the structure of these body representations with the multitude inside the zombie, then a single zombie as well as the whole zombie population is being created from bodies within bodies. They all create a metaphor of the multitude as if the state were created from a horde of zombies. The difference here is that in a potential zombie state, there is no hierarchy of its parts.

The belief in the separation of body and soul persists in contemporary culture and religion. Some reject the immaterial or transcendental nature of the soul. For these thinkers (as with Epicurus's materialist model), the soul is an effect of mere matter and comes to an end at the moment of death. However, for others, the body is inhabited by some ineffable element that cannot be defined or pinned down. This soul, or rational mind, escapes the body at the moment of death and the body becomes nothing more than a cadaver, empty matter that is destined for decomposition. Some Baroque paintings represent the souls of the dead as abstract forms or even materialized as figures of infants—for example, *The Burial of the Count of Orgaz* (1586–1588) by El Greco in which the soul rises to heaven to indicate that the deceased has been selected by God. As we have seen, the idea that the zombie is a body lacking a soul is based on a long philosophical tradition that separates and abstracts the soul from the body. This same tradition marginalizes the zombie, as it did with indigenous peoples, due to a lack of religiosity, free will, and gender, or, as we will see later on, due to its incomplete body.

When the zombie resuscitates, it is no longer the same person. Firstly, it has lost its cognitive capacity, its memory, and its analytic function—all that we understand as "soul." As we read in Ecclesiastes (450–200 B.C.): "The living know that they will die, but the dead know nothing; they have no more reward, and even the memory of them is lost. Their love and their hate and their envy have already perished; never again will they have any share in all that happens under the sun" (9:5–6).[18] This loss of memory or consciousness aligns with this biblical text, though affirming that the zombie's mind/spirit is completely lost can be problematic when analyzing seminal zombie films such as *Dawn of the Dead* by director George Romero in which zombies retain traces of their memories, as illustrated by the way they return to their usual consumerist customs and begin to congregate at the mall.[19] In *Land of the Dead*, there are a number of zombies playing instruments such as the saxophone and the tambourine; others know or quickly learn how to use guns.[20] In the same movie, a gardener remembers how to keep moving his lawnmower down the street, though he is no longer mowing grass. In *Versus*, zombies retain their ability to shoot guns and are still looking forward to killing their murderers.[21] In *I Am a Hero*, a Japanese film based on a popular manga series by artist Kengo Hanazawa, one zombie retains the physical abilities that distinguished him as an athlete, and he is able to perform amazing physical feats.[22] One of the other infected protagonists of this film can access memory and speech and is able to control his urge for cannibalism. Another waits for the train, as though he were reliving his morning commute. In this film, it is interesting to see that those zombies who seem to possess "memory" are considered to be the happiest, because they retain a link to the past. They seem to be more complete individuals whose bodies and souls show a kind of Epicurean pleasure. Following Lucretius's *De rerum natura* (*On the Nature of Things*), as well as Aristippus of Cyrene's writings (c. 435–c. 356 B.C.), Epicurus defined ultimate happiness as achieving the coincidental states of *ataraxia* (lack of fear and anxieties) and *aponia* (absence of bodily pain). Most of the zombies, one can say, have reached both states: they don't seem to have pain in the body (although they are physically damaged and may be missing parts of their bodies), and they have a stress-free soul. Compared to humans who are not infected, who are guided by fear and desperation and are always on the move, zombies don't appear to suffer.[23] Some romantic zombie comedies such as *Warm Bodies* even reverse the zombification of a person through the commodification of pleasurable affects activated by memories.[24] Zombies return to their normal state of humanity and are able to "cure" their disabled bodies thanks to images of love they consume.

The Zombie Collective

In its shambling, voracious presence, the zombie is a body that feeds itself on many other bodies—it feeds off multitudes. This idea of the power of the multitudes can be aligned with the Spinozian view clarified by Esposito, who explains the difference between Hobbes and Spinoza: Spinoza believes that "the human body requires, in order to conserve itself, many other bodies."[25] For Hobbes (per Esposito) the political survival of man is dependent on the separation of the self from the other.[26] When a zombie bites a human, it is accumulating other bodies inside its body. Like the bodies it leaves in its wake, the zombie is a mutilated body, a subject that depends upon the absorption of other corpses into itself, in repeated acts of cannibalism. As Mel Y. Chen states, by biting and feeding upon the bodies of society, zombies perpetuate their state of eternity and are assured of their own immortality as they confer the state of eternity upon those they devour.[27] As the zombie collects bodies inside of itself, it becomes a representation of the multitude. Each zombie, in effect, is a multitude.

But what sort of multitude does the zombie become? Following Hardt and Negri's *Empire* (and later Hardt's *Multitude*), we can consider the zombie to be a political subject.[28] They define the multitude as a product of globalization and a reaction to the network of control, conflict, and war imposed by the levers of power. The multitude is like a counter-network, one of cooperation and collaboration "in which all differences can be expressed freely and equally, a network that provides the means of encounter so that we can work and live in common," and which makes democracy a possibility.[29] Further, the zombie does not exist alone. Not only does the zombie traditionally become some part of a horde but through its cannibalism it amasses many bodies in one, a multiple subject that depends on others to survive. Hardt and Negri describe a state of siege of the global order that can also depict the zombie scenario, a state of exception in which any type of violence can occur. The liberation of capitalism as a devastating leveling force in a globalized world puts the zombie subject in a situation where its only concern is the struggle for survival, and that mere subsistence is in itself a method of resisting capitalism. To understand the type of capitalist environment we are talking about, we should look to Sayak Valencia's term "gore capitalism." We live in a world where biopolitics have given way to necropolitics, and capitalism has taken an even more violent turn. Gore capitalism controls the conditions of life in such a way that bloody violence controls the economy.[30]

Whether we consider the zombie to be fully conscious or barely connected to instinct, the fact remains that it does, at minimum, select food sources that are living and not infected. What does this selectiveness mean? We might suppose that a healthy living body not only satisfies zombie hunger but perhaps allows it not to decompose so rapidly. As far as we can tell, the zombie doesn't defecate—the zombie is dead and bodily functions are suspended—but somehow the uninfected body is absorbed, transformed, and retained within the zombie. This cannibalistic act allows the corpse to use this source of energy. This is a natural option for the perpetuation of the zombie body, and as asserted by Chen, eating allows for the reproduction of the zombie condition, its disability. The lack of defecation, however, highlights the racialization and otherness of zombies; they are not only impaired in function but are full of filth: shit, piss, menstrual fluid, and so on.[31] According to Kristeva, they are subjects who have not abjected; that is to say, they have not eliminated any bodily residues.[32] For the spectators, zombies have become the abject, not only because they are repulsive to the viewers but also due to the fact that they upend the system, its order, and our identities. Zombies are cadavers that are neither dead nor alive; they represent the object from which we would need to separate in order to become subjects. Spectators feel attracted and fascinated by those cadavers because somehow they remind us of our own mortality.

Considering Bakhtin's notion of the grotesque body, it becomes clear that zombies modify the grotesque.[33] For Bakhtin, the grotesque body emphasizes its openings in such a way that allows a certain kind of communication between the interior of the body and the exterior. All bodily orifices such as the mouth, the nose, the anus, the eyes, the ears, and so on produce fluids that are expelled. Zombies, however, ingest and retain. It is only a one-way communication, for they do not share with the exterior. We do not see urine, semen, shit, or menstrual blood. Everything, if produced, remains inside of the bodies. And yet, sometimes we can see their open viscera; their monstrosity is shown to us by opening the body and not closing it. What was supposed to be a communication between the exterior world and the body becomes an interaction between the former and the organs themselves, oozing and unnaturally exposed, in a sort of hyper-grotesque.

Halley, however, provides us with an alternative to the hyper-grotesque.[34] The conscious zombie Alberto refuses to eat meat, and when he is urged on by a friend to do so, he later is obliged to manually remove the meat from his esophagus so that it doesn't rot inside of him. Not eating meat is not the solution to his zombie condition, however: we see him continue to rapidly decompose by means of maggots that can be seen under the skin. At the end of the film, he seeks to exile himself to a cold climate to slow his decomposition. There he intends to avoid resurrection; he wants to be free of his eternal condition.

For Esposito, the body is the only thing that allows for the metaphysical conflict between the person and the thing to be resolved, since the body is the only space in which we can visualize the union of our individual and collective experiences.[35] This is precisely what happens within the zombie body. There is a literal interaction between the individual and the collective, starting with the body, but the zombie is not *just body* or *just thing*; it retains some tenuous link to its mind/soul. As a thing, it is considered disposable, but it is not only a thing since it contains a brain, nor is it only a person, nor is it only a body, though it is a mutilated, destroyed, displaced, and disabled body. The fact that people have conceived of zombies as soulless beings does not mean that they are.

The Allegorical, Political Zombie

It is also important to underscore the eschatological aspect of the zombie genre. Its focus on the final destination of man beyond the moment of death brings us closer to an allegorical understanding of history in the Benjaminian sense. If we think of his concept of allegory described in his tract on sixteenth- and seventeenth-century *Trauerspiel* (Passion Play), he aids us in understanding the parallel between the concept of history and the end times.[36] But it is precisely his allegorical method of interpreting history as the history of salvation that obliges us to see the instability of salvation in the model of zombie narratives. If these creatures resuscitate immediately after being infected, without awaiting any judgment, the certainty of some final redemption is lost to humanity.[37] No final reward is possible if the dead arise before that final day. We can recall

Dr. Logan from *Day of the Dead* attempting to train the zombie Bub by tricking him into obedience as we were tricked with the promise of an ultimate reward.[38] The zombie, therefore, is itself proof of the deception. It can be seen as a neo-Baroque or even postmodern allegory since it represents the uncertainty of history and the impossibility of salvation.

As Benjamin asserts, the most important symbols of the Baroque are ruins and skulls, the latter generally contemplated by some melancholic subject within a landscape of decay and decomposition of nature.[39] In both symbolic images, we can visualize death. Remember that the "final" death of the zombie is only achieved through destruction of his brain and skull. There is no preservation of the zombie's skull, and as a consequence, its Baroque traces are destroyed. No one can save humanity; there is no savior or deus ex machina that will guarantee entrance into paradise. The zombie genre achieves the secularization of the end times. This rupture in salvation logic destroys the guaranteed economy of salvation. Upon resurrecting before the Final Judgment, this promised salvation enters into a condition of doubt and death, which only serves to emphasize the transitory nature of life. Likewise, in many films of the genre, the scene is set within an environment of decay, both of nature and of the icons of history. As in Benjamin, the ruins of the apocalyptic world present us with a secular version of history in which humanity finds itself in tension with death. The Benjaminian perspective forces us to consider the viewer of the zombie film as the melancholic Baroque subject, as one who contemplates the eschatological films of this genre and reflects upon the transitory nature of life and the end of time. In this way we can visualize a parallel between the Passion Play and the zombie film: if for Benjamin, the Passion of Christ presents a world that is equivalent to a funeral shroud, zombie films also are based in a world that is littered with figurative shrouds, creating a stunning image of destruction. In *Juan of the Dead* (*Juan de los muertos*), the zombie attack precipitates the physical destruction and collapse of state buildings, leaving a landscape that looks like it has been the target of a terrorist attack.[40] The pain of *Trauerspiel*, for Benjamin, is caused more by a lament over the transition to a capitalist modernity. The Baroque allegory comes at the beginning of this transition to capitalism, which is a fundamental element of the zombie genre as well, in which capitalism is the basis for exploitation and the end of the world.

The Argentine film *What's Left of Us* (*El desierto*) is another example of the type of allegory proposed by Benjamin.[41] The character of Axel begins to tattoo himself with tiny images of flies, and over time, they begin to cover most of his body. Real flies are also present throughout the film and can often be spied crawling and flying all around these characters. The aural effect of the drone of the flies helps to create an environment in which death and decomposition are always present. The buzzing of the flies even plays through the credits, getting even louder in the silence, in a metaphysical nod to the spectators; the flies

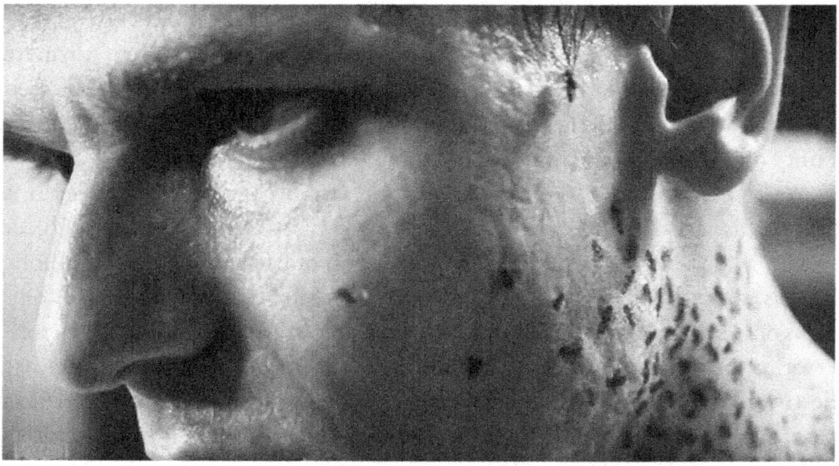

Axel in *What's Left of Us* covers himself in fly tattoos. (Credit: Cristoph Behl, *What's Left of Us* (*El desierto*), 2015.)

follow them out of the experience of the film. Axel's tattooed body also evokes the feel of *vanitas* paintings, a genre of painting that begins in the Middle Ages but finds recurring popularity in the Baroque period. Take, for example, the work by Valdés Leal entitled *Finis gloriae mundi* (1670–1672). In this painting we see the scales of justice that weigh the vices and virtues of the dead. The corpse, however, is covered by maggots and other necrophagous species that crawl in and out of the body. In this way, the image presents the corruptibility of physical matter and evokes the transitory nature of life. Though this particular work does specifically reference Judgment Day through its use of the scales of justice, the rotten cadaver is foregrounded. Axel's body serves a similar function in *What's Left of Us*. Both bodies are covered with flies, and thereupon, the atoms of their physical matter undergo a transformation. The process of tattooing the multitude of flies on his body, one by one, has the effect of preparing us for Axel's final exit. When he is completely covered, we understand that he will die and become a zombie. In stark contrast with the Baroque allegory, here Axel is the author of his own death. He decides when he will die, as does Ana (the focal point of the twisted romantic triangle) when she allows herself to be bitten by their captive zombie and, in effect, become a thing bound up in chains.

For Benjamin, monuments constitute the ruins of a city, precisely because they are representatives of the past in the context of the present. Also, "Allegories are to the realm of thoughts what ruins are to the realm of things," he says.[42] If allegory allows us to see zombies as subjects who secularize history, they can also be perceived as ruins. The zombie is not only a cadaver or an empty signifier without a soul; it is actually a ruin full of its own past, and it is up to the spectator to recognize this as an example of what Benjamin calls a *dialectical image*. Such an image, states the German philosopher, is equivalent to a moment of mutual recognition between the past and the present. In this understanding of history, spectators of zombie movies are allowed to reconstruct the past. Zombies, therefore, could be viewed like the monuments of a city, its ruins that are in constant dialectic with our own memories.

The Necrotic Zombie

For Heinz Bude, the "black box of the self" that is studied by cognitive psychology allows us to trace the way that individual structures mold themselves to social structures. The concept of fear can give us a vision of how society is changing. Bude asserts that sociology cannot discount the principle of fear, which exists in every corner and level of society. Moreover, citing famed sociologist Niklas Luhmann and his system of functional equivalents, Bude argues that fear is the only principle that is given absolute validity over the relativization of every other factor.[43] To further complicate the matter, fears are multiple and multitemporal. It is important to focus on fear, since it can illuminate the ways in which the apocalyptic sentiment transmitted by zombie narratives make spectators into subjects that experience multitemporality: through the horror aspect of this genre viewers feel fear about the present, about what has happened in the past, and about the uncertain future and apocalyptic end times. And it is especially true in this neoliberal era, when most states do nothing to alleviate citizens' fears with respect to labor security, health and disability, the environment, and other minimum requirements for human life. As Bude observes, these conditions are achieving exactly the opposite of what was proposed by Franklin D. Roosevelt. In other words, far from being calmed by the state, the citizenry is inundated with apocalyptic films that are popular precisely because they reflect the fears we already are experiencing in society.[44] Paul Virilio, on the other hand, argues that fear, and in this particular case terror, can spread globally with the speed of technology and be felt all over the world thanks to synchronization of emotions on a global scale.[45] The spread of news (e.g., COVID-19) creates a "community of emotions." In this way, localized fear becomes globalized affect. Throughout z-narratives, noninfected people are always afraid of becoming zombies: "Don't let this happen to me" is the typical reaction expressed in response to what Priscilla Wald calls "outbreak narratives" that simultaneously spread fear and fascination among members of a society. In her book *Contagious: Cultures, Carriers, and the Outbreak Narrative*, Wald demonstrates the way these narratives not only create a community that gathers around fear of contagion but also have a local and global impact regarding survival rates and routes of contagions. By the same token, they "promote or mitigate the stigmatizing of individuals."[46] The noninfected are afraid of contagion not only of the original virus that produced the appearance of zombies but also of their bites and their hyper-grotesque condition as eternally wandering corpses.

The animated film *Seoul Station* (*Seoulyeok*) (2016) by the Korean director Yeon Sang-ho presents this fear as a result of a capitalist utopia.[47] In a gory and explicit style the film exposes societal threats at every level: the lack of humanity attributed to homeless people, the lack of resources to provide for the most basic needs of the most vulnerable of society, guns in the hands of the state, communicable disease, exploitation of the female body, and so on. This film is effective in its use of animation because it creates a certain distance from the characters that allows us to make a parenthesis in the aesthetic pleasure of horror. The spectator's "safe space" allows us to better visualize the horrors Bude writes of: fears that the state has not been able to eliminate among the citizenry. When the young protagonist escapes the brothel where she had been exploited and moves in with her boyfriend, he attempts to set her up as a sex worker—she still needs to sell herself in order to survive, and her boyfriend intends to profit off of her. During the zombie attack, she is in arguably more danger from the hierarchy of sexual exploiters threatening her. In this film, the zombie plague starts among the homeless and most vulnerable, and the horror they (and the audience of the film) experience is paralyzing. Here we can visualize the power of the genre as a narrative of protest and resistance. Being a zombie is the only method for the most marginalized—the homeless, sex workers, the elderly, and the sick—to find a kind of hope for defeating the capitalist Empire as described by Hardt and Negri. Here the zombies become subjects of resistance.

In order to define what a zombie is, Amparo Cano and Miguel Ferreira refer to a group of three apocalyptic works that are not expressly zombie-genre, *The Matrix*, *Avatar*, and George Orwell's novel *1984* (1949), in which they identify the creation of a transhumanism with capitalist ends.[48] While the *Matrix* series depicts the conversion of life into virtual energy for the machines, *Avatar* creates a perfect transhumanism that attempts to penetrate the secrets of a more "primitive" society with the intent of extracting minerals from its forests. On the other hand, Orwell's novel depicts a social hierarchy that creates a class of persons similar to the living dead in order to perpetuate the power of the elites. As Winston says to Julia in *1984*, "We are the dead."[49] Here it is extractive capitalism that creates these zombie-like transhumans.

In this sense, zombies are used to represent the capitalist efforts of the elites and the destruction of society through neoliberal ambition. The Ecuadorian philosopher Bolívar Echeverría, following Weber,[50] has identified the Calvinist ethic that exemplifies the impulse toward productive rationality that promotes labor-based success.[51] But it is the belief in that success being the basis for, in effect the equivalent of, happiness that is a hallmark of neoliberalism. The zombie narrative negates happiness as an objective within a capitalist system. The zombie doesn't consume, does not participate in the market as a buyer, and in fact denies the fetishization of merchandise. It is an anti-capitalist and anti-happiness narrative. As a multitude, zombies participate as political subjects that reject capitalism.

A traditional zombie's disability is also physical: it has lost its ability to speak, think, remember, and, usually, even walk and move as humans do. Zombies are a perfect metaphor for the imaginary Other when these are considered inferior: they are disadvantaged bodies, marginalized, deformed, wounded, and torn, and they have lost many of their functions. Depending on the particular narrative, this disability is the result of an environmental disaster or a virus spread within a neoliberal economy. The zombie embodies the pathologization of the body and the soul and is a vehicle for the explicit expression of society's fears. In most zombie narratives, their movement shows the effects of any injuries they have suffered, they don't sleep, and at times they must simply drag themselves. They generally don't manipulate door handles or locks, only gaining entry to places they can break into with brute force. In general terms, the zombie embodies a *necroprotest*, in which we are forced to consider the treatment of disabled bodies, racialized and rationalized as a product of gore capitalism and neoliberalism.

Cano and Ferreira insist that in order to understand disability we must note the changes to what has qualified for the title of "disability" throughout history. If in Greco-Roman society disability functioned under the model of disposability (of the disabled subject), in the Middle Ages it was believed that disability was a form of divine punishment. In modernity we began to speak of illness, of individual deficiencies and deviations that were viewed through the lens of disciplinary power (Foucault). In postmodernity, disability is seen, following contemporary sociological theories, from the viewpoint of the context in which the subject exists, and the environment of the disabled is seen as faulty, as ableist, since it does not adapt to the disabled subject. These authors propose that in order to resolve the problem we must focus on modifying social structures.[52] Zombie narratives help us to visualize these societal conflicts. Spanish director Juan José Patón's *Zombie World* (2013) creates a different setting for the relationship between zombies and humans.[53] In this film, the world is ruled and inhabited by zombies: they reproduce like humans, adjust to a capitalist and heteronormative chrononormativity, buy, consume, read, work with technology, and so on. Nothing seems to have changed to accommodate their zombiness. The only difference is that they are slower due to the fact that their bodies are disabled (according to our "normal" perspective). In this society, an outbreak starts and suddenly zombies are converting into wild and cannibal humans. The future that Patón's movie proposes is reverting to humanity but without significant changes to what we consider normal human behavior. In that sense, the movie falls short at envisioning a posthuman world.

If disability is considered from the perspective of a futurism where it may become "cured," then the disabled body will always remain disabled; it must achieve this "cure" to be considered "normal." But if we consider the disabled body through a *crip* lens, as proposed by Alison Kafer, we can imagine a different future, one that includes the disabled in a new conception of temporality.[54] As of now, zombies propose a new futurism that is not based on sexual reproduction. As previously mentioned, and as Mel Y. Chen also proposes, zombies reproduce their eternal condition through their bite, through eating.[55] Crip temporality approaches time from a queer perspective, but it also takes into account disabled bodies and subjects.[56] Using this perspective, zombies can also have a different future that is not necessarily based on traditional human reproduction. Disability, as proposed by crip theory, needs to be seen not as a fault of the body but rather as a structural fault of society. Only then can we consider zombies not "crippled" subjects, but crip subjects. In addition, they are allegorical representations of intersectionality. To view the zombie from a crip perspective is to consider the connections between race, disability, gender, and class and all categories of otherization that contribute to notions of a subject's (in)ability to participate fully in society.[57]

The Hungry Sovereign Zombie

The cannibalism of the zombie further marginalizes zombies. Zombie cannibalism that first appeared in Romero's *Night of the Living Dead* is another manifestation of the zombie as soulless savage that harkens back to the subjugated peoples of the colonial imaginary—those who were denied their liberty under that system along with free Haitians who were perceived as threatening to the continuation of imperial supremacy.[58] In Romero's film, the Black hero/protagonist, Ben, is assassinated by members of a state war machine because they mistake him for a flesh-eating zombie. In the American context, it is natural for the audience to assume that the color of his skin played a part in the decision to shoot him, especially since throughout, before coming to that tragic and pointless end, the film has illustrated the racial tensions of the late 1960s. As a crip body, the marginalized person of color is killed for his resemblance to the savage and the contaminated. But, in fact, we have already watched a full-length film in which Ben leads the group of White survivors with whom he is trapped, doing his best to protect them. Therefore, this ending exposes a double tension: the color of his skin disables him in the eyes of hegemonic power, and this disability is the cause of his murder. Additionally, it bears mention that the group of men that kill Ben and haul his body to the pyre of zombies to be destroyed is made up of White vigilantes working in concert with the state-sanctioned police force, a phenomenon we continue to see today in the participation of some police officers in nationalist militias and paramilitary groups in the United States.

As Carlos A. Jáuregui asserts, during the conquest of the Americas the concept of cannibalism developed a type of semantic affinity with the American continent and has been a constant descriptor for colonial alterity; in fact, it has been resemanticized in various ways, from the Conquest to the present.[59] The trope is deployed at various times between the African continent and the Caribbean such that Pliny's cynocephalic (dog-headed) African monsters become the savage cannibals indigenous to the American continent in the sixteenth and seventeenth centuries. Later on, they reappear as justification for enslaved labor visited upon both populations, only later to be revived as images of rebellious uprising slaves during the Haitian Revolution of the eighteenth century.[60] In fact, the fear of cannibals was used to justify the conquest of the Americas. The Spanish words *Caribe* (Caribbean) and *caníbal* (cannibal, from the Latin *canis* for "dog") were nearly interchangeable. Columbus had already heard of dog-headed monsters that devoured the flesh of other tribes. As Jáuregui points out, the European imaginary of the Other had already configured those monsters.[61] For example, we may look back to the creatures in the Book of Revelation that John uses to symbolize the decadent Roman Empire. The teratologic characteristics of these monsters were used to show the deformation of the oppressive imperial regime. This same descriptive tactic was turned from the oppressors to the oppressed, inverted to describe the indigenous peoples of the Americas as soulless and demonic monsters in order to facilitate their exploitation and the theft of their lands. People were reified as tools to extract the precious metals of their own land. In his *Discourse on Colonialism* (1950), Aimé Césaire, the politician poet of Martinique who contributed to the founding of the *négritude* movement of Francophone literature, asserts that the objective of colonization was never benevolent, nor was it ever meant to improve the lives of the colonized.[62] For Césaire, the colonial encounter deliberately destroys the past to reinvent and "civilize" the colonized. The objectification of colonized individuals dehumanizes them and treats people as soulless animals in order to turn them into merchandise. Using their own imported law as pretext for laying claim to superiority, colonizers destroyed existing civilizations and formed societies based on racial and cultural hierarchies. This is what happened to both indigenous Americans and the allegorical zombies. Thanks to their purported cannibalism and their American origins, they participate in the resemantization of the soulless, savage cannibal, victim of the capitalist interests of the European.

Another important aspect of the z-genre is the identification of narrative space: this includes both dystopian narratives and dystopian spaces because everything is either destroyed or on its way to destruction. What do we understand by "dystopian" and what is the role of zombies within these spaces? Let us start with the apocalyptic frame because this is crucial for understanding the main referent of a dystopia. As we already know, the biblical revelation of the apocalypse can be read as a reaction to Roman imperialism. It was originally written to relieve the suffering of oppressed people by promising that the just would one day triumph. In this way we can see that dystopia was created as a form of resistance that would permit marginalized groups to embrace a hope of surviving imperialism: that after dystopian suffering, the Second Coming of Christ would bring an endless utopia. The dystopia/utopia dialectic is necessary for understanding zombies. The zombie apocalypse immerses us in dystopian worlds headed for total destruction. For many theorists, the emphasis on the apocalypse is a cultural manifestation that serves as a reference to the religious end times described in Revelation and, paradoxically, is a state that makes survival of dystopian chaos possible. In the case of Mexican literature, for example, Sánchez Prado proposes that the apocalyptic novels of the "Crack" generation mark the collapse of the concepts of nation and modernity that defined the culture and politics of postrevolutionary Mexico.[63] For him, these narratives constitute an imaginary of disaster that becomes a strategy of resistance to a neoliberal economic attack.

We define this strategy of resistance through the "presentified" figure of the zombie. Its corporeal form, which humanity has created, is a type of reflection of ourselves, of our own discourse and ideology. This idea is clearly represented in *Pontypool*, the Canadian film in which the zombie virus is communicated and spread through language.[64] The film problematizes all forms of communication, from DJ Grant Mazzy's radio broadcast to official state announcements, and even personal and individual communication. Speaking imperial English and using any words to communicate ideas or feelings is problematic because the speaking and understanding of words is precisely how the zombie contagion is spread, creating violent cannibals out of regular citizens. In *Pontypool*, our ideology and discourse is *monstrified* through the figure of the zombie. In this film, when a person hears verbal communication and internalizes it without consciously considering its untruth, the virus is transmitted. In fact, speaking a foreign language, such as Armenian or French, can protect one from this transmission because then the dominant code is no longer being used and understood by the majority. There is a double critical reflection being used by English speakers in the act of using a second-language code. When subjects are infected, they are instantly limited to repeating a single word or phrase. They are reduced to their own echo; their existence is a performative act that displays the relationship between language and identity. *Pontypool* allows us to see zombies as the "presentification" of how our own infected discourse and ideologies don't permit trustworthy communication. As Kirsch and Stancliff have observed, there are monsters "that underwrite the survival and dominion of the state, but also—and this is what sets *Pontypool* apart in its language-focused sub-genre—of potentially any spoken word in which understanding becomes a felt thing, near enough to touch or bite."[65] The scene in which the character of Sydney Briar communicates with Mazzy by writing "We are here" on a notepad coincides with the arrival of the zombie horde to the station, and the zombies begin to pound on the windows. This scene allows us to see the connection between ourselves and our own monstrified reflection. With *Pontypool*, we can conclude that the zombie is a cultural production that we ourselves have created and upon which we have conferred a (racialized, monstrified, savage, disabled) identity. It is the zombie that, with its condition of eternity and its distinct future, shows us the infected nature of our empire and of our own imagination.

How can we define zombies vis-à-vis sovereignty? Zombies, as sovereign subjects who are not afraid of death in the Bataillean sense, become subjects of resistance to human biopolitics by creating a state of exception that constitutes a paradigm of the oppressive government, where the Other becomes the living dead. Moreover, according to Bataille, sovereign subjects only die to be reborn.[66] Sovereignty means to free oneself from the fear of death that makes humans subordinate to the future. The philosopher distinguishes between the political/religious sovereign and the authentic sovereign. The authentic sovereign refuses to be a servant by rejecting all property. It loses itself in the sense that it delves into excesses that allow it to communicate with other beings. Achille Mbembe's "Necropolitics" defines sovereignty as "the right to kill."[67] If biopower decides who can be allowed to live and who must die, zombies, by biting noninfected bodies, are simultaneously killing them and allowing them to live for eternity. In principle, zombies have taken over the state's biopower, but they themselves have been reduced to what Agamben calls the bare life.[68] For him, bare life needs to be seen in relation to the abandonment of natural life to sovereign violence or the unconditional power of death. Zombies then can be seen as subjects exposed to this violence who become sovereign subjects themselves. They personify the savages of the colonial order, the liberated slaves who have undergone a revolution, and yet, following Mbembe, have lost their political status, their home, and the rights over their bodies.[69] For Agamben, the state of exception is analogous to the right to resistance.[70] Although Italy considered including the right of resistance as part of its constitution, it ultimately failed. Article 20 of the German constitution, however, includes it, provided there is no other way to save democracy.[71] The U.S. Department of Defense defines a resistance movement as "an organized effort by some portion of the civil population of a country to resist the legally established government or an occupying power and to disrupt civil order and stability."[72] Carl Becker affirms that the second article of the Declaration of Independence included the "right of revolution" but that this meaning was in decline as soon as the Constitution was adopted.[73] The Constitution includes a bill of rights, but there is no explicit mention of the right to resist. Zombies in global cinema become agents of resistance with their own dead bodies and sovereign subjects of necroactivism who can very well follow Bataille's general economy.[74] While a restrictive economy only considers activities whose goals are gains, acquisition, usefulness, and conservation, Bataille's general economy includes activities that lead to waste, loss, exuberance, destruction, and so on. Zombies protest against the restrictive economy whose neoliberalism subjugates human beings. These fictional characters are waging a revolution that we, as beneficiaries of capitalism, probably won't.

In his essay "El monstruo político" (The Political Monster), Antonio Negri develops a genealogy of power and shows us that, since classical metaphysics, this genealogy is linked to the concept of eugenics.[75] Eugenics assumes that only those who have a good birth and are therefore beautiful and good are destined for positions of power. This understanding of eugenics actually excludes the monstrous and ends up justifying slavery. In the world of antiquity, the monster could only be accepted through some kind of mythology of metamorphosis. Modernity, however, heralds the return of the monster as a metaphor, as a sort of Leviathan figure. By doing this, asserts Negri, the monster apparently transforms itself into a sovereign, rational monster, an instrument of power and a deus ex machina who can control the multitude.[76] This genealogy gave monsters the quality of rationality. Therein lies their power. Beginning with capitalism, the monster becomes present within the system, and the system itself becomes a conceptual monster, a beast that sucks blood, exploits and absorbs people. The monster's actions spark resistance as an inevitable consequence. Masses of people protesting become a new type of monster, and these people keep protesting a suffering that becomes more and more gore. The monster protests, the monster resists, lives the bare life, a state where bodies encounter eternal danger.[77] This is how we can see zombies, as defeated subjects, expelled from humanity and made into objects, but who themselves become subjects again. They can be defined precisely at the intersection of people, things, and bodies. Zombies live the bare life. They are necroactivist subjects that resist biopolitics, subjects who reject an economy of happiness, suffer gore capitalism, and, therefore, open up a new posthuman futurity in which the eugenic nature of humanism can be rejected for eternity.

Freaks of Death

The first zombie movies that appeared at the beginning of the second half of the twentieth century are undoubtedly linked to the perception of minority groups as the Other, as weird, different, dangerous, savage, and contagious. The tendency to define ourselves in opposition to exoticized identities and extraordinary bodies has existed since antiquity. However, as Rosemary Garland Thomson notes, the interpretation and contemplation of the rare or atypical body took a turn in the passage to modernity. She asserts that what she calls the "freak discourse genealogy" illustrates a transition as "what was once sought after as revelation becomes pursued as entertainment; what aroused awe now inspires horror."[78] From the nineteenth century until the first half of the twentieth, freak shows and the exploitation of extraordinary bodies were extremely popular in the United States. P. T. Barnum's founding of the American Museum in 1841 contributed to the transformation of the freak show into a "coordinated business venture enhanced by advertising, promotional materials, and celebrity appearances."[79] Among the most famous and popular freaks we have Ota Benga, a Batwa Pygmy from Central Africa or Sarah Baartman, called the *Venus hotentote*, a nineteenth-century South African woman who was paraded as a sexual object throughout Europe. Other examples include the Mexican Julia Pastrana, who was very popular in the sideshows from the nineteenth century due to her hirsutism and gingival hyperplasia. Roger Bartra's reading of these spectacles confirms that they were constructed as savages. Some of them had physical disabilities (the Aztec Children), but others just came from exoticized places. Presented as cannibals, they were shown with their traditional garb, sometimes eating repulsive meat (repulsive to the taste of the American public). Rachel Adams explains that "'racial freak' and 'wild man' were interchangeable to refer to a particular kind of exhibition that linked the spectacle of ferocious wildness to racial and national difference."[80] While usually the disabled (dwarfs, fat women, giants, racialized White women, bearded ladies, pinheads) were able to interact with their audience and lecture them about their bodies, the "wild men" (usually people of color) were deliberately presented as "inarticulate and undomesticated."[81] Rosemarie Garland Thomson describes this phenomenon of collapsing categories (race, disability, nationality, and extraordinary physical features) as "freakery."[82] Freaks, like zombies, were considered dangerous. Positioned on elevated platforms, the public was told: "Hold back, ladies and gentlemen, what you are about to see will shock and amaze you!"[83] Freaks were real people—extraordinary, disabled, or simply racialized—and they were treated like animals from which to profit; their *freaked* bodies actually generated money even after death. Edward L. Schwarschild considers Charles Wilson Peale (1741–1827) to be an early American freak showman because his introduction of taxidermy for display in American museums (including mummified animals) exposed the dead to the public, presenting the vulnerability of life and the inevitability of mortality. Schwarschild cites Peale as a showman who wanted to "tame and display death for posterity." Just as taxidermy displays dead creatures for entertainment, zombies visually represent the awkward limits between death and life on screen for the public to consume.[84] According to Bartra, who follows the life of Pastrana, including her posthumous freak show even in 2005, contemplating deformed bodies brings up something hidden that provokes racism and sexism.[85] Freaks were usually conceived of at the intersection of human and animal. People affected by hirsutism were called "gorilla-man/women," and "monkey-child." Ota Benga was placed in the zoo next to the orangutan in order to equate her with the animal. Julia Pastrana was supposed to have descended from the hairy Root-Diggers, also presented as a hybrid from which her human features prevailed over her "orangutan side."[86] It is also important to mention that *geeks* (hired people acting as freaks) were very common because few disabled people would agree to being publicly exploited. *Geeks* were usually homeless, alcoholics, or other vulnerable people who worked for money by performing freakery. Zombie cinema has replaced *freak shows* and they have become the source of horror and fascination by which neoliberalism represents victims of capitalism and marginalized groups and creates a spectacle of the Other. Like freaks, zombies exist within a narrative that props up homogeneity and vilifies difference. Zombies do not represent real historical people, yet they are a representation of human exploitation. It could be said that zombie cinema is a continuation of freak shows in the twenty-first century and that geeks are some of their ancestors, while at the same time, they are representing resistance.

The Once and Future Undead

Zombies have surely undergone a series of changes over the decades that have captured the cultural imagination. William Seabrook depicted the undead working in the sugar mills. Their existence was created around slave labor, and at the same time it was an attempt to recolonize African descendants. Haiti achieved its independence after the Haitian Revolution in 1804, while in the United States, slavery had been abolished only sixty-four years prior to the publication of the *The Magic Island*. Famously, Romero resuscitated the cannibalistic ghouls that popularized the genre in the United States toward the end of the twentieth century. *28 Days Later* introduced us to the faster-moving rage monsters that dominated the genre in the early 2000s. Over the decades, these genre films have begun to present the viewer with more complex zombies with a changing set of rules. Some of them have consciousness; others are even more intelligent or talented than the average human. *Land of the Dead* presents us with zombies that can communicate among themselves. They organize their attacks, navigate territory, and target their victims. Then there is the case of *Halley*, the Mexican film whose zombie protagonist Alberto retains his capacity for reason, including his ability to adapt to the capitalist system, establish relationships, and even contend with his own physical and emotional needs, all while experiencing the decomposition of his body. The fact that he even continues to desire is particularly important in *Halley*, since it is rare for a zombie to display any physical need other than hunger.[87] In *Zombi Child*, Mélissa experiences a kind of inherited, legacy zombie state, directly passed to her by her Haitian grandfather who was one of the original zombies and who was able to escape that fate but not the generational repercussions for his offspring.[88]

Other representations of zombies bring us to a more abstract, almost ethereal, conception of the soul. In the Spanish film *REC*, a faux "found footage" film, the zombies are part of an infection that stems from the demonic possession of a Portuguese girl named Tristana Medeiros.[89] Here the spirit has become flesh, but unlike the Platonic ideal or the incarnation of Christ, the spirit is demonized. Demonic possession is depicted as a zombie state in *The Wailing*, in which a Japanese stranger disrupts a small Korean village, as a reminder of the colonial past and the damage inflicted in it.[90] In *Atlantics* (*Atlantique*) the zombies are women temporarily possessed by the spirits of their dead boyfriends, drowned in a failed attempt to emigrate and returned to extract their revenge on the capitalist state that was the cause of their deaths.[91] In *Savageland*, a film about the border crisis between the United States and Mexico, the viewer never sees the zombies, only the ethereal photographic representations taken during the attacks.[92] These images are used as allegories that refer to racialized and fantasmagoric spectres that return within the imagination of a nation, especially in a border space controlled through necropolitics. We are able to visualize the spectral zombies as conceptual metaphors that represent both the obvious racialized capitalism of the border as well as the marginalized subjectivities that stubbornly continue to make themselves present.

But, above all, the zombie is a subject of queer temporality[93] in opposition to modernity's chrononormativity and Christian theology.[94] It is one of the dead, who has arisen before the scheduled Final Judgment, and whose corpse wanders the streets in search of flesh to consume. The only way to kill a zombie, we are told over and again, is to brutally destroy its brain, thereby eliminating the only trace left of what used to be the depository for its thought and mind/soul. If the zombie is only truly dead when the brain is wiped out, the brain remains central to undead existence, and we should consider the possibility of there remaining a trace of human consciousness left in that organ even after zombification. In fact, we must question whether it is precisely the presence of this repository of mind/soul that makes resuscitation possible. As Esposito proposes, the binary division between persons and things that has persisted for so long has always excluded the body: in the arena of law, the field of philosophy, and Christian theology, the person has been separated from the concept of body and reduced to an idea.[95] The fact, therefore, that the zombie maintains this phantom connection to his brain even after having lost all cognitive function is one more piece of evidence for this dependency between mind and body, body and mind. The mind needs the body to exist as a person, but the body needs the mind to be alive. This may be why we see so many examples of trace moments of what seems like memory or recognition in so many of the most recent zombie films.

We can also see a tendency toward posthumanist zombie movies. These films depict zombies and zombie-like behavior as a stepping-stone to the development of a new way of existing, one that rejects Enlightenment humanism and all that has resulted from it. In a way, the development of zombies as posthuman is the remedy to the ills that created the problem of the undead. Posthumanism offers a way to transcend the morbid effects of late capitalism, the endless wars and state of siege, and the effects that both have had on life on our planet.[96] *Descendents* (*Solos*) by Chilean director Jorge Olguín introduces a new generation of children who are immune to the virus infection but who develop gills and are drawn to the ocean, having evolved into a new version of humanity.[97] Similarly, in *The Girl with All the Gifts* (2016) we are presented with a zombie that looks healthy and normal and, though treated as a science experiment by uninfected humans, is as fully capable of thought and reason as its human captors, if not more.[98] It represents a human-zombie hybrid that will inherit the earth. The Portuguese *Mutant Blast* significantly changes the zombie genre, making a zombie outbreak the precursor to the creation of a breed of mutants, whose "humanity" is explored respectfully despite what at first appear to be hideous transformations. By using different filming techniques, the director Fernando Alle places the viewer behind the mutants' eyes—adjusting the angle of the lens so as to present the perspective of a mutant. He says in an interview with Erich Ortiz García, filmed outside the Cineteca Nacional de México, that this film is his love letter to the genre and also his breakup letter as his love for zombie movies transforms into something new.

Nobody can foresee the zombie of the future. The "rules" of the genre are constantly changing, as the genre itself has stretched to include comedy, romance, and social commentary along with horror. As a necroactivist political subject, zombies are fighting for inclusion within an equitable system that considers race, class, gender, disability, and the environment. They might become our new superhero-freaks as they reflect and expose injustices of our neoliberal system. As we have mentioned in the introduction, theories of horror have made us aware of how similarly people react in real tragedies versus reading or watching good horror stories. As infected/mutated superheroes who catalyze horror and hold up a distorting mirror, zombies can also show us the way to cope with the tragic realities of the COVID-19 pandemic, the threat of climate change, a looming economic downturn—and whatever comes after.

2

Mutilate the State!

Nation, Race, Power

The zombie first appeared in the Caribbean, as Haitian folklore that reflected the brutality of the lives of the enslaved in the seventeenth century. As we touched upon in the previous chapter, it was created through rituals of vodou, a syncretic religion rooted in repressed West African beliefs held by slaves who were forced to convert to Christianity. The Haitian zombie would become the soulless slave of the *bokor* that made him and would behave as if in a trance while carrying out his master's wishes.[1] In this early version of the zombie we can see the objectification of the subject of forced labor and the "death-in-life" that is slavery's effect on the enslaved. In early U.S. zombie literature and film, we can see the ways in which the zombie myth is appropriated and, in effect, colonized in the United States for popular consumption in the same way that the bodies of the colonial and enslaved laborers were appropriated and commodified by colonizing powers. There has been a significant amount of work done in describing the zombie phenomenon in the Americas as commentary on the historical legacy of slavery (Sarah Juliet Lauro) and the cannibalistic nature of capitalist society (David McNally, Jean Comaroff and John Comaroff). In following the development of the zombie, we can trace the evolution of the themes responsible for the creation of the zombie myth: imperialism, exploitation of the marginalized, imbalance of power, and racial and national identity. Zombie lore was born in the Americas, and it is inextricable from the coloniality of power as put forward by Aníbal Quijano. Our modern concept of race, according to Quijano, didn't exist before the colonization of the Americas, and its reason for existence is to distinguish social identities and grant "legitimacy to the relations of domination imposed by the conquest."[2] By following how our modern American capitalist system and movement toward globalization grows from the conquest and colonization of the Americas, we can trace ideas of race that still linger as zombies have developed from slave labor to terrifying, cannibalistic "other" and understand the way in which the zombie fits into ideas of nation, race, and dynamics of power.

The Birth of Z-Nation

The Haitian zombie is a perfect example of slavery taken to its extreme. The human body is stripped of its soul, its identity—all that makes it human—and is converted into a labor machine, one that is under complete control of a master. The zombie works without any of the requirements necessary for sustaining human life, because it is, in effect, no longer considered human. As such, it is a perfect portrait of the abject misery of slavery. But the zombie is also an eerie and menacing figure, containing the threat of violence, an inhuman drive to continue to function mechanically, almost robotically, and an absence of reason. Sarah Juliet Lauro points out that the contemporary understanding of the zombie myth was formed by "the colonial oppressors, slaveholders, and French and Spanish monks and chronicles in the exaggerated travelogues of curious travelers,"[3] explaining how representation of the myth was appropriated by hegemonic power nearly from the start. Well before it was converted into a money-making entertainment, it was part of a salacious propaganda campaign to otherize oppressed peoples and justify the violence against them. But beneath the push and pull of fascination and disgust present in the oppressor's interest in zombies there remains that underlying dread of the unruly automaton that, while it does the bidding of its master, refuses to comply with the laws of nature. Though it is controlled externally by an exploitative power that subjugates it, the zombie's very existence is a threat to order and reason. Thus the zombie is a metaphor for the effects of the cruel abuses of power while also inherently resisting against it.

Lauro has argued that the zombie simultaneously represents the slave and the slave-in-revolt: that while the zombie is in helpless thrall to its master, it is also breaking with the bonds of death. Furthermore, she reminds us that "demonstrations of agency aside from overt rebellion are worthy of consideration as acts of resistance. . . . [E]ven the docile slave is sometime a rebel and the free man, sometimes still a slave."[4] Sometimes resistance is best achieved from a position that looks like submission, since the ultimate expression of rebellion—outright denial—is a guarantee of death. In this way, the act of ending one's own life on one's own terms—choosing death—becomes an act of rebellion, but one that includes the ultimate loss. This tension between the right to live and the right to die, between biological life within the symbolic death of slavery on the one hand and the freedom of choice that ends in actual death on the other, locates the enslaved in a liminal existence. And as the post-Romero filmic genre has evolved to embody the modern conception of zombies as gore-hungry shambling corpses, it remains at once a slave to its own impulses and a menacing threat to existing power structures.

Necropower and Slavery: Black and White Zombies

Michel Foucault explains that suicide was once considered a crime because it assumed the *right* to end one's own life and was a theft of that power to cause death that was the sovereign's alone to exercise. He writes of the ancient rule of *patria potestas* that afforded the Roman father the absolute right to end the life of his children and the slaves in his care. But, in his description of the notion of biopower, Foucault describes how this "ancient right to *take* life or *let* live was replaced by a power to *foster* life or *disallow* it to the point of death."[5] Foucault explains that, beginning in the seventeenth century, an *anatamo-politics* of the human body as machine, governing its docility and utility, gave way to a *biopolitics*, which sought to regulate the population through the functions of life, health, birth, and longevity, changing the terms of sovereign power to a focus on extending life instead of dealing death. In his "Necropolitics," Achille Mbembe examines issues of sovereignty and biopolitical power. He assumes from the start that "the ultimate expression of sovereignty resides, to a large degree in the power and the capacity to dictate who may live and who must die."[6] He considers the contributions of Foucault, Schmitt, and Arendt among others on the case of Nazism as the direst example of the *state of exception*, in which the sovereign is obliged to operate outside the rule of law for the sake of the "public good," when the public good is defined as outliving (and therefore murdering) a designated Other. But Mbembe insists, differing from those theorists referenced above, that the roots of necropolitics actually lie in slavery and colonialism, pointing out that race is the basis for colonialism as well as slavery. In the name of so-called civilization, European powers (which recognized only their European neighboring states as countries, and therefore as "enemies" on equal footing) looked across the waters at territories that contained peoples unlike them in racial features and organization and deemed them "savages," "animal," and therefore less than human—thereby justifying any "savage" deaths incurred in the business of colonization and slavery. Taking all this into account, the zombie becomes an apt symbol of the results and lasting damage of a hemisphere full of American nations founded on the doubled violence of slavery and colonization. As Mbembe observes, "because the slave's life is like a 'thing,' possessed by another person, the slave existence appears as a perfect figure of a shadow."[7] He describes slave life as a "death-in-life": the enslaved have had their homes and rights over their bodies taken from them; they have been left with no political status. These losses result in social death. This shadow, a figure between presence and absence, whose borders are permeable and difficult to define, is indeed similar to the modern-day zombie. If we take this argument as our foundation, we can see the ways in which the zombie began the work of decolonization from its birth as a myth spread among vodou followers and later disseminated by the same hegemonic forces that inspired it. The zombie can be seen as an echo of the atrocities of the past that have never fully been reckoned with. As Jennifer Rutherford points out, the zombie "doubles the trauma of the past. It signifies a past that awaits; a past to which one can always be returned if . . . one loses the right to being an individuated subject in a free society."[8]

The earliest Hollywood-produced zombie production illustrates the subtle shadowy qualities of early zombies. As discussed in chapter 1, *White Zombie* followed William Seabrook's book *The Magic Island*, which explains that to make a zombie, one has to "go to a fresh grave, dig up the body before it has had time to rot . . . then make of it a servant or a slave . . . setting it dull heavy tasks, and beating it like a dumb beast if it slackens."[9] Halperin's film uses precisely this conception of the zombie, and in fact opens the film with the spectacle of a burial taking place in the middle of the road in order to protect the newly dead from grave robbers, just as described in Seabrook's text.[10] In the film, we catch a glimpse of a zombie master's cane mill, which is entirely run by undead labor. The vacant stares and slow plodding movements of the workers have the effect of making them into the mere machinery of the mill. They operate in shadows, not speaking or interacting in any way, entirely bereft of human affect. In *I Walked with a Zombie*, the White plantation-owning family and the young White woman who comes to serve them as a nurse are the protagonists of the central drama of the film.[11] But the action unfolds surrounded by the presence of the descendants of slaves, their generational scars, and the culture of vodou. The ghost of slavery haunts the plantation in the physical form of "Ti Misere," the figurehead of a slave ship modeled on St. Sebastian, pierced with arrows. Even the plantation owner, contemplating the statue, concedes that everything they have is built upon the misery of the slave. When the final tragedy of the film befalls this privileged family, the same figurehead looms over the final scene, implying that the tragedy was earned and that the family, whose fortunes were built on suffering, are doomed to suffer themselves. The titular zombie of this film is the wife of the plantation owner, who drifts about in diaphanous robes. But there is another zombie, Carrefour (played by Darby Jones), whom the nurse encounters in the fields as she searches for a cure. He is a Black man, tall and angular, his exaggerated bulging eyes are wide but otherwise unresponsive. His sudden presence in the field startles the nurse, almost as a scarecrow wards off birds, and is clearly meant to be a titillating scare for the viewer of the film. He appears out of the darkness in the night, is an ominous presence in the shadows of the plantation, and later acts as as an observer when the zombified wife is murdered by her lover, though it is unclear if he can see anything at all through his clouded and unmoving eyes. As the figurehead of the slave ship is a witness to the horrors of the colonial and slave-owning past of the island, Carrefour is present during the violent fall of the descendants of enslavers.

The zombies of these two early films share little in common with the rotting, flesh-eating zombies of contemporary cinema, but they are an apt precursor to those harbingers of apocalypse. They at once illustrate the death-in-life of the slave and the narrative of death in that necropolitical structure that does not disappear with the end of legal slavery. These figures also firmly plant the origins of the zombie in the concept of race. Following Foucault, Mbembe grounds what he calls "the phantomlike world of race" in the division and subdivision of humanity into groups, creating a "biological caesura" between them, an imaginary distance created to justify their death.[12] In these two early films, the identification of zombie with slave, or ex-slave, underscores this biological caesura and indeed widens it as the zombie operates outside of the realm of the functions of biology itself.

But it must also be observed that there is another type of power dynamic at play in these two early films, one that revolves around gender, control, and Whiteness. In the case of both films, the zombie myth that has sprung up from Haitian folklore has been turned around to menace a young, White heroine, and, in zombifying her, to place her body in the control of someone else and to negate her consciousness and her will. These films, made for the entertainment of a White North American populace, exoticize the menace of vodou ritual and Black Haitian culture further by offering up the victim in the form of a helpless young White woman. It is significant that the role of the zombie, still very much associated with slavery in this early form, is twisted to explore a different dynamic of gendered power. Of course, it is important to remember that plantation slavery also included sexual enslavement of its victims. The use of White zombie heroines in these films is used to titillate White audiences with the suggestion of an exotic threat hanging over White culture as opposed to addressing the very real crimes committed against enslaved women.

The 2015 Mexican film *Ladronas de almas* (whose title can be translated as "Soul Thieves") offers an update and a corrective to some of the themes we have observed in those early films.[13] It combines the Haitian zombie with the cannibalistic post-Romero living dead and explores themes of colonialism and gender relations through horror tinged with humor. Taking place in the nineteenth century, during the war for Mexican independence, the film centers on the Cordero family, once-rich, landowning *criollos* (Mexicans of mostly

European descent) that, after having been raided by the *realistas* (Royalists, fighting for Spanish interests against independence), have struggled to survive and isolate themselves during the war. In the raid, their matriarch was murdered, their father gravely wounded, their gold stolen, and their eldest daughter María bound and kidnapped. When she attempts to escape, she is caught and surrounded by soldiers and about to be killed when local zombies attack. She plays dead to avoid being bitten while most of her captors are killed. Indalesio, a Black Haitian in the family's employ who is the protector of the Cordero sisters, explains that these local zombies were created in Mexico when his people migrated there and brought their zombie rituals with them. The undead were kept in the mines as slaves, but now, during the violence of the revolution, they have been abandoned by their masters and have turned feral. Indalesio's grandfather, a Haitian *bokor*, held the secret to creating zombies, and now Indalesio shares that secret with María and her sisters. They turn the captain of the *realistas* into a zombie under María's control and set him to guard their gold. Thus, the zombified slaves in the mines kill the representatives of the Spanish Crown, and the royalist captain, as a walking dead man, is consigned to their same fate for eternity. When more mercenary soldiers come in search of the gold, they kill Indalesio, rape María, and attempt to rape her sister. The three sisters get their bloody revenge by killing most of them and keeping two more as zombies, using the skills learned from Indalesio. In this film we not only see the abused and abandoned laboring zombies rising up to attack representatives of a crumbling colonial power but also the Cordero sisters' feminist revenge for the use and abuse of their bodies. In this way, *Ladronas de almas* works as a feminist revenge fantasy, as well as an intersectional commentary on the cruelties of the colonial system.

Siege Mentality: The War against Zombies

While Mbembe asserts that slavery must be considered as a foundational example of biopolitical experimentation, he goes on to address contemporary wars as a further expression of necropower, typified by a closing of territory, a technology of surveillance, and a *state of siege*, in which daily life is militarized, and which is related to the *state of exception*. He claims that contemporary wars are faster in their onset, dependent on mobility and technological advancements in speed. State armies are no longer the sole arbiters of war: war is now a commodity; military force is bought and sold where militias, private armies, security firms, and state armies all claim the right to deal in death and terror. Mbembe describes the necropolitical power being exercised in these contemporary wars as "more tactile, more anatomical and sensorial" than in colonial wars and the effect on civilian bodies more drastic, as the new technologies of death are less interested in discipline than in massacre.[14] But when death is not achieved, Mbembe describes the effect of physical wounds, scars and amputations that do perform a degree of discipline through presentation of mangled bodies: "their function is to keep before the eyes of the victim—and of the people around him or her—the morbid spectacle of severing."[15] This description echoes the physical characteristics of twentieth-century zombies—the shuffling corpses, dripping with gore, that we find in the immensely popular TV series *The Walking Dead*, for example. Though these more recent zombies differ greatly from the eerie automatons of the *White Zombie* and *I Walked with a Zombie*, they follow in a direct line of evolving power relations that, like coloniality, survived the end of colonization.

The creature that began as an echo of colonialist and slave terror now serves as a reminder of the inhumanity of the necropolitical effects on populations in successful films such as *World War Z*.[16] The film, based on the novel by Max Brooks, follows one man, Gerry Lane, as he and his family attempt to survive a zombie plague. The first indication of trouble occurs while the family members are sitting in a taxi, stuck in traffic in their home city of Philadelphia. First there is the unexplained appearance of frenzied police, rushing to an emergency, then an explosion is heard, and people are seen running from some unseen danger. Though the scene is not set in New York, these elements of chaos in an American city can't help but call to mind the attacks of 9/11 that had occurred just over a decade prior to the making of the film, and even recall the live footage made by the people who were at Ground Zero on that day. Gerry, a former investigator at the United Nations, is called upon to help uncover the origins of the plague, and his work takes him to South Korea, where he visits a military base and sees the carnage of the initial outbreak, viewing (un)dead bodies, some burned but still moving, strewn within and without the compound. Finally, Gerry travels to Jerusalem, which in the film has been walled off in advance of the outbreak. The film's reliance on situating the action of the plot to these sites: a northeastern U.S. city, South Korea, and Jerusalem—all sites of extreme violence, war, and terror within the last half century—illustrates how, even without referring to the war and attacks associated with those places, the film maintains a connection between (un)dead and mutilated bodies and sites of necropolitical machinations.

The final example of Jerusalem is particularly interesting in a consideration of Mbembe's assertion that "the most accomplished form of necropower is the contemporary colonial occupation of Palestine" in which the cutting off and splintering of territories under a militarized *state of siege* is a condition of daily life.[17] Furthermore, it is an occupation built upon the presumption of the state's divine right to exist in a territory where more than one monotheistic culture has sacred claim to geography, and based upon the horror of the historical mass murder that was the Holocaust. In the film, officials in a fortified Jerusalem begin letting refugees inside their walls, acknowledging that "every human being we save is one less zombie to fight." And it is this act, this blurring of the necropolitical divisions between peoples, that is their fatal mistake in the film. As Palestinians and Israelis come together in celebration, singing and dancing together as they unite, finally, against the ultimately more dangerous, more Other, undead enemy, the sound of this reunification is what agitates the horde as zombies crawl over each other to attack the city, forming a kind of corporeal tidal wave that spills over the walls. Once the walls are breached, the city falls, and the zombie attack quickly results in more piles of dead and dismembered bodies. The suggestion here is that reunification, as the end of the colonial project (itself the result of thanatopolitical genocidal acts), will bring about the end of the world, an apocalypse that is the end of history. In a landscape that has been read as the eventual site of the biblical apocalypse to come, we are given the message that humanitarian kindness is dangerous, and ruthless exclusion of the Other is the way to safety.[18]

In chapter 1 we touched upon Romero's seminal film of the zombie genre and its importance given its sociopolitical moment. *Night of the Living Dead* was released in 1968 in the United States, at the end of the civil rights movement and during the Vietnam War and the Cold War with the Soviet Union. This was just three short years after the murder of Malcolm X; in fact, the movie's theatrical debut was in October of that year, only seven months after the assassination of Martin Luther King Jr. The sudden and unexplained rising of the dead to torment the living in this film has been read in a number of ways: as a critique of capitalism, as an expression of Cold War anxieties including fear of nuclear annihilation, as a commentary on resistance and repression, and as a parable of race. Most of these readings have in common a reaction against biopolitical sovereign power. The hero of the film, Ben, is clearly the most capable of a group of survivors and very quickly takes up a leadership role. He is the only Black survivor in a house beset by the cannibalistic dead (who are, by and large, all White). As the majority of the (White) inhabitants of the house fall to the zombies due to weakness or foolishness, only Ben survives the night. In the morning, he hears barking dogs and gunshots, which to him raise the possibility of salvation, indicating the presence of other uninfected humans. The sheriff and his deputized mob approach the house, shooting the undead as they go. They are filmed in a low-angle shot, with particular focus on their German shepherd police dogs and long rifles. They loom over the spectator menacingly, not exactly the cavalry coming to save the day. As Ben approaches the window to see who is coming, he is preemptively shot between the eyes by one of the police in the final scene of the film. The credits roll over Ben's sudden and unheroic end as film stills appear on the screen, continuing the narrative through a series of images. These images are reminiscent of crime-scene or news photography: foregrounding the hooks used to drag Ben's body to a pyre and contrasting the angry White faces of the mob with Ben's face in death. To the spectator at the time of the film's release, having so recently lived through the historical assassinations of Black leaders and witnessing civil rights protests that ended in violence, these end credits would look like photographs of those events: scenes of violence contrasting Ben's unresponsive, supine body with the police force bent on disposing of the uncontrollable dead.

The racial implications of this scene, coming as it does at the tail end of the unrest of the 1960s in the United States, cannot be ignored. In fact, these end credits create what Adam Lowenstein calls the *allegorical moment*, "a shocking collision of film, spectator, and history where registers of bodily space and historical time are disrupted, confronted, and intertwined.[19] As spectators of this scene we cannot assume that the militarized police presence, here represented in a state of siege, can be trusted to save the living; they only manage the disposal of the living and the dead they have slaughtered. Mbembe has described the ways in which "weapons are deployed in the interest of maximum destruction of persons and the creation of *death-worlds*, new and unique forms of social existence in which vast populations are subjected to conditions of life conferring upon them the status of *living dead*." George Romero's iconic pulp horror film provides a visual element to the idea of death-worlds: one that has resonance in nearly every contemporary zombie film.[20] It was *Night of the Living Dead* that gave the zombie genre that inevitable, contagious element of apocalyptic weight and threatened to spread the infection over the whole world.

Michael Hardt and Antonio Negri contend that though imperialism is dead, a power they call Empire has replaced it: a global network of power that includes the larger nation-states, multinational corporations, supranational institutions, and other organizations. This "network power" naturally contains inequalities and hierarchies, and therefore, divisions and disputes, visible from a global to a local scale, resulting in a state of perpetual war. Many of these wars are being carried out, as we have seen, by organizations that are not necessarily representatives of a particular nation, as the sovereignty of nation-states is declining in general. Hardt and Negri maintain that the attacks of 9/11 did not create this phenomenon but did cause the world to take notice of it.[21] These conflicts, taking place all over the planet, are considered by the authors to be civil wars within Empire, and are all connected by the global imperial system. As the authors assert, "these are not isolated wars . . . but a *general global state of war* that erodes the distinction between war and peace such that we can no longer imagine or even hope for a real peace."[22] Therefore, proliferation of these militarized groups, be they official representatives of nation-state, mercenary, terrorist, or paid security, and the violence they are prepared to enact upon populations, help to inspire a global state of anxiety and fear.

The state of exception has become permanent: there is no exception to the exception. We exist in a state of siege. Through this lens of anxiety and fear we can examine a trope common to countless zombie movies: the menacing and corrupt military. As the zombie threat exacerbates a state of siege, the military/police/SWAT groups become the only hope for fighting the monsters and protecting survivors, but in z-films, they usually either fail to protect or actually become another threat to civilian survivors. We find many examples of this in the films made in the Americas. For example, in *Juan of the Dead* (*Juan de los muertos*), a satire focusing on a motley crew of zombie-killing entrepreneurs in Cuba, the protagonists are stopped by the military, searched, stripped and inspected for bites, and thrown into the back of an army vehicle full of naked and chained men.[23] They are told that they have been rounded up as part of an effort to arm the uninfected survivors and conscript the builders of a new society. This plan goes awry within minutes as one of the men has been infected and bloody mayhem ensues. In Robert Rodriguez's *Planet Terror*, a corrupt and unstable army lieutenant and his men are actually the cause of the zombie outbreak, having released a biochemical agent into the air in a Texas border town.[24] They reserve all the antidote for themselves and imprison a group of survivors that appear to be immune to extract some kind of cure from their bodies. They torment these survivors, showing their cruelty and predatory nature before being killed by their prisoners. The Chilean film *Descendents* (*Solos*) depicts an army lining up suspected zombies against a fence, bound hand and foot and with a white hood over each of their heads. They are then each shot in the head, executed in a manner that recalls the state-imposed violence of the Pinochet era (1973–2000). These images, along with those of terrified people being shot at from helicopters, remind the audience of torture methods used at Villa Grimaldi.[25] Similarly, *Block Z* references violent Philippine history, specifically, the rule of Ferdinand Marcos, whose tenure lasted from 1965–1986 and was characterized by corruption, embezzlement, and repression of political opponents.[26] Marcos's declaration of martial law in 1972 had the effect of suppressing civil rights and freedom of the press: many reporters, activist students, and opposition leaders were persecuted, tortured, and killed. In the film, which takes place at a university, a military-enforced quarantine is imposed, and when panicked students try to escape, they are shot ruthlessly whether they are infected or not, in the interest of containing the virus. This recalls the targeting of student activists under martial law and suggests that the students themselves are as dangerous as the deadly outbreak. The military unit that has welcomed survivors in *28 Days Later* with promises of protection from the cannibalistic rage monsters that have overtaken much of Britain turns out to have lured them there only to acquire women with whom to repopulate the earth against their will. In so many zombie films of the last couple of decades the presence of the military adds to the dangers of the outbreak, turning its violence on nonzombies with almost as much zeal as it does the undead.

The Corpse Politic: State Control of Unruly Bodies

In the South Korean film *Seoul Station* (*Seoulyeok*), the police, when begged for help, at first don't believe the zombie crisis is real, thinking that the infected are just the homeless hordes that they are usually blind to and who disgust them on principle: they can't see the difference between a flesh-eating living corpse and a poor and unhoused person.[27] When the protagonist, a marginalized and displaced young woman, finally finds a safe zone guarded by militarized police, she is kept out since she is deemed to be disposable due to her low social standing and therefore is suspected of infection. The marginalized victims and ravenous zombies in *Seoul Station* are indistinguishable from each other in the eyes of the police, since they are all walking dead and only serve as cautionary tales to help legitimize a positive public opinion of state power.

An article by Linnemann, Wall, and Green examines how "dispossessed, non-white and working poor subjects" can be "zombified" as a justification for brutalization by police force by examining the 2012 case of thirty-one-year-old Rudy Eugene, shot dead by police as he attacked a homeless man on a deserted Miami causeway.[28] He was found biting the face of his victim, Ronald Poppo, in a bizarre and bloody attack. Linnemann et al. describe the way that Eugene, a Black man of Haitian descent, was dubbed the "Miami Zombie" and his case was sensationalized and spectacularized by the media as part of the media's tendency to capitalize on the most gruesome news. It bears considering that Eugene was unarmed and naked at the time of his shooting. His exceedingly violent attack on Poppo appeared to be completely out of the blue—completely inexplicable to those who knew him. Family and friends were shocked and could not explain how he could have transformed from the man they knew to this publicized monster. The zombification of Rudy Eugene that was splashed across the media was based on a focus on his "abnormal normality" (the idea that this could happen to anyone through ingestion of drugs), "the transformative power of illicit drugs" (which were thought to confer "superhuman" strength), and "the supernatural Gothic" (in the perceived demonic nature of the attack).[29] These narratives were used to justify a messy and panicked shooting that also left Eugene's mauled victim injured by police fire. This "zombification" narrative functions as part of an ideological structure that frames police shootings in the media as necessary and protective, while smearing victims of police shootings as "suspects" at best, and supernaturally evil at worst. While Eugene's case is horrifically violent, we can see in this case the way that narratives of the "killability" of those suspected of crimes are used to normalize and justify state violence, especially when directed at elements of the citizenry that are considered less "alive" than others.[30] After all, the article points out that it was not until Eugene's homeless victim was given the status of "grieveable and resilient" that he "became anything more than a member of the walking dead in his own right."[31] And in the worldwide state of siege, as financial collapse looms and environmental disasters are common occurrences, our collective anxiety is explained and normalized in sensational media and state narratives that attempt to reinforce the existing social order of race and class dominance.

This biopolitical control of the public body is explicitly depicted in the film *Z-O-M-B-I-E-S*, produced by the Disney Corporation in 2018.[32] In this musical comedy the rules of zombie life are laid out clearly and with a minimum of gore, since the target audience consists of children and young teens. The town of Seabrook is divided by a giant wall (the film was released two years after Trump's proposal of a "big beautiful wall" at the border with Mexico): the "normal" people of Seabrook live in contented, orderly pastel-hued conformity on one side, and the zombies are ghettoized in "Zombietown" on the other.[33] This is where we find a community of zombies whose conduct is regulated by a magnetic "Z-Band" they wear on their wrists, which controls any violent impulses. Even though they are surveilled and controlled, they must live under certain restrictions as imposed by humans. There is a strict segregation of the populations: businesses display signs proclaiming, "No Zombies." The police force in Seabrook is simply called the "Zombie Patrol," indicating that the racialized zombie population is the only group that requires policing.

It appears that their Z-bands not only control their aggression but also mute many of their talents. In order to compete with the human kids, the zombies learn to "hack" their bands, so they can be stronger, faster, and smarter. When our zombie protagonist, Zed, hacks his Z-band to win a football game, he becomes vulnerable to a predatory group of human cheerleaders who gain control of his wristband, and thus, gain control of him. They allow him to become *agitated*, and Zed begins to appear unstable and aggressive, though he is making attempts to control himself. Before he can hurt anybody or do any damage, he is taken down by the Zombie Patrol and taken to Zombie Containment (prison), where he receives a software update (it is a Disney film, after all). Mel Y. Chen proposes the study of *agitation* in issues of security, medicalizing discourses that racialize disability, and the "disabling" of race.[34] The term "agitation" has been used to describe psychomotor or neuromuscular movement that connotes tension, disturbance, and results in gestures that must be treated with psychiatry or pharmaceuticals for the sake of control. Agitation is unexpected, unpredictable, and pathological. She also acknowledges that, often connoting aggression, the agitation is frequently used to justify the need "for violent suppression, to the point of intentional killing, by state or security agents," including "the continuing sequence of viewable Black deaths at the hands of police."[35] The history of agitation as a political term is linked to dissent and the action of opposition to dominant forces, and it helps to explain how agitation can be read as a rebellious choice instead of an uncontrolled reaction.[36] This would explain how green-haired, racialized zombies in this Disney production are seen as incapable of integration. Zed hasn't committed any crimes when he is arrested—he is being arrested for *who he is* and because the perception of zombies as wild subjects must eventually lead to their incarceration.[37] In a way, Zed's attempt to compete with the mild citizens of Seabrook was his first gestural wrong, for which he was eventually punished. In her article Chen describes other "gestural wrongs" that are punished with state control or street-level execution: cases of speaking Arabic on a plane, having a traumatic brain injury or autism and reacting to shouted police orders in unexpected ways. We have unfortunately seen the horrific results of police misinterpretation of gestures in the proliferation of cases of police shootings of unarmed Black and brown subjects. This injustice can't exist in the world of Disney, however. When the zombies are all controlled again, and given upgraded software, the once-scornful human teens are invited to a dance party in Zombietown, for the happy ending that extolls the wonders of unity—as long as all are properly controlled by the state.

This is a disingenuous depiction of the effects of state control on bodies. Frantz Fanon's concept of "combat breathing" gives us a different perspective: "There is not occupation of territory on the one hand and independence of persons on the other. It is the country as a whole, its history, its daily pulsation that are contested, disfigured, in the hope of a final destruction. Under these conditions, the individual's breathing is an observed, an occupied breathing. It is a combat breathing."[38] In 2011 an issue of *Somatechnics* was dedicated to the term as a description of a somatic response to state violence. In the introduction, Suvendrini Perera and Joseph Pugliese explain that "for Fanon, to be on the receiving end of state violence is always to be reduced to a body in question."[39] This target body is reduced to such vulnerability by the somatically "interpenetrated" effects of state force that every bit of their energy is dedicated to survival—to breathing—which guarantees that the subject will not have the energy to expend subverting the power of the state. This reduction of the existence of a target subject to just the act of breathing is echoed in the words of Eric Garner and George Floyd, two unarmed Black men killed by police in the United States in 2014 and 2020, respectively, while being detained on suspicion of minor infractions. Both lives were extinguished after they told officers they couldn't breathe. These cases occur in a national context where the media and state propaganda has primed the public with stories of violent crimes perpetrated by racialized subjects and ended by police intervention, and the buying and selling of cigarettes becomes a gestural wrong equivalent to the incomprehensible Miami Zombie attack. For Garner and Floyd, and countless other victims of state violence, the attempts to subdue their (mis)perceived agitation resulted in actual death, not "correction" as suggested by the Disney fantasy in which a happy ending is equal to submission to the state. If we take this phrase of Fanon's and apply it to a zombie context, combat breath reduces any possibility of resistance to mere breathing. Perhaps as undead political subjects, zombies subvert this form of state control by doing away with the need for breathing, freeing their bodies to act in protest and agitation, but at the cost of their humanity.

Survival Tactics at the Border: Multitude and Gore

The common thread in the films discussed above is that a militarized group or security force is set in opposition to a heterogenous group of desperate survivors. Though the prime cause of terror and distress is the wave of once-human monsters that hunt and kill the survivors, the militarized group is a secondary source of danger and anxiety, either mishandling the crisis and failing to help what remains of humanity or, worse, actively attempting to cause harm to them with predatory cruelty. In this state of exception, often cut off from the rest of civilization by the ensuing apocalyptic panic, martial authorities find it easy to follow their baser natures to necropolitical ends—deciding who may live and who must die. In these narratives, the rule of law is doubly suspended, regular law is replaced by martial law, and martial law breaks down to survival of the fittest (or best armed). This calls to mind the double *exceptions* identified by Hardt and Negri. The first of these is the constant state of exception that exists in Empire's unending global wars. The second is a reference to U.S. exceptionalism, which they see to have two incompatible meanings: one being "*exception from the corruption* of the European forms of sovereignty . . . as the beacon of republican virtue in the world," and the second, newer, meaning being *exception from the law* as the United States "increasingly exempts itself from international agreements . . . and claims its military does not have to obey the rules to which others are subject."[40] This rogue attitude is reflected in these films in microcosm, with the military or police, as the most powerful and armed of the survivors, assuming this freedom from restraint. As Hardt and Negri explain, the "exception" refers to the double standard enjoyed by the most powerful—that is, the notion that the one who commands need not obey. If we take as given the breakdown of the sovereignty described in the concept of Empire, and the network of power described in it, then this sense of *exceptionalism* can apply to any group that is the most powerful in its locality, and who thus can claim the moral superiority of the powerful.

Importantly, in most of these films, the group of survivors pitted against this militarized power includes social outcasts or otherwise marginalized figures, while the military figures are much more homogenous. This is not only an echo of the racialized origins of the z-narrative but can also be seen as illustrative of what Hardt and Negri term "multitude." The multitude is a growing alternative to Empire's technologies of control (bio- and necropower) and also a result of globalization's increased circuits of communication and collaboration. The authors claim that in the multitude, a new worldwide kind of democracy can form. They assert, in opposition to those who bemoan globalization's homogenizing effects, that in the multitude participants can remain "themselves": "In the multitude, social differences remain different. The multitude is many-colored, like Joseph's magical coat."[41] As these zombie films and stories play out, as in any apocalyptic narrative, the suggestion is that the cataclysm has opened the way for a new reality, since the old order has been upended. This theoretical multitude is similar to the observation of Hisup Shin, that in zombie films, survival patterns "often take the form of communal bonding forged by the need for mutual protection beyond any racial or ethnic categories. The sense of local specificity or cultural belongingness is either blurred or entirely suspended."[42] The zombie apocalypse turns every survivor into a stateless refugee. These small bands of survivors, then, represent the future in this new world, and as their fortunes go, so do those of the whole planet. That they must first clear the hurdle of a threatening military is significant, and, as we have seen, repeatedly appears in this genre.

If the stand-in for the crumbling authority of the sovereignty of the nation-state—the military—claims the moral superiority to rule over survivors, on what is this power based, besides having the most guns? Interpreting Hardt and Negri to address this question for our purposes, this feeling of moral superiority may rely in part on the revulsion they feel for both the monsters and the civilian survivors, for the "monstrosity of their flesh." Hardt and Negri describe the multitude as a "living social flesh that is not a body [and] can easily appear monstrous. For many these multitudes that are not peoples or nations or even communities are one more instance of the insecurity and chaos that has resulted from the collapse of the modern social order . . . the unformed and the unordered are horrifying."[43] Hardt and Negri also suggest a possible figure to express this monstrous flesh: the vampire.[44] Their conception of the vampire and our zombies share many attributes that terrify those nostalgic for a previous institutional order: an indiscriminate desire for the flesh of either gender, a singular form of reproduction (the bite) that undermines the heterosexual union, a subsequent destruction of the need for the nuclear family. But in contradiction to the vampire, the zombie lacks an erotic element. The zombie's flesh does not inspire a necrophilic desire; it is a rotting reminder of the vile physical properties of death. From this perspective, the disordered and chaotic nature of roving bands of survivors is a repudiation of an imaginary previous order of homogeneity. The threat contained in this repudiation is as monstrous as a zombie to the agents of control. It inspires a nostalgia for order that is, Hardt and Negri assert, the basis for the re-emergence of right-wing populism around the world: "Newly dominant reactionary forces call for the return of national sovereignty, stoking the flames of racism and violence against migrants."[45] The awakening of the multitude as a potential power inflames an equal and reactionary movement that seeks to strengthen traditional divisions and ideas of national purity.

This tension that exists in a globalized world of porous borders, looking backward to an imaginary past of racial purity, is the subject of the 2015 faux documentary *Savageland*, codirected by Phil Guidry, Simon Herbert, and David Whelan. The film foregrounds race and the value of bodies in areas where privileged and nonprivileged spaces meet and is set near the Arizona-Mexico border. Here, the zombie attack is at first presumed to be a mass murder, and the main suspect is an "illegal" immigrant, Francisco Salazar, a quiet laborer. The town where the bloody acts take place, Sangre de Cristo (Blood of Christ), is identified as the home of the cooks, maids, and laborers (all of Latin American descent) who work in the neighboring majority-White town of Hinzman. The locals in Hinzman refer to Sangre de Cristo derisively as "Savageland." The White law force comes down hard on Salazar as the murderer of an entire community until his own photographic evidence of the attack comes to light, revealing the shadowy figures that slaughtered the population of the town. Throughout interviews with White locals from nearby, and especially the racist sheriff, the fear and disgust that the accused mass murderer inspires in them is racially tinged. As one of them says, "Salazar is *la raza*. They've come to wipe us from the map." All this in spite of the fact that forty-seven of the forty-nine victims were Mexican or Central American immigrants. The real population that is being wiped from the map is the most legally, politically, economically, and physically vulnerable population. But here, the less powerful, othered population, used for labor but kept separate and in poverty by representatives of the state, is transformed. It is assumed, since no bodies are found, that the missing have become part of the menacing and bloodthirsty horde. In the film, it is implied that the zombies come from the south, from the desert at the border between the United States and Mexico. This is terrain that undocumented border-crossers must face at the risk of their own lives: thousands of migrants have died there.[46] What we are seeing in *Savageland* could be an invasion of the dead who create and incorporate more dead to add to their numbers. Or, it could be the embodiment of the violence the undocumented endure on their journey and as a result of their status within the United States. It remains open to interpretation. What is certain is that these are monsters that the authorities fail to see and refuse to believe in, ultimately placing all of the blame on the scapegoat Salazar.

*Un*doctrination: "We Don't Need No Education"

In the case of Salazar, his supposed inferiority and lack of power in the eyes of the U.S. courts in which he is tried, and the denial of the photographic proof he created, is based on relations of power that find their roots in the process of colonization and the modern conception of race. The fact that Salazar's conviction and execution takes place within a system of knowledge that cannot accept as reliable any evidence that comes from outside of its own concept of truth and provability can be taken as support for the coloniality of power, as suggested by Quijano. He asserts that globalization, which benefits Eurocentric capitalism, is the culmination of the process that began with the colonization of the Americas, and that therefore the "model of power that is globally hegemonic today presupposes an element of coloniality."[47] Quijano contends that the modern concept of race was based upon supposed differences in biological structure that were manipulated in order to prove superiority of Europeans and inferiority of non-European groups in a way that would allow European colonizers to feel naturally, logically superior. In part this was achieved through the imposition of a Eurocentric concept of temporality. This process was imposed in three stages: the expropriation of the cultural knowledge and production of the colonized group for the benefit of the imperial power; the repression of the production of meaning and symbolic expression of the colonized; and finally, the imposition of the dominant culture to replace the stolen and repressed culture, belief system, and symbolic universe of the marginalized. In this way, "the Europeans generated a new temporal perspective of history and relocated the colonized population, along with their respective histories and cultures, in the past of a historical trajectory whose culmination was Europe."[48] By destroying the means of the continuation of the culture in question, that culture was necessarily relegated to the past, as only a stepping-stone on the way to European world hegemony.

"The imposition of dominant culture," as described above, is an example of epistemic violence and is achieved in part through the educational system, not only during conquest and colonization but in the centuries that followed, in order to cement the place of the colonized into a less "civilized" past and protect the dominance of the colonizing culture. The French film *Zombi Child* addresses this process. The film follows Mélissa, a Haitian student who has moved to France after the 2010 earthquake. She is the only Black student in an elite school exclusively for the daughters of recipients of the Legion of Honor medal. Mélissa's mother apparently was given the award for her work fighting against Duvalier's dictatorship. We first see her in a history class, where the professor is talking about the ideals of the French Revolution and how they led the world at the time but have not since lived up to the goal of providing justice for all. Later, the superintendent tells the girls that their magnificent school is based on "national values" of merit, hard work, and reason. Another teacher asks the students to write about the "consequences of the People's Spring," and Mélissa's aunt, a tutor, teaches a boy about the history of the Roman Empire in terms of the life of Christ. All of these educational snippets that populate the background of the film laud Enlightenment ideals and the dominance of

"Western culture." These are the "colonial legacies, national languages and disciplinary foundations in the education system that teaches us . . . how to think."[49] Meanwhile, Mélissa is asked to join a secret sorority, and as her audition, she recites René Depestre's poem "Cap'tain Zombi," which begins, "Listen up, white world / to my zombie roar!" When she talks about vodou, she describes her family and community and tells the other girls that "vodou is real, and beautiful. Life and death are inseparable." But the girls only have the exploitative Seabrook-style zombies as a reference, after watching a movie called *Voodoo Possession* on their phones when Mélissa is not around. They have too-effectively internalized the narrative of the colonizer. The scenes in France are intercut with scenes from the life of Mélissa's grandfather, who is named Clairvius Narcisse.[50] Clairvius is poisoned and becomes a zombie, but he manages to eat some meat one day in the fields and begins to recover from his zombie state. He wanders the Haitian countryside for decades, until he is recovered enough to return to his wife and family. Mélissa and her aunt (who is a *mambo*) both seem to carry some effects of their patriarch's zombification, carrying it with them as part of their cultural inheritance.[51] When one of the French girls, Fanny, decides to hire Mélissa's aunt to perform a ritual that will cure her of her heartache over a failed affair, her attempt to bend vodou to her own selfish cause is doomed because she doesn't understand the culture. The ceremony appears to have disastrous effects for both Fanny and Mélissa's aunt. In this film we see the toxic effects of the nation-building style of education that represses the production of meaning of the colonized group while imposing and reinforcing the tenets of the dominant culture.

Mélissa's education in France is much more sophisticated than the indoctrination Melanie receives in her prison/school in *The Girl with All the Gifts*.[52] The basic education of the child "hungries" (human-zombie hybrids) in this film consists of content-free recall of facts, since "these are wards of a state that has no interest in their future beyond their utility."[53] Melanie is told the story of Pandora's box by the teacher she loves, a cautionary tale, but one that at least includes the possibility of hope. When Melanie decides to prioritize her mutant generation over the survival of humanity, she keeps that favorite teacher, now locked in a bubble, to teach her and her cohort. But now Melanie is in control, and her education is on her terms. In a sense, she rejects the doctrine of the value of human life above all other lives, and in doing so, *un*doctrinates herself, refusing the narratives of those that would control her, use her, and kill her to save themselves.

Flipping the Script: The Real White Zombies

The experience of indigenous children in Canada exemplifies this culture-destroying relationship between the educational system and marginalized communities. An amendment to the Indian Act in 1894 mandated that First

Nations children attend residential schools, located far from their families, where they would be given a settler-style education. The schools, which were intended to "civilize" indigenous children and suppress the passage of indigenous cultural knowledge from generation to generation through familial separation, didn't see final closure until 1996. This system and the abuse suffered in it by indigenous children had long-lasting, damaging effects on generations of First Nations families. We can see the effects of this process and other methods of biopolitical control of minoritized populations in the recent Canadian film *Blood Quantum*.[54] The title refers to the method of quantifying "Indianness": literally the percentage of "Indian blood" one must have in order to be classified as First Nations. Based on ideas of biological racial differences, it was a system imposed by federal governments in order to control who could and could not consider themselves citizens of a tribe and therefore lay claim to any rights, benefits, or identity that membership implies. The way First Nations choose to use or change that rule today is controversial and carries with it great questions of what it means to be native. On the one hand, it can be seen as a method of preserving a vanishing foundational culture that has suffered genocide in the Americas; on the other hand, it is a problematic tool for controlling populations. Federal governments, seeking to shorten their obligations to Native peoples, assumed that through intermarriage and assimilation, it would take approximately three generations for American Indians to "breed themselves out." Now it appears the law is having exactly that effect, as many Native youth do not qualify for enrollment, though they "speak their language, practice their traditional religion and, in fact, represent the future for their nation."[55] As Breny Mendoza notes in her comparison of decolonial theories, children of mixed European and indigenous parentage were treated differently in North America than in Latin America, where *mestizaje* was created as a category of mixed offspring. Mendoza explains the North American situation by comparing it to the "one drop rule" used to enforce "Blackness" in which even one drop of African blood conferred Black identity (and enslaved status) to children. She indicates that the opposite was true of indigenous populations in settler colonies, in which one drop of White blood erased indigenous identity and conferred Whiteness: "in these racial politics, indigenous blood seems easy to dilute, while African blood is credited with extraordinary polluting powers."[56] These rules existed for the benefit of White settlers and slave owners: all children with any West African blood were added to the supply of slaves, while dilution of the Native community was used to justify the expropriation of their land. Blood quantum laws, effective biopolitical tools that they are, paradoxically attempt to quantify and define indigeneity, while at the same time represent a record of its erasure.

In Barnaby's film, blood quantum is the key to who can survive the zombie pandemic, turning the title of one of the earliest zombie films into a truth: there are only "White zombies"—the disease affects only White people. With this starting point, this director, himself Mi'kmaq, racializes Whiteness and centers indigenous identity. He creates a powerful metaphor of colonization as disease. The film takes place in 1981 (a significant year, as we will explain) in the fictional Mi'kmaq Red Crow reserve, which has been barricaded against the White zombie horde that has destroyed civilization outside of the barricade. The story centers around a family composed of the sheriff of the reserve, Traylor; his ex-wife, Joss; their son, Joseph; Joseph's pregnant White girlfriend, Charlie; and Traylor's half-White son, Lysol, from a previous relationship. Traylor, Joseph, and Charlie are accepting uninfected White refugees from the outside, taking them in and protecting them. Lysol, in a rejection of his White half, resents this dangerous intrusion into their fortress. He is an emotionally tortured character: as a typical outsider he feels his rejection by his father keenly, and he both loves and resents his younger half-brother Joseph for his Mi'kmaq identity and his close relationship with their father. These emotional traumas result in some psychotic behavior, and eventually Lysol's attempt to murder Joseph. Lysol hangs dead-alive zombies around the reserve, dismembered and helpless but still viciously biting at passersby. They are his warning to stay away as well as a warning of what could happen to any White person unwise enough to come near enough to be bitten. Importantly, Lysol is immune to the virus, just like his father. This detail indicates that it is native blood that is more powerful than White blood, indigenous immunity is the dominant trait, and it cannot be erased.

This delicate balance is shattered when, inevitably, a White refugee hides the fact that she has been bitten and eventually infects the 150 refugees inside the reserve. Natives, if not torn limb from limb, flee. They remain immune but have lost their safety and their land. Very few make it to the end of the film. What small ray of hope is implied by the birth of another immune child after Charlie delivers her baby is overshadowed by the fact that her lover, Joseph, must shoot her in the head to keep her from turning into a zombie herself. The symbolism of the White "civilized" world descending into cannibalism and mayhem is powerful, especially when read as the toxicity of a culture built on genocide and violent bloodshed. What matters is that this apocalypse signifies the end of that Eurocentric temporality that was constructed on the ruins of colonized peoples. Here the colonized are placed outside of that history, immune to its effects but forced to deal with its consequences. Before the catastrophe hits the reserve, one character says that the earth was alive, and the Whites never understood that, so She made them into something She could use to destroy them. "Who says we're immune?" he says. "Maybe the Earth just forgot about us." The native peoples are freed from the European temporality in which they had been relegated to the past, but at the same time they have been untethered from their own temporality, through the process of colonization that occurred hundreds of years ago. This so-called zombie apocalypse comes to them hundreds of years after their people's first apocalypse—the arrival of the settlers. In a way, it is a repeat of that original catastrophe. The birth of one more infant, immune to the virus and possessing mixed blood, implies a hope for the future, but at what cost, now that both native and White populations have been ultimately wiped out by the toxic effects of colonialism? This film flips the zombie trope of the horde as marginalized Other on its head by centering the indigenous characters and point of view and exposing the pathology of colonization.

Early in the film, the immune survivors blockade a bridge to protect themselves from the zombies: they set up a zombie-grinding contraption that reduces each zombie that stumbles into it into so much splatter. This scene takes place on the very bridge that was the site of a real act of resistance and, ultimately, state violence when in June 1981 (the same year as the setting of Barnaby's film) there were two raids on the Mi'kmaq people by Quebec provincial police (Sûreté du Québec) in an attempt to limit their fishing rights—while not imposing any limits on commercial fishing companies that fished in the same waters. By the time the second raid started, Mi'kmaq were prepared and blockaded the bridge with trucks and sandbags, supported by other First Nations peoples who traveled to support them. This historical event was recorded in Alanis Obomsawin's 1984 documentary *Incident at Restigouche*, which was an influence on Jeff Barnaby as a child.[57] Obomsawin's documentary opens with an elder explaining that when the raid occurred, he took out an axe and drew a line in the ground that he told the police not to pass. This same spirit of resistance is echoed in *Blood Quantum* in Sheriff Traylor's father, Gisigu, who was the first to notice the zombie virus in a fish caught in those same contested waters. At the end of the film, the old man fights off the last wave of attacking zombies so his grandson can escape. He appears to be taken down by the horde, but later, in an animated sequence, we see him triumphant, holding up a gore-dripping decapitated head, declaring, "None of you are getting past this line!"

We see another interpretation of the pathology of Whiteness in the colonial context in the Australian film *Cargo*.[58] In this film, the indigenous peoples are not immune to the virus but are much more prepared for survival. The film follows Andy (played by Martin Freeman) who is infected with the zombie virus. He has approximately two days before the transformation becomes final, and an infant daughter for whom he must find caretakers within that time. He goes to a hospital to find help only to learn that the funding for this isolated location, serving mostly indigenous Australians, had been cut drastically, and there is not much there. The sole inhabitant, a White teacher, tells Andy that her students are gone, "living in the old ways." She indicates that there are mobs from all over the area coming together, going back to live in their country. There are scenes of them luring mostly White zombies in with loud noises, then

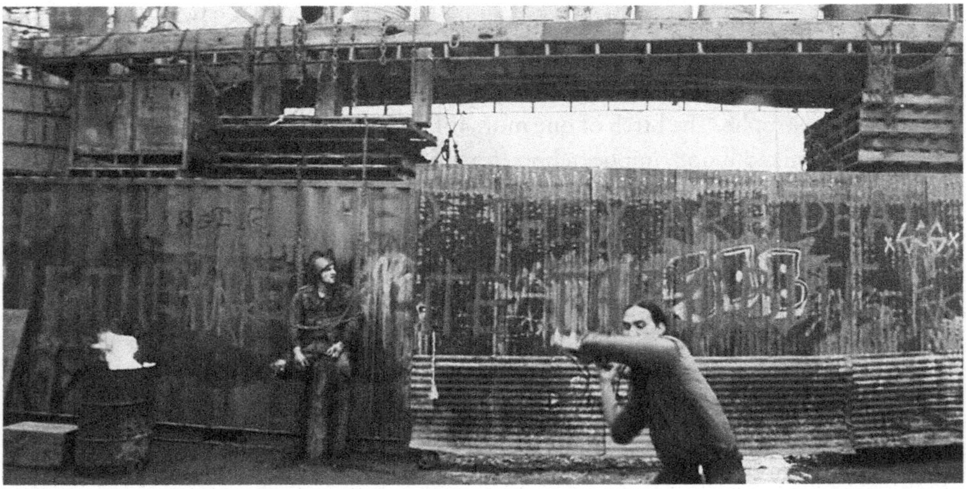

In *Blood Quantum*, Natives build their wall to keep the zombies out. Graffiti reads, "If they're red they are dead, if they're white they bite." (Credit: Jeff Barnaby, *Blood Quantum*, 2019.)

killing them and burning them, cleansing their land of the infection. At first, Andy is reluctant to seek them out, since he doesn't belong to their group. He helps another "white fella," Vic, but quickly learns that Vic is caging healthy indigenous people to attract zombies, who he then kills, stealing anything of value the undead happen to have in their pockets. Vic is hoarding now-useless goods, looking forward to a future in which things have gone "back to normal." He is unable to understand that the neoliberal post-colony Australia no longer exists. He cannot face the reality of the destruction of a culture that he understood, and he reacts with violence. A young indigenous girl, Thoomi, reluctantly begins to trust Andy and promises to take his infant daughter back to her people, where she can survive. The film presents a vision of an indigenous future, one that relies on indigenous knowledge and culture for survival.

Both *Cargo* and *Blood Quantum* cast White characters as carriers of disease and as a racialized group that is less equipped to deal with the virus it is spreading. To close this chapter's exploration on the themes of race, nation, and power in zombie films, we turn to the observations of Nell Irvin Painter upon the election of Donald Trump to the presidency in the United States.[59] As Trump ran on a promise to "Make America Great Again," Painter observes that it was "a phrase whose 'great' was widely heard as 'white.'"[60] She writes that "thanks to the widespread analysis of voters' preferences in racial terms, white identity became marked *as a racial identity*." Explaining that as non-White minorities came to capture higher visibility in popular culture, gaining political power until the election of a Black president with a Black first lady, that the election of Trump was an attempt to "take us back to the time of unmarked Whiteness and racially unmarked power," but that the event had the effect of racially marking Whites. Whites, according to Painter, had traditionally enjoyed a freedom from racial identity, and a focus on individuality, before Trump further marked his followers as a racial group by not explicitly rejecting the support of White nationalists, effectively infecting all his supporters with White nationalism, even those who would vehemently reject that label.

On January 6, 2021, during what should have been a routine formality of the counting of the electoral ballots cast for the presidency of the United States, a horde of insurgents stormed the Capitol building in Washington, D.C., where legislators and the vice president had gathered for the event. The violence and destruction of the riot, which ended in 5 deaths and 140 injured police, were described by two different witnesses who experienced it in zombie terms. Jim Lo Scalzo, a photographer for European Pressphoto Agency said, "all at once, it became like a zombie movie, there were people smashing through doors and windows . . . rampaging through the Rotunda."[61] Kevin Dietsch recalled, "it was like something out of a zombie movie. Where hordes of these rioters just kept coming and coming. It seems like one after another . . . they slowly started coming toward us."[62] The use of the same comparison between the insurgents and a zombie horde shows how deeply we have internalized the tropes of the genre. But the use of the metaphor to describe a violent, politicized group that had been instigated by political agents who fed them a diet of propaganda and lies about a stolen election, including President Trump, who encouraged them to march on the Capitol, is not just a rhetorical device.[63] It is an example of a racialized group who has been intentionally agitated. Some of them believe in apocalyptic conspiracy theories (QAnon) that tell them that their savior (Trump) would enact righteous vengeance against those they perceive as evil, killing them in the public square. *Blood Quantum* and *Cargo*, as films made in (mostly) English-speaking nations that grew out of colonialism, find their echo here. In those films, White zombified characters are tainted with disease, violence, and a failed culture. They are a group that needs to be monitored, and if infected, destroyed. The racialization of the zombie figure, who developed as a metaphor for the victims of the slave trade and colonial capitalism, has come full circle in its many expressions in popular culture and flipped the hegemony of power on its head. Ultimately, the zombie virus doesn't discriminate; it can infect us all.

Zombies begin as reminders of an inhuman past, and as such, embody a decolonizing influence. Imperialism has given way to a globalized capitalism, but the borders between privileged and marginalized spaces continue to be zones of violence and the worst cases of institutionalized bodily harm, whether

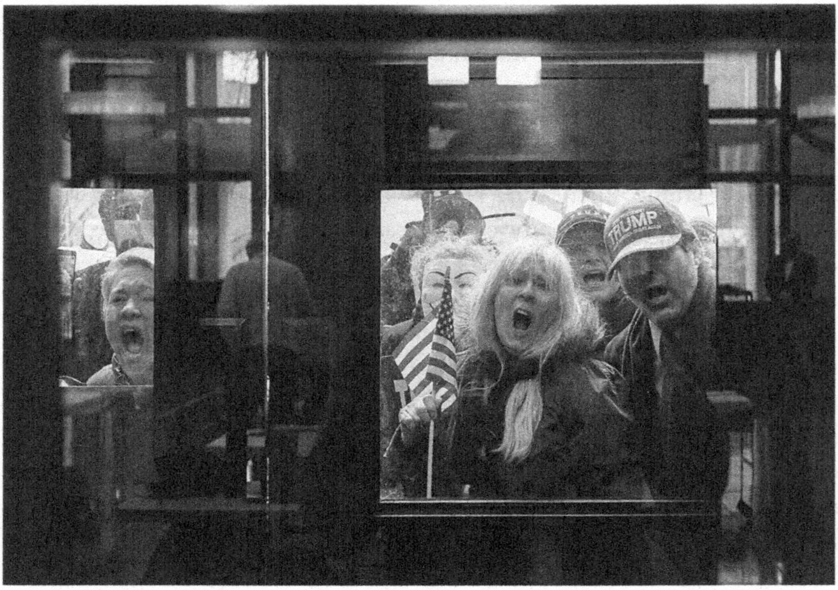

Anti-shutdown protestors at the Ohio Statehouse during the pandemic on April 13, 2020, captured in a photo that echoes classic zombie film imagery. (Credit: © Joshua A. Bickel—USA TODAY NETWORK.)

criminal or state sanctioned. Wealth inequality continues to expand, consigning millions to lives of labor that do not afford them the basic necessities of life. Global conflict and black-market forces conspire to turn living bodies into dead merchandise or cannon fodder in endless wars. The persistence of racialized state violence continues to haunt our reality. The zombie remains, lending flesh to the biopolitical and necropolitical churn, both as an echo of historical violence and a symbol of the continuing state-of-siege mentality, in the actions of nations built on the foundations of colonialism, genocide, and slavery. Born as a result of the worst abuses committed in the building of American nations, the zombie is a symbolic reminder of the infection inherent in the levers of sovereign power that make up the state. Whether the zombies in question are representative of oppressed peoples, whose bodies are acted upon by the state to guarantee its capitalistic and political ends, or the undead remnants of the settler mentality that has transformed the land and poisoned the original inhabitants, the theme of necropolitical power is visible everywhere in the genre. As centuries have passed, the zombie returns, sometimes dormant, to rear back up from a shallow grave ready to mutilate that which is the cause of its condition and expose the emptiness of the state promises of safety and order.

3

Devouring Capitalism

As a result of catering to the interests of capital under neoliberalism, free rein has been given to corporations, giving them an outsized power in the global order as the sovereignty of the nation-state has declined. Human populations have served to feed the interests of multinational corporations through labor forces that become disposable as they are subjected to harmful working conditions, low wages, and a lack of access to health care. This state of affairs has only been amplified by the global pandemic of COVID-19, highlighting the ways in which all nations, their populations, and their economies are intertwined. In the United States, in particular, the failings of neoliberalist capitalism have been exposed by the dire effects they've had on the population. The most truly essential work has been shown to be the labor of the most vulnerable: farm laborers and meat-processing workers—largely immigrant and undocumented laborers—who are underpaid by employers and persecuted by the U.S. administration; warehouse workers deprived of union protections; grocery store staff; public school teachers and administrators; medical and emergency workers; and delivery and public transport drivers. The failings of the nation's profit-based health care system that ties health care to employment have also been exposed, as has the greed of the pharmaceutical and biotech companies who have profited on the bodies of the sick and dying. The effect of shutdowns on the labor market in the context of a weakened economic safety net caused a spike in unemployment; early in the pandemic, failing small businesses are emptied out and boarded up as city streets were abandoned, giving a glimpse of apocalyptic imagery familiar to anyone who knows zombie films.

In the previous chapter we examined the colonial roots of the zombie as a figure and its relation to the enslaved and colonized subjects. The appropriation of the genre for pop cultural profit is a fitting metanarrative of the fate of the original undead creature and a metaphor for the death-in-life that is enslaved labor and existence as human commodity. In this origin story of the zombie we can see the beginnings of its use as an allegory for abused labor forces—as the unpaid, raped, impoverished, and exchanged subject. The cannibalistic shift in the z-narrative in Romero's films intensifies the complexities of meaning embodied by the zombie by adding "rabid consumer" to its field of meaning. As we have seen, recent films use the zombie as a signifier for social unrest (*Juan of the Dead*, *World War Z*) and even as the carrier of the plague of colonialism itself (*Blood Quantum*). In this chapter we hope to trace out these lines of meaning to explore how the ever-growing genre is playing with ideas of neoliberalism, labor, and (quite literal) consumption.

Mabel Moraña begins her discussion of Karl Marx with an analysis of the ways in which his description of capitalist society tends toward the gothic. Marx used the bloodsucking image of the vampire to describe the process by which the minds and bodies of laborers are converted into commodities representing dead labor—"a monstrous, alchemical and dehumanizing process that implies the subordination of the living to the power of the dead."[1] Marx was writing at roughly the same time that vampire literature had captured the European gothic imagination, beginning with the 1819 publication of John William Polidori's *The Vampyre* and culminating with Bram Stoker's *Dracula* in 1897.[2] The vampire, symbolic of a decadent aristocracy that gorged itself on the labors of a captive lower class, is an apt symbol for the workings of Marx's *Capital*.[3] The vampire as representative of the oligarchic rich, reliant on the disposable bodies and lifeblood of the poor, was a menacing figure through which to express the anxiety rooted in this unjust caste system. This fear, inspired by a system in decay, repeats itself in the ebbs and flows of opulent societies in economic distress. The classic cinematic and literary trope of the haunted house, for example, is strongly linked to the image of a Victorian-style mansion, these being the favored "McMansions" of the newly rich during the Gilded Age, proliferating in order to display wealth in their ornate construction and decoration. These homes, abandoned and decaying in the wake of the Great Depression, became associated with terror based on their symbolic link with the death and despair that lingered after economic collapse.[4] Frequently, these rotting husks were converted into rooming houses for the nearly destitute, having fallen from the heights of ostentatious wealth to the reality of the existence of the working poor. Similarly, the tradition of the haunted plantation house vital to the Southern Gothic aesthetic is a symbol of the terror of the enslaved and the cruelty upon which the enslaver's wealth is built and the system that was left in ruins after the Civil War. The continuation of racist systems of displacement of the Black population and the alienation of southerners bereft of the system that buoyed them most likely contributed to the genre.

Zombies at the Market and at Home: Zombie Malls and Abandoned Homes

Our own late twentieth- / early twenty-first-century moment of globalized capitalism and ever-growing wealth disparity might find its own gothic aesthetic in other abandoned physical spaces that once were temples to consumption, privilege, and ostentation but now are falling victim to the changing business models of a bloated economy: the shopping mall. Although shopping malls across the country have been typically occupied by populations of differing backgrounds and economic strata, the common activities of consumption and desire for commodities supported the dream of upward mobility. As brick-and-mortar stores are shuttered across the country, shopping malls are also failing, and an aesthetic of "haunting" images of these vast, empty constructions is forming.[5] Termed "the retail apocalypse," this failure of a cornerstone of the American dream of consumption as the road to happiness and fulfillment has led to the possibility of a new gothic economic disaster.[6] This very setting, the abandoned shopping mall, was presciently and effectively used in Romero's classic 1978 *Dawn of the Dead* and may have contributed to the feeling of dread that accompanies the sight of the abandoned market in the popular imagination. Romero's zombies, deadly as they were to the dwindling survivors, were often played for laughs, going through the motions of their habits in life, shopping for entertainment, driven by faded memories of consumerism. But the small band of survivors, holed up in the mall before the zombies' attack, similarly succumb to the allure of the material, raiding abandoned shops for luxury goods that they could not have afforded before the zombie catastrophe. This blind compulsion to consume forms the basis of Romero's cultural critique: the American consumer, driven to mindlessly feed the soul with the dead labor of empty merchandise, is the (figurative) zombie. Both voracious consumers and the workers who produce merchandise (probably abused, international, and completely unseen at the mall) feed the elites (either by shelling out money to afford the merchandise or producing the goods on subsistence wages) while "feeding" themselves with their objects of desire. In the mall, the zombies can be seen to be taking their revenge, by attempting to replace the stolen vitality of dead labor—symbolically, while returning to the malls where they "fed" in life—and literally, as they consume the bodies of the living humans to continue their "walking dead" existence of meaningless hoarding.

Steven Shaviro has recognized that capitalism "seeks . . . to rationalize and normalize [death], to turn it to economic account" but that Romero's zombies cannot be controlled and put to work, and so they "mark the rebellion of death against its capitalist appropriation."[7] For Shaviro, zombies are not representative of workers but "figures of nonproductive expenditure."[8] In some films and series the zombie pandemic is the result of a marketplace catastrophe in which a desired product has gone horribly wrong,[9] a government-commissioned bioweapon is stolen or misused,[10] or an unrelated vaccine mutates and endangers the planet.[11] Even when this is the case, the ravenous consumers that result from the capitalist disaster are helpless slaves to their own desires—once desirous of merchandise, they now seek to consume human flesh. This is representative of the ways even participants in capitalism are used by the system to perpetuate itself, and the ultimate fruitlessness of a system whose end point is the swallowing up of resources with no view toward their replacement. The monstrous quality of the system is shown in the decaying corpses who are never satisfied, always in a desperate rage of consumption, until all are infected and nothing remains. The z-narrative, if played out to its tragic ends, provides no solution to the problem of supply and demand: supply will run out and demand remains unfulfilled. This is an end to which we are immediately propelled in a zombie pandemic. Society and all the sophisticated systems that are in place to protect civilized commerce breaks down: communication, transportation, and monetary and supply chains abruptly end and a savage battle for resources immediately replaces them, in a man-eat-man world. It is free market capitalism taken to its cannibalistic extreme.

The retail space as a location for the zombie showdown has been replayed in countless films and television adaptations: where shots of shambling zombies approximate the brain-dead consumers of hollow merchandise, searching for items that will "feed" their existence. Aside from Romero's *Dawn of the Dead*, Jim Jarmusch's 2019 film *The Dead Don't Die* shows recently turned zombies wandering in and out of abandoned stores, mumbling the names of the products and commodities they wanted most in life.[12] The retail space also is useful as a plot point in many films: the survivors, now driven out of their homes and starving, are forced to break into the abandoned market and sift through the often ruined or rotting merchandise for usable supplies to sustain bare life and must contend with the hungry dead that occupy those spaces. In other films, the zombie emergency inspires a variety of marketplace reactions: for example, survivors may protect themselves through consumption of product (the supermarket panic in Argentina's *Phase 7*) or may offer entrepreneurial mercenary services (*Juan of the Dead*).[13] The fight for survival immediately becomes a fight for resources, and most frequently, survivors are pitted against other survivors in this fight. The Romero-esque trope of zombies at the mall reappear in numerous films and contains equal parts horror and comedy, taunting the modern consumerist viewer with the meaninglessness of the pursuit of accumulation of goods in what has become a ridiculous shopping mall context. These examples cross national and cultural boundaries and include Hong Kong's *Bio-Zombie* (*Sang Faa Sau See*) and Japan's *I Am a Hero*.[14]

But the mall is far from the only communal or public space to appear in zombie films as plot points. Recent zombie films have expanded the use of symbolic public spaces that add interesting commentary to the contrast of that empty signifier of humanity—the undead—with spaces that we connect to modern life, success, and enjoyment. For example, *Warm Bodies* depicts a zombie population that occupies an abandoned airport—once the symbol of global connection, movement of freight, and freedom and ease of movement for those who could afford it.[15] Now the airport is filled with bodies that simply wander about, going nowhere, accomplishing nothing. Emphasizing the metaphor for the emptiness of modern life in capitalism, the zombie narrator, in voice-over, remembers a time when "everyone could express themselves, and express their feelings, and just enjoy each other's company," over a flashback image of crowds of people silently bent over their devices, ignoring the humanity around them while in thrall to that one great commodity that serves as an empty "black mirror" of the modern soul, the smartphone. While this sight-gag is played for laughs, it is a reminder that the modern subject is already a zombie, compelled to feed from the empty rewards of social media to satisfy the hunger for belonging.

The empty domestic space is also a trope that appears again and again in the zombie narrative. Abandoned suburban housing developments become a space where monsters lurk and survivors shelter, among the discarded possessions of the former residents. When society collapses and humanity disappears, all that is left are these husks, monuments of day-to-day existence that no longer retain any meaning. Aarón Rodríguez Serrano also points out that, especially in films appearing after the global financial crisis of 2007–2008, the house "has gone from being the domestic space *par excellence* to the ultimate emblem of the crisis," due to its simultaneous relationship with both traditional connotations of safety and familial permanence and the reason for the endangerment of that safety and permanence—the housing crisis of 2008.[16] When whole neighborhoods emptied out in response to the inhabitants' inability to pay the inflated prices they had borrowed to pay for their homes, "ghost town" suburban areas were filled with the shambles of "middle class" daily life. The empty houses that appear as temporary refuge/scavenging grounds in films like *Warm Bodies* and series like *The Walking Dead* and *Black Summer* display some of this haunted quality, revealing evidence of lives upended and abandoned in crisis.[17] In other cases, the lure of the defunct domestic space proves difficult to abandon: in the French film *The Night Eats the World* (*La nuit a dévoré le monde*),[18] the lone survivor of an overnight zombie apocalypse never ventures out of the Paris apartment he was in when it happened. Instead, he systematically clears nearby apartments of flesh-eaters while scavenging among the possessions left behind to create the daily routine of his survival. This dependence on his domestic space and the things within it are a sort of death. He will not actually be living until he ventures out of his (relatively) comfortable isolation and confronts the possibility of dying while pursuing a real life, one that includes a search for other survivors. He will need to sever his relationship to the abandoned domestic space and its collection of quotidian objects to continue some semblance of life in the world.

The need for survivors to defend and inhabit spaces like abandoned homes and shopping malls also feeds the need for a feeling of normalcy under catastrophic circumstances, according to John Edgar Browning. He points out that groups of survivors can successfully inhabit these "survival spaces" when working together, but "are drawn into self-destruction, typically after one or more of the group's members attempts to re-privatize the enclosure."[19] Therefore, the need for private ownership, to maintain one's connection to possession, is what causes their demise. Browning also notes that in the post-millennium, z-narratives have more often set their bands of survivors to move from place to place as nomads, having freed themselves from the spaces of domesticity and consumerism that once were the definition of normalcy. The arc of the protagonist of *The Night Eats the World* is a fine representation of this process of letting go of the material comforts of home in order to find some kind of hope. But the need to consume and possess sometimes appears to linger, as we shall see, even after death.

This persistent relationship with objects that represent the ruins of modern life appears to much different effect in the 2017 film *Ravenous*.[20] This film's band of survivors are in rural Quebec, and they, like all survivors, find the need to acquire and accumulate items that will help them to survive as they attempt to flee to what they hope will be a safer existence in the city. But it is the film's zombies who retain a particular relationship to the things they and their victims have left behind. These Quebecois zombies retain uniquely human reactions to being hurt and attacked. They cry out when injured and their vocalizations express a rage and sadness not frequently heard in zombie cinema. Additionally, they appear to be collectors of things, the common items of their previous human existence, out of which they fashion huge totemic sculptural towers. They are creating categorized piles of now-useless objects: a pile of chairs, for example, a tower of televisions, a smaller pile of discarded toys. They are often seen stumbling about with objects in their hands: a doll, a wooden chair. These zombies then gather, somewhat reminiscent of the classic horde stumbling through a mall, around the base of these object-towers, apparently mesmerized.

This fascinating detail is never explained or addressed explicitly in the film. Is the act a function of memory, an inexplicable worship of the items they have

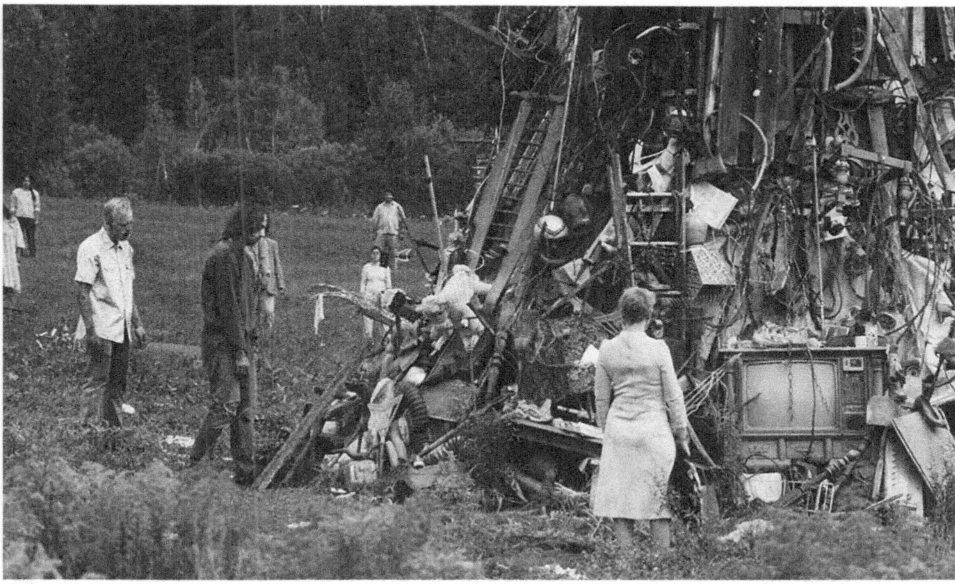

Ravenous zombies create their towers of discarded objects. (Credit: Robin Aubert, *Ravenous* (*Les affamés*), 2017.)

accumulated throughout their modern lives of acquisition and consumerism? Are these items a totem to their lived pasts that they are unable to let go and yet are incapable of understanding? Are they building traps for their prey, attracting them with what they perceive to be most appealing and important to them, these end products of dead labor, so the living will be tempted and can be ambushed, attacked, and consumed in their turn? These items that can no longer be used by the living dead who collect them are just as dead as the zombies: an object's usefulness declines precipitously when there are no longer human hands available to use it—the objects have become useless, empty signifiers of what they once were. They are the surplus rubble of a destroyed community based on a capitalism that can no longer survive beyond the breakdown of the social contract of exchange and use of objects and capital. Peter Schwenger, explaining Walter Benjamin's views on ownership of objects, describes a kind of paradox of possession, in which objects, "absorbing the psychic investments of their owners, . . . paradoxically possess something of their possessors." The owner of the objects "lives in them," as Benjamin asserts, which has the effect of objectifying the person, who becomes little more than "the sum of his objects."[21] Further, he relates this objectification to the concept of *vanitas*, a reminder of the inevitability of death and the "futility of amassing material things, and of the Last Things that await everyone."[22] The zombie is humanity reduced to its objectified form, the corpse that used to house a consciousness, but now is the reanimated biological debris of a life once lived. Here we see hints of the zombie as dedicated consumer of things, who, like Benjamin's rag-picker, repurposes the fragments of abandoned lives, concerned with "the salvation of objects and people from the oblivion of forgetting," perhaps sensing a bit of humanity's obsolescence.[23] However, the towers that are built by the zombies in *Ravenous* are collected and assembled by beings that no longer have the power to own things or to use them. They merely stand and stare at this lost debris of participation in life, family, and society, experiencing a sort of zombie nostalgia.

(Dis)Possessions

In chapter 1, in our discussion of zombies as persons versus things, we pointed out, following Robert Esposito, that Roman laws regarding rights of possession were central to who or what can participate in personhood.[24] Dawn Keetley, following Hardt and Negri, points out that humanity is still tightly bound to the idea of property: having property defines the condition of being a "free individual" in the West, and we exercise proprietary rights over our own bodies.[25] We not only own property but we also are (our own) property. She points out that in the z-narrative, the zombie's loss of selfhood coincides with its loss of property, and that both are felt to be equally catastrophic. She connects this "propertyless multitude" with the response common to the human survivors in zombie narratives: that of claiming, hoarding, and defending new property from other humans who are in the same dire straits as they.[26] Keetley notes that this same violent struggle to claim property in the postapocalyptic reality is what brings out the monstrous in humans, who risk losing their so-called humanity in their efforts to survive. Altruism is rarely seen in zombie narratives, and when it is indulged, it is frequently paid back in violence, an exaggeration of the neoliberalist idea that the requirements of the market trump the value of human life and human relations.

The link between humanity and ownership of commodities resemanticizes the abandoned malls and suburban spaces full of objects that have lost their value. The zombie malls are the physical world's echo of filmic zombie hordes—empty and purposeless, wasted space and capital that is haunted by the passion plays of desire for material goods that used to occur there. This link also strengthens the connection of the zombie multitudes to the poor, the other, the literally dispossessed and marginalized, and the process of dehumanization that the allegory entails. Zombies are usually depicted outside, in the streets or lurching through the landscape, unless they are trapped in what used to be their home or enter a large public space (such as a mall or a train station) to hunt. They require no shelter; they are no longer subject to the discomfort of extremes of temperature and are no longer afraid to roam in the night, as time and the rhythms of life have lost all meaning. In *Seoul Station*, the very first to fall to the virus that will later spread to the business commuters in *Train to Busan* (*Busanhaeng*) are the homeless people who gather in the underground station at night.[27] They are already halfway to being zombies (in the perception of those who walk past them during the commute), having no personal property and possessing no domestic space of their own, and are therefore more vulnerable to the infection. Later in the film, human survivors set themselves up in luxurious model apartments, which are in pristine condition because their purpose is not to house people but to be useless and empty and to advertise the idea of status that wealth can confer to the upper classes of the city. The protagonist, Hye-Sun, is delighted to have found such a place, having struggled all her life in desperate poverty. The space is beautifully depicted in this animated film, but its emptiness confers an eerie quality, with echoing hallways and gothic shadows adding to the possible dangers that may be around each corner. Unfortunately, it is there, in the setting she always had dreamed of one day occupying, that Hye-Sun is subjected to a danger far greater than the infection from which she has fled. The man she went there to meet, thinking it was her estranged father, turns out to be her murderous pimp. The film thus enacts a common theme in modern zombie films, that we, the living, are the greater monsters. After she becomes a zombie and murders her tormentor, she will lose all pleasure she may have taken in her surroundings, and we can assume she will return to the streets to join the other infected creatures.

If possessing makes us human, the act of being possessed gives meaning to objects as well, while dispossession strips away meaning. As Keetley notes, the zombie has not only lost its possessions but has also lost "property in itself," having lost its selfhood. These dispossessed undead hordes have no rights to property and are actively antagonistic toward property and the humans who claim it. This possession of the self becomes important when we discuss the market value of the human body, both living and, especially, dead. The original Haitian vodou zombie lore has clear connections to the practice of dehumanizing capitalist forces that considered humans to be property and is, in fact, a rebellion against it. The consideration of the market value of the human slave is the most obscene version of profiting from human life and death, but echoes of that consideration exist throughout the practices of global capitalism. The value of the living body is evident in Marxist analysis of a workforce that, having no access to the means of production, is underpaid for labor (life force that is used to create merchandise or provide services) but whose life force continues to be devalued over the life of the product, which comes to represent "dead labor." Herein lies the basis for Marx's vampiric allegory: the lifeblood of the working class is sucked away by the owners of the means of production to hoard it into their own fat stores. Though in industrialized, and now postindustrial, society, the labor force is not literally, legally the property of the business owner—we can say that they are, at least, owners of themselves and are considered to be persons, endowed with rights. However, as their labor is always paid in less than the value that can be gleaned for their product on the market, as their labor is stolen in a context in which they are powerless to demand fair pay, can we really say that they are owners of their own life force and vitality? Zombies then become representative of bodies that have been emptied of their life force and have been reduced to the hunger for what has been stolen from them. They are, of course, monstrous, being a threat to the status quo and upending the market itself. They render possessions meaningless and invalidate the personhood of the human participant in a society in which humanity is predicated on possession. They are a grotesque mirror for a frivolous materialist humanity and a reminder that the end will come for each and every one.

This scenario of materialist revenge of the exploited dead upon the living beneficiaries of society takes place in a genre that often foregrounds matters of race, gender, and class as part of the zombie narrative.[28] The earliest Hollywood zombie films focused on the lives of the rich landowners and depicted the Haitian zombie as a phenomenon of the (ex-slave) laboring class. Romero's fourth *Dead* film, *Land of the Dead*, adapted the class distinction for a modern, American context.[29] The human survivors, occupying and defending the city of Pittsburgh, are divided between the rich, who live in a luxury tower complex called "Fiddler's Green" (a traditional Irish name for a pleasant afterlife), while the rest of the survivors live in squalor. Any attempt to organize these poor survivors is put down ruthlessly by Paul Kaufman, the plutocrat that controls the city. The zombies occupy the suburbs and rural areas outside the city, where the humans scavenge for supplies, while some zombies are captured and used for entertainment and as violent weapons: a sex worker is forced into a cage match with zombies as punishment for helping the political organizer, Mulligan. When Kaufman is killed, the poor are led to safety by the rabble-rousing Mulligan. The exurban zombies who invaded the city, led by an African American zombie who appears to be regaining his intelligence and consciousness, allow the survivors to go free. In this film, the villains are not the undead but those humans who hoard wealth for themselves, shutting out poor survivors and zombies alike.

Zombies in Service: Repurposing the Dead

There are several films that feature zombies who are trained for menial labor and represent an unwilling and completely unpaid working underclass. While their physical exertions are bought and sold for profit, they are also tightly controlled as a possible source of danger, should their strength be turned against their masters. The final scene of *Shaun of the Dead* gives us a hint of what commercial uses zombies can be put to, such as subjects of exploitative *COPS*-style and reality-spectacle television shows and "recruitment for the service industry."[30] Japan's *Miss Zombie*, far from being a comedy in the vein of *Shaun*, depicts a poor creature that is bought by a wealthy family as a domestic servant, and thus is literally enslaved.[31] *Fido*, on the other hand, shows an institutionalized zombie labor market (used for gardening, door attendants, delivery, and babysitting), each zombie controlled by an electronic collar that deters its aggression.[32] Similarly, the Swedish short film *The Unliving* (*Återfödelsen*) depicts a zombie workforce (from menial servitude to talented entertainers) that is controlled through devices implanted in their brains.[33] In this system mercy killings of the infected are forbidden since mercy would involve the destruction of capital: the zombie body. The grotesquerie of these productive corpses synthesizes their function as exploited labor class, dispossessed poor, and existential other while exhibiting the traces of the literal and figurative violence that placed them there. They embody the useful object of the bourgeoisie while being an ugly reminder of the futility of objects and of the very act of possessing them.

According to Marx, the capitalist is able to turn "past, materialised, and dead labour into capital, into value big with value, a live monster that is fruitful and multiplies."[34] He writes that "capital is dead labor, that, vampire-like, only lives by sucking living labour, and lives the more, the more labor it sucks."[35] We can see the effects of this capital vampire embodied in the corpse of the zombie, that has been sucked dry by monstrous capital, especially in the context of industrialized societies that have mechanized labor and devalued the importance of the laborer. Like the objects collected in towers in *Ravenous*, the manual laborer is in danger of becoming emptied of its significance, becoming zombie. James Tyner has argued that "the relations between labor and capital necessarily inform the relations between life and death," and indeed we can see an antagonistic relation between the demands of capitalism and the conditions needed for the sustaining of life, brought about by the diminishment of the value of labor, which point to the emergence of what he calls *necrocapitalism*. "Capital values those bodies deemed both *productive* (e.g., in a position to generate wealth) and *responsible*, with responsibility conceived of as the ability to participate fully as producers and consumers in the capitalist system. . . . Those individuals who are deemed nonproductive or redundant, based on an economic bioarithmetic, are disproportionately vulnerable and increasingly disallowed life to the point of premature death."[36] Tyner here updates the necropolitics of slavery as proposed by Mbembe with a necroeconomics that devalues the life of workers without the obvious, extreme dehumanizing cruelty inherent in slavery. It is a commodification of death, in that "those conditions that facilitate death [are] being increasingly recognized as sites of capital accumulation."[37] It is a necroeconomics that also devalues the life of every member of the economic system, to the extent that every participant can be used to feed the machine.

The 2018 award-winning[38] short horror-comedy film *Zombied*[39] illustrates the bleak situation of the lower rungs of essential workers by precisely equating it with zombie existence, providing pointed commentary while clocking in at only fifteen minutes. The protagonist, Jordan, hates her job as a grocery clerk at Priced-less Supermarket. Complaining of low pay, lack of vacation time, and generally bad treatment, she says, "We deserve to be treated like people." Her co-worker admonishes her that this job is all the low-skilled laborer ("highschoolers and burnouts") can hope for, and that the job only requires "compliance, silence, and servitude." After being attacked and bitten by a zombie on an unauthorized smoke break, Jordan experiences what the film sets up as the six stages of zombiehood: denial, hunger, festering, brains, acceptance, and reintegration. As she realizes she must succumb to her ravening hunger for human flesh, she remains human enough to reject the idea of eating the deliciously chubby baby of a store customer or one of her beleaguered colleagues. Instead, she rushes out behind the strip mall and attacks a homeless man sleeping among the garbage bags, indicating that this man is essentially disposable, sacrificing the only human she can find that ranks below her position in capitalism. The film quickly jumps ahead to the aftermath and reintegration step of her journey. In voice-over (Jordan appears to have lost the capacity for speech, and any speech would be impeded by the Hannibal Lecter–style mask all zombies must now wear to protect society from their bites), we hear Jordan explain that after the outbreak and vaccine, society needed to contend with the zombie question. A zombie rights campaign was founded, and Jordan has finally won the workplace respect she desired all along, having been given more credit for subpar work, a raise, and even being named Employee of the Month. The rights that she was not able to demand in the capitalist context, being a living and opinionated being who participated in the workplace, have been conferred upon her only when she is dead, silenced, and can be expected never to ask for more than that of which she is deemed to be worthy. Though the market demands the labor and life-energy of a human being to be able to function, it really prefers the source of that labor be an interchangeable corpse, but reanimated: the zombie is again the perfect laborer.

In comparison with *Zombied*, the earlier full-length film *Fido*, presents a much darker vision of a zombie labor force, despite also falling within the genre of horror-comedy. It opens with a propaganda reel reminiscent of 1950s-era educational film, being shown in the classroom where Timmy, the protagonist, is a student. The reel promotes ZomCon, the company that organizes society and keeps all the (living) occupants safe in special planned cities that keep out the zombies that roam the "wild zones" outside the fences. The company has been able to control flesh-eating zombies with "domestication collars" that can be manipulated with a remote control to deliver painful electric shocks as punishment. The film declares, "Thanks to ZomCon, we can all become productive members of society, even after death," and promises "a better life through containment!" All appearances point to ZomCon being the highest authority, a company that has replaced government and appears to control the life and death of all the occupants of the town. Death is a constant in this place, and ZomCon sells expensive funerals "to those who can afford it" that provide separate "head coffins" that ensure a permanent rest after death. These funerals provide a way for the richest families to ensure that their bodies will not be exploited posthumously, and since they are being provided by the very same company that threatens to profit from their corpses, they amount to an elaborate form of extortion.

Though life in Willard is a lovely well-groomed version of a 1950s ideal, death is ever-present. While the dead help the children as crossing guards, milkmen, and newspaper delivery in this suburban heaven, the young learn how to kill zombies in Outdoor Education, singing, "In the brain and not the chest / Headshots are the very best." Timmy's father, Bill, is obsessed with ZomCon funerals and has spent all the family's savings ensuring that he, his wife, Helen, and Timmy each will get one. In fact, when his wife becomes pregnant and tries to tell him about the new life, his mind goes immediately to death, "I just don't think on my salary I can afford another funeral." Meanwhile, ZomCon holds the necropolitical power of life and death. It will sell you a domesticated zombie, but if you allow it to malfunction and hurt someone, the company will repurpose it (one character says it would never waste a good zombie) and send you out to the wild zone to become one yourself, appropriating your home and belongings. The elderly are treated with suspicion and fear: the retirement home is in the old prison building, since age is a physical condition that brings one closer to death and the elderly must be vigilantly surveilled. Life is devalued unless it is in support of production or consumption of capital in a film that eerily seems to presage some of the discussions around the elderly as a vulnerable and disposable population in the age of COVID-19.[40]

Corpse Economies: The Dead as Commodity

The materiality of the human body, that being the only element of the body left after death, is key to understanding its long history as an object of value. David McNally's work on the subject traces the connection between monster stories such as *Frankenstein*, vampire lore, and zombie film and the anxieties that arise from the commodification of human labor.[41] McNally writes of the corpse-economy of England from the sixteenth century onward, explaining how those who refused to work for wages but instead resorted to theft, poaching, or vagrancy could be penalized by imprisonment or corporal punishment, which included the phenomenon of "punitive dissection."[42] Those bodies that were available for dissection by anatomists included hanged criminals, abandoned bodies of the poor, even those that were unclaimed after being subject to violence, which led to outright murder in order to produce or sell a body, particularly in the case of street youths. This led to a movement by the working class to save the bodies of the executed and otherwise protest against this corpse-economy. McNally strongly ties this culture of grave robbing to the publication of Mary Shelley's *Frankenstein* as an expression of the fears that were rampant at the time, which included exploitation of the poorest segment of the population at the hands of the landed class, and in pursuit of a scientific power of life over death. This element of class struggle in British history is evident in the 1966 Hammer film *The Plague of the Zombies*, which was released a scant two years before Romero revolutionized the genre.[43] The obviously decaying zombies of *The Plague of the Zombies*, which reach out to attack and maul humans, may be seen as an interim stage between the mostly harmless, hypnotized zombies of *White Zombie* and Romero's *Living Dead* films that introduced the cannibalistic element. In *The Plague of the Zombies*, young, working-class men are sickening and dying of a mysterious illness. The antagonism between the families of the dead and the landowning squire of the village is evident throughout the film. We discover that this aristocrat, having spent significant time in Haiti, has learned to create zombies and that there is no plague—he is robbing the graves of those he has "killed" through ritual in order to create a workforce for his shuttered tin mine, which was deemed too dangerous for human laborers. In this case, the bodies of the poor are being stolen and their labor converted into capital; they produce tin for their master.

This power of life and death that the rich and powerful wield over the poor to make live or to allow to die is the basis for theories of biopolitical power. As we have seen, James Tyner explains in his bioeconomic terms the way in which capital denies life to the working class and to the poor, whose well-being will be endangered by lack of regulation of economic power. Tyner in fact argues that "premature death is an intrinsic, systemic condition of necrocapitalism" since neoliberalism values profit and "health" of a corporation over the physical requirements of its workers, as well as over the lives of the society at large, the poorest of which will be hardest hit by the market's failure to comply with safety and environmental regulation.[44] This necrocapitalism finds its extreme expression in what Sayak Valencia calls *gore capitalism*, in which spectacularized violence and death itself are the end products in a neoliberal system. She locates this gore capitalism in border spaces: areas where extreme wealth encounters zones of extreme poverty, and which move the allowance of premature death into the active performance of violence upon the body to produce capital—the corpse as capital and the commodification of mutilation and murder. It is a "capitalism that simultaneously produces capital and destroys bodies, a capitalism founded on the speculation of bodies-as-commodities" that trades in narcotrafficking, human trafficking, a black market in organ sales, and murder as a method of intimidation and consolidating power, as well as murder-for-hire.[45] Gore capitalism refers to a dystopian market that mirrors the logic of accepted neoliberal market strategies. It is driven by hunger (desire) and spreads like a virus, one that Valencia indicates radiates from the United States. "The US takes its culture to every corner of the globe through technology, mass media, networking, advertising, and consumption; creates consumerist desires even in those places where it is difficult to satisfy those desires legally; and strengthens and reinforces the Market as the New Nation that *unites us*."[46] This desire is carried globally through the information bloodstream. Like contagion, corporations know no borders. It is created by neoliberalism in the global poor that occupy what the First World[47] sees as "*Spare-Part-Factory-Countries*," useful as sources of cheap labor.[48] The hunger for the consumption of that which cannot be obtained within acceptable methods, therefore, creates a criminal class that will resort to violence to satisfy its voracious urges, especially in a context in which legal satisfaction is not available. Valencia warns that we must pay attention to this form of capitalism that, as she says, exists in "so-called Third World countries as well as throughout Eastern Europe," but also encourages us to be less exoticizing in our approach, mapping out "conceptual bridges" to include the ways she warns it is already affecting, and will continue to affect, the centers of power.[49] In addition to the borders between supposed First and Third World nations, there exist other liminal spaces that can function as border spaces—borders between the rich and the poor (as the commuter station in *Seoul Station*) and between urban and exurban spaces (as in *Land of the Dead*). In both of these we see also symbolic use of high and low spaces, those that live in towers and those underground.

The 2011 Spanish/Cuban film *Juan of the Dead* (*Juan de los muertos*) features a satirical commentary on gore capitalism.[50] *Juan of the Dead* explores the Cuban context, which is very different than the Mexico/U.S. border, but still a place where poverty can inspire the kind of hunger that Valencia references.[51] Juan (Alexis Díaz de Villegas) and his buddy Lázaro (Jorge Molina) are petty criminals who make their marginal living just outside of the law. Juan calls himself a "harvester" of opportunity, who has been able to get by without working by selling black market whiskey and stealing stereos from cars. He is content, though those around him dream of migrating for a "better" life, having fallen prey to some of that desire for what U.S.-style capitalism might provide. When the zombies arrive in Cuba, their advent is not explained. They appear to be coming from the sea, in a reverse migration pattern, perhaps from the United States (like a plague of materialism), perhaps from elsewhere, but they are outsiders. The government broadcasts regarding the phenomenon put the blame on U.S. evil influence and describe the zombies as rioters and outside agitators, dissidents and insurgents. Juan and Lázaro, along with their adult children and a couple of their friends, Primo and China, take the opportunity to become entrepreneurs of violence, starting a zombie-disposal business: "*Juan de los muertos, matamos a tus seres queridos.*"[52]

Valencia points out that the *endriago* subjects of gore capitalism, though performing dystopic and violent actions, cannot necessarily be seen as *illegitimate* in the context of neoliberalism.[53] Entrepreneurs identify an opportunity and organize a business in order to enter the economy, and "in this definition of entrepreneur, based on following neoliberal logic, we find no restrictions on the type of companies the entrepreneur can create."[54] This new business the gang creates represents the most traditionally successful moment in their lives, and they all have quite a talent for this exhilarating labor. In fact, they become so comfortable with this blood-soaked work they sometimes leave human non-zombie casualties in their wake: Lázaro kills an uninfected neighbor because he owed him money; when they inadvertently kill one of their customers, Juan's only concern is being paid; they leave an elderly man to die because they need his wheelchair to transport crates of stolen rum (sacrificing the disabled/aged in favor of capital). And when Juan finally must kill China, who has turned zombie, he appears to take a grotesque delight in smashing her head to bits. Before the zombie invasion, Juan seemed content, but this catastrophe gives him the chance to have more economic security, prove himself a good father figure and provider to his estranged daughter, and advance his position in society. We see him and Lázaro, relaxing in their usual spot on the roof of their building after a day of gruesome work, and when a building collapses in front of them (in a scene eerily reminiscent of 9/11), they only notice that their view has improved. The destruction around them, the infection on the island, and the opportunity to mutilate bodies for money, have given them the life they have always desired but could not achieve otherwise—a life that includes leisure, status, and economic advantage. Finally, the gang of survivors fashions a ramp out of a pile of corpses to clear the wall and escape the island in their amphibious vehicle, literally launching their futures from a mound of the bodies they killed. Juan stays behind, saying he'll be alright, he likes it here. Before the credits roll, we see him perched upon a gory mountain of the dead, facing down a new horde, and leaping toward the camera to attack, literally throwing himself into his bloody work.

How Zombies Bite Back: Hauntology and Necroactivism

Juan of the Dead is an aggressive satire: a Cuban film that satirizes socialism and capitalism and is ultimately anti-imperialist and iconoclastic.[55] Juan is the (anti)hero in this film, and the comedic performance by Alexis Díaz de Villegas is charming and relatable; we remain on his side throughout. While this allows us to refrain from passing moral judgment on his actions, he and his band of *violence specialists* are missing one element of gore entrepreneurship that Valencia defines as key to understanding gore capitalism: the performance of cruelty to inspire terror (which is transferred from the bodies undergoing mutilation into those that are spectators of this violence) and ensure intimidation (which converts the graphically injured body into the commodity itself, due to its role in the accumulation of power). Juan is indeed turning corpses into profit, but most of them are already (un)dead. We see the most extreme version of this type of violence among rival bands of survivors in the genre who torture and mutilate the living in order to accumulate power: for example, the characters Negan and the Governor in *The Walking Dead* television series, *Land of the Dead*'s Paul Kaufman, or the members of Unit 631 in *Peninsula* (Sang-ho Yeon's follow-up to *Train to Busan*).[56] In these cases, the zombie outbreak has converted the world into a vast "Third World," where no effective currency exists to regulate economic power and these characters take advantage of their talent for gore to establish themselves as the chieftains of the new dystopia. Another example of gore capitalism is present in the Mexican film *Tigers Are Not Afraid* (*Vuelven*), which deals explicitly with narco-violence and human trafficking in an unnamed Mexican city, and the children who are orphaned by that violence.[57] These dead are the same ones that Valencia identifies as the victims of "the necropolitical commercialization of murder": their dead bodies *are* the commodity.[58] The spectacularization of disemboweled, dismembered corpses, the rivers of blood they leave in the street, are used to consolidate and maintain power in a show of necroempowerment.[59] We consume the spectacle of death as part of the market of the media, news reports, and cultural production. We internalize the meaning of the gore aspect for, as Valencia has said, "The message written on the body of another is a message for oneself, is it not?"[60] In the film the members of the cartel pursue the children of murdered victims because they have stolen a phone that contain photos and videos of murder—the visual representation of these deaths is the currency that is in most demand. Though the film is not what we would traditionally deem a zombie film, having no threat of contagion or outbreak narrative, its ghosts include briefly reanimated corpses who lure the head of the drug cartel to his death. They are reminiscent of the spectral zombie horde in *Savageland*, an economically exploited population of disposable and easily replaced surplus labor that appears to be moving north to wreak havoc in the power centers of the United States.[61] We can see these examples in *hauntological* terms, or the social and political effects of haunting.[62] Avery Gordon asserts that haunting lays bare the mediations between the individual and the institutions and social structures in which they exist: "in haunting, organized forces and systemic structures that appear removed from us make their impact felt in everyday life in a way that confounds our analytic separations and confounds the social separations themselves."[63] Hauntings lay bare the framework that is the context for trauma, by being a relentless reminder. The presence of the dead in *Tigers Are Not Afraid* or in *Savageland* is a revenant memento of those whose bodies have become the source for the economic advancement of another (gore capitalism) and the dispossessed surplus labor of the migrant world. The violence of their (first) demise is repeated as the specter of fear that traces the violence enacted for the sake of the market. In *Savageland* they are spectral zombies, unable to be captured in Salazar's photographs, but which leave a trail of gore to mark the violence they impose on the population of Sangre de Cristo. In *Tigers Are Not Afraid*, they are fleshy ghosts, like zombies; they are terrifying in their grotesque corpse-like appearance and, though not cannibalistic, still able to destroy the man who tormented them.

The French/Senegalese film *Atlantics* (*Atlantique*) plays on this hauntological presentation of the zombie while also taking it back to its pre-Romero, and even pre-Haitian, origins.[64] Sarah Juliet Lauro traces the historical and etymological origins and development of the zombie and theorizes that though it is impossible to trace the exact origins of the myth, it may have its oldest seeds in the belief in "soul capture" hailing from West Central Africa.[65] The zombie-like figures in *Atlantics* are not the soulless bodies of the dead but rather living women temporarily possessed by the souls of their dead partners; therefore, they are more similar to the earliest version of the zombie, whose actions are compelled by another. The film begins at a building site in Dakar, where young construction workers have come to demand pay that has been withheld from them for months. They are mostly young men, who haven't made families of their own yet but who work to help support their parents—not only is their future at stake but also the well-being of the prior generation. The tower they have helped to construct is the only high-rise in the area, and it looms over the Atlantic coastline—again, the high-rise representing the unreachable heights of wealth to which these men contribute but can never achieve for themselves, especially since their labor has gone unpaid. In desperation, the whole crew of young men set out to illegally emigrate to Spain to find work. The Atlantic Ocean is a presence in the film: though it is the opposite of the hostile terrain of the Sonoran Desert the migrants must have crossed in *Savageland*, it is just as deadly. We see it sparkling in the sun when, in voice-over, the protagonist, Ada, tells us of the drowning death of the emigrating young men. As the women mourn the absence of the men, they begin to fall ill with fever, and eventually they awaken in the middle of the night with the clouded eyes we associate with zombies, possessed by the souls of their missing boyfriends. They gather in the street and silently go to the house of the developer that owes them. They menace him and threaten to burn down the tower. They also compel him to dig all of their graves, laughing that "now he's doing real work." The film represents a hauntological revenge fantasy in which laborers are paid what they earn even after death and thus still provide for their families. The route that these characters attempt in the film is a real-world path of migration and is truly as deadly in life as in the film: in late October 2020, two separate shipwrecks resulted in at least 290 deaths. Migrants are willing to risk death on this route, which has been nicknamed "Barcelona or die" due to extreme desperation.[66] In the same way, *Savageland*'s phantom zombies could be the result of the crossing that Mexican and Central American migrants continue to brave in the deadly Sonoran Desert, where more than 9,000 migrants are believed to have died since the 1990s and where the flow of migration has been directed through the 1994 U.S. policy of prevention through deterrence.[67] The spectral zombies of these two films that focus on the migrant experience raise those lost to that desperation from their unmarked graves to confront a ruling class that would rather forget them.

In *Atlantics*, the returned souls that temporarily zombify the girlfriends of the lost crew are not the figures of the abused and exploited laborers (though abused and exploited they may have been in life) but rather the eerie and undead reminders of the sins of the rich developer, who cannot rest until he has made restitution. The origins of the zombie, the sub-Saharan lore that mixed with the experience of the African diaspora in Haiti and then influenced popular culture in the United States, are being reinterpreted around the world to reflect the changing realities of economic and cultural globalization, and zombies are evolving in the process. The dead do return, but instead of their bodies being reanimated without consciousness, it is their memory and souls that temporarily take possession of healthy, live bodies to make the wealthy pay with currency and labor: in this way, they represent a form of *necroactivism*. Eunjung Kim has described necroactivism to constitute "the undoing—and the return of—the disposed-of 'necropolitical labor,'" also referred to as "disposable populations" and "wastes," or "individuals whose experiences of suffering and injustice do not provoke social, political, and legal recognition and remedies and are subject to further violations as their presences are seen as transgressing."[68] These "wastes" are treated as just more raw materials that have been appropriated by industry, used up, and cast aside either dead or disabled, in order to feed the logic of capitalism. If corporations have as their primary goal the accumulation of shareholder wealth, the well-being of the human beings who make that accumulation possible is the very least of their concerns, considering that the flow of labor is endless in a globalized economy where so many suffer from poverty and unemployment. The construction crew in *Atlantics* were indeed not recipients of any kind of legal remedy after being drained of labor and not remunerated. They were not paid because the business that hired them had no incentive to pay them as an easily replaceable labor force, and they had no societal power to demand payment. The threat of the hunger and displacement of their families drove them to a dangerous search for illegal labor, which ended in their deaths. Their only possible remedy had to come from beyond their watery graves, and the living bodies of their zombie/possessed girlfriends were the tools they used.

However, this spectral, suggested presence is not the only way that zombies are subjects of necroactivism across the genre. We propose that the very presence of the zombie, the rotting, dismembered body that carries its viscera on the outside, a presence that contains its own absence and represents the ruin of humanity, *is a political subject of necroactivism in and of itself.* The zombie is a walking corpse that refuses to lie down, to curb its hungers, to hide its wounds. It demands that the spectator confront the consequences of the hegemonic force of a neoliberalism built on the commodification of life, and that created the context for its violent death. It pierces our conscience through the horror that its gore aspect engenders. It is similar to Adam Lowenstein's concept of the allegorical moment touched upon in chapter 2, but the horrors that are confronted here are not relegated to the past. They are current and continuous—they are happening now, seemingly unstoppable, and too close for comfort. Sayak Valencia has written that the seed for *Gore Capitalism* was the shock of seeing a real dismembered body fall off a pickup truck in Tijuana: "That dead man shook me out of my spectralized and comfortable idea of death, ripped me out of the mediatized logic that tells us that bad things always happen to Others. The body makes me realize that I am the Others. . . . That dead man tells me that I am also responsible for his dismemberment, that my passivity as a citizen is crystallized in impunity."[69] The metaphorical presence of the zombie attempts to cause the same shattering of complacency in us, in the same way this horrific experience affected Valencia. We see *ourselves* in the destroyed body and jarringly are forced to accept some of the responsibility for its destruction.

Let us return to *Savageland*: after the rampage and disappearance of the spectral zombies, Salazar is sentenced to death as a mass murderer. Though he is innocent, the state must find a scapegoat, publicize his presumed guilt, and provide the spectacle of capital punishment. The last shot of a living Salazar is through an interrogation room window, where the camera closes in on his bandaged hand. It is a clue of what is to come: he has been bitten in the attack. After his death, we hear a clip from right-wing radio: "You know what made my morning? Hearing that some group of unknown patriots found where Salazar's grave was and dug it up. The body is gone, my friends. And good riddance." The state had made a gore spectacle of Salazar's punishment, and society wants to hide the corpse, disappearing it right from the grave and from their conscience, negating his existence. But of course, the grave was not robbed. Some damaged "found footage" appears to show an undead Salazar, in his prison jumpsuit, attacking campers, and news reports give evidence of so many similar attacks that he cannot be the only creature perpetrating them. In death, he can retaliate for the injustice of his execution, and in the closing credits we see that he has indeed become a folk hero of resistance. Chicano youth are

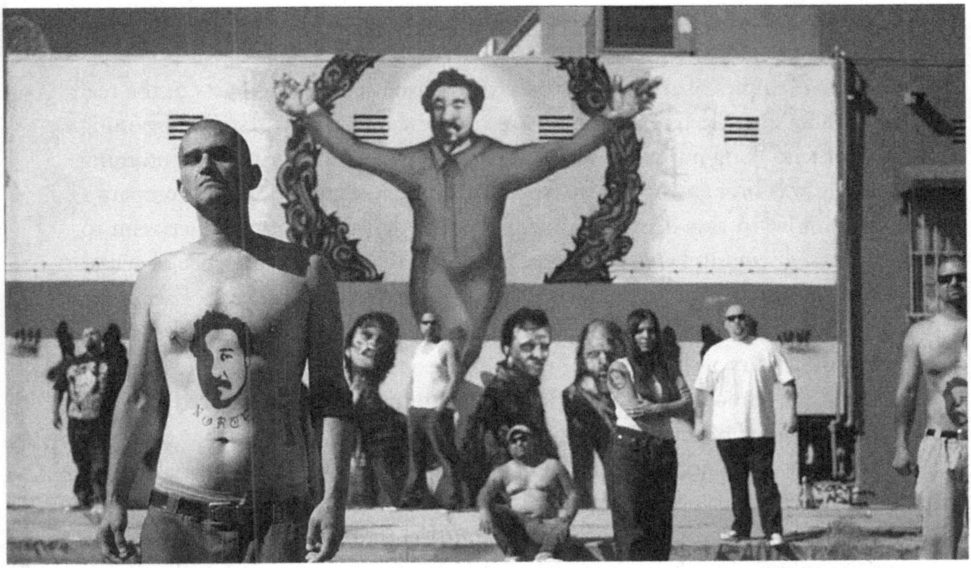

Savageland's Salazar: the zombie as folk hero. (Credit: Phil Guidry, Simon Herbert, and David Whelan, *Savageland*, 2015.)

shown sporting Salazar tattoos in the shadowed, stylized mode of the Che Guevara pop art print, defiantly posing in front of a mural in which Salazar is heroic and leading a formation of zombies.

In the Australian film *Wyrmwood: Road of the Dead*, after a meteor shower, anyone who doesn't have type A-negative blood is turned into a zombie within a day.[70] As a side effect, zombie blood and exhalation are flammable and can substitute for gasoline to power vehicles; their blood and breath literally power the machines of their oppressors. Brooke, a woman with resistant blood, is taken by a military group and experimented on by being injected with zombie blood in a nightmarish lab that looks more like an abattoir. As a result of this abuse, she develops the ability to control zombies telepathically, and she soon has hordes at her disposal, which she uses to rise up against her tormentors. In this way, Brooke and Salazar are following in the footsteps of Carrefour, the catatonic zombie in *I Walked with a Zombie* who appears to witness the sins of the plantation-owning family with his blind stare. They are akin to Bub, the zombie who kills the violently reactionary Captain Rhodes in Romero's *Day of the Dead*, or another of Romero's creatures, Big Daddy, the zombie leader in *Land of the Dead* that attacks the privileged profiteers of catastrophe. *Juan of the Dead*'s "insurgent" hordes, *Shaun*'s working-class British slackers, *Fido*'s paternal zombie who reorganizes the nuclear family, *Miss Zombie*'s abused domestic worker who frees her sister in servitude, the brutally conscripted miners of *Plague of Zombies* who eventually descend upon their master, the dispossessed masses of *Seoul Station*—all of these are subjects of necroactivism that struggle against the coloniality of marginalized existence.

These examples of zombie necroactivism have their counterparts in the real world. Kim's article refers to the corpse protest over the industrial poisoning death of Kim Pong-hwan in South Korea in 1991, in which the coffin containing the body was brought to the workplace to force recognition of the company's responsibility in this death. Kim expands the definition of necroactivism to include *mourning* and *objects representing death*, as well as the presence of actual corpses, in making claims for justice. Taking just the eventful year of 2020, we can see various examples of this phenomenon. In January 2020, activists placed hundreds of pairs of shoes in the Zócalo in Mexico City, each one representing a victim of the femicides that have plagued the country, each painted red to evoke the blood spilled in these gruesome crimes.[71] Amanda L. Petersen has observed the way in which objects such as these shoes can "reveal the shape of the absence" caused by femicide and "point towards a possible specter of justice" without replicating the bloody images of the actual murders that are the media's obsession (and contribution to the gore economy).[72] In June 2020, protesters in Brazil dug one hundred graves marked with black crosses on Copacabana's beach (in front of a luxurious hotel) to protest President Bolsonaro's mishandling of the coronavirus in favor of lifting restrictions that would harm the economy. In July of the same year, the body of U.S. representative John Lewis of Georgia was carried across the Edmund Pettus Bridge in a flag-draped coffin as part of his funeral procession, crossing on a bed of red rose petals to represent the blood he and others spilled there in 1965 during a voting rights march where his skull was fractured by state troopers and he nearly died.[73] This gesture came in the same year that the United States was dealing with a wave of political protests led by the Black Lives Matter movement reacting to police violence against Black people, and was therefore laden with even more meaningful symbolism. In New York City, in August 2020, teachers protested being forced to go back into the classroom during the COVID-19 pandemic with mock caskets, gravestones, and skeletons, as they felt their lives and the lives of their students' families would be endangered. "I do not want to be an experiment," one of them told reporters.[74] Each one of these performative death-protests are an attempt to break with the status quo that brought us to this state and to call attention to the value of lives and the causes and necropolitical motors of death.

In *Otto; or, Up with Dead People*, Otto is a young zombie with an identity crisis who becomes involved with a director who is making a film about a zombie uprising featuring "the gay Che Guevara of the undead" in protest of "the gluttonous, mindless consumers of the developed industrial countries who have buried the Third World in an avalanche of putrescence and decay."[75] We follow along as the filmmaker character, Medea Yarn, explains her film in long, expressive monologues excoriating the unjust, heteronormative, and capitalist modern world. In

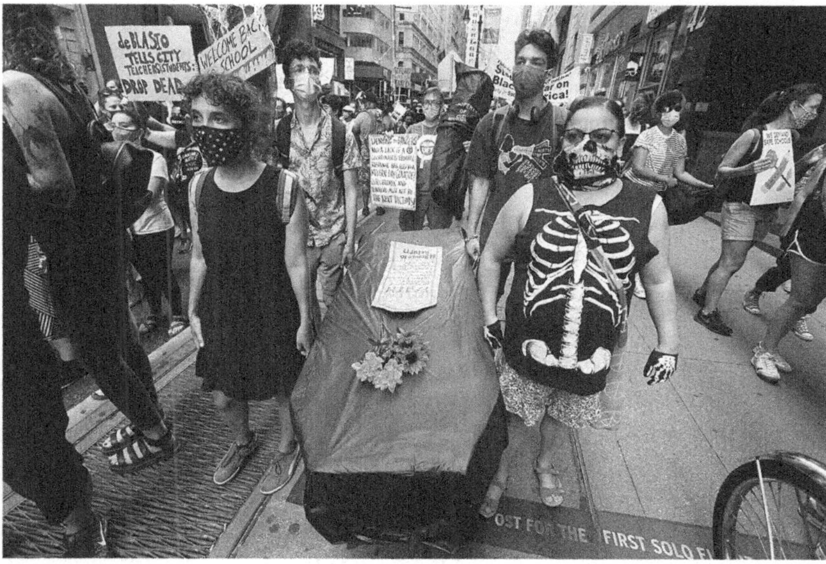

In August 2020, New York City teachers protest being sent back to the classroom during the coronavirus pandemic. (Credit: Dan Herrick.)

one scene, she directs Otto as he approaches a slaughterhouse: "As a zombie, you are intoxicated by the lewd perfume of bloody carnage. . . . For you it is . . . a symbol for mankind's quest to turn the earth into an industrialized wasteland of casual extermination and genocide." When Otto enters the building, we are presented with footage of faceless workers chopping piles of what looks like chicken, as Otto is drawn to the raw meat and begins to consume it. Among the many targets of this film, the meat industry comes under attack for its environmental impact, animal cruelty, and human consequences. Some of these consequences unfortunately were illustrated by the COVID-19 outbreaks in meat and poultry processing plants across the United States, in which some 200 workers had died of the virus by September 2020, some 87 percent of which occurred among racial and ethnic minorities (these communities representing the majority of the labor force for the industry).[76] Considered "critical infrastructure," these businesses were blocked from closure by executive order by President Trump, a move that protected the corporations involved from liability for the sickness and death occurring inside their plants. This aligns with Tyner's necroeconomics that profit from the premature death of those deemed redundant. As Medea tells Otto, who as a zombie hungers for human flesh both on and off the movie set, "Focus on meat because the world is meat. *We are meat.*"

Themes of corporate greed and their effects on the bodies of "disposable populations" are also evident in films that include the effects of corporate profiteering from human experimentation under the cover of supposed health benefits. Zombie films that involve viral narratives often include storylines about cures or vaccines and the devastating effects that medical experimentation can have on populations, in an echo of McNally's historical description of the "corpse economy." In *Resident Zombie* the search for a cure for AIDS leads one company to experiment on "small ethnic communities in a restricted area," which goes wrong and causes the zombie outbreak that is explored in this anthology film, illustrating how ethnicity becomes a factor in identification as a disposable population. In *Altered Skin*, a pharmaceutical company sells a patch that can treat, but not cure, a rage virus and profits from it, controlling the infected populace.[77] In patients, the patch eventually ceases working, at which point they are put into induced comas, except for a handful of patients who have been allowed to develop beyond the safe phase, becoming monsters that are kept alive strictly for researching new mutations. All these patients—the ultra-sick, the comatose, the patch dependent—represent profit for Ingenec, the company that makes the patch. By the end of the film, it is revealed that the company has had an effective cure for years but held it back at the behest of its acquiring U.S. corporation to maximize profits, adding a globalist element to the critique of the pharmaceutical industry as a neoliberal death cult.

As Comaroff and Comaroff note in their 2002 study of the economic basis for the preoccupation with zombies and the demonization of immigrants in Africa, it is the "*experiential* contradiction at the core of neoliberal capitalism in its global manifestation: . . . it appears to offer up vast, almost instantaneous riches to those who control its technologies, and simultaneously, to threaten the very livelihood of those who do not" that gives rise to these spectral appearances of the zombie, both in popular culture and in cultural beliefs and practices.[78] As the technologies of neoliberalism have accelerated, the perception of labor, earning power, and human value has continued to evolve. The so-called gig-economy leaves a segment of the population in an unprotected, haphazard economic state. Data mining makes consumer's online activities another source of profit for corporations, making the user into the product—a commodity-addicted, consuming product that recalls *The Dead Don't Die*'s zombies forever in search of the products and tech they gorged on while living.[79] All these developments have widened the wealth gap internationally, to the extent that the global pandemic, its effects, and the restrictions it has made necessary has been devastating to the working class but enriching for the wealthiest, leaving world economies teetering on the brink of disaster. Though this catastrophic event may not be the *Kill Bill 2*–style "attack on the global capitalist system" that Slavoj Žižek suggests it may be, it is beyond doubt that the long-lasting global economic effects of the pandemic have yet to be seen, and the value of human life, human activity, human bodies, and human death are still being negotiated on world markets.[80]

4

Bodies That Splatter

Queering and Cripping Zombies

We have explored the many ways the zombie is used to represent othered populations in terms of race, nationality, and economic power. But the zombie's presentation, as an ailing, decomposing reminder of our biological humanity, has other associations that make it an easy symbol for categories of identity that are discriminated against, put down, hidden, or forgotten in ableist, heteronormative, misogynist culture: categories that are based in the body, its gendering, its characteristics, its disabilities. In this chapter we will talk about the zombie as a queer and disabled body that distorts societal notions of what is "natural" and "good" with its confrontational biological presence and its refusal to engage in "productive" labor or heterosexual reproduction. We will address how the above categories have gained their power through systems of coloniality and how they can be disrupted. The zombie causes a disturbance in how we see the world and ourselves. It is an uncanny and dark mirror that invites us to question how we arrived at the accepted perspective on humanity that has taken Western cultures centuries to develop.

Countervisuality against Ableism

In *La perspectiva invertida* (Reverse Perspective), the art historian Pável Florensky demonstrates that over the last seven centuries, we in the West have been made to believe that linear perspective is the "natural" way of seeing.[1] Linear perspective assumes the placement of a unique vanishing point at the apex of a visual pyramid. Following linear perspective, objects that are closer to the spectator seem larger while other objects diminish in size the farther away they appear.[2] Similarly, bodies should either follow the proportions of the Vitruvian Man by Leonardo da Vinci[3] or represent the golden ratio[4] typically found in Western art since the Renaissance. In this way, it can be said that Mona Lisa's face, and other figures in da Vinci's art, represent the ideal human form. Florensky shows us how the creators of Byzantine Russian icons did not limit themselves to linear perspective, though they were quite familiar with it. This is why when we look at the faces of those icons we have the sensation that one eye may be bigger than the other or that the face may look ill-formed. But it is in this type of art that we can observe what Florensky calls reverse perspective in compositions that contain proportions that don't necessarily correlate to what the West understands to be linear perspective and the golden ratio.

Florensky's conclusions are important in understanding how Western cultural training for over six centuries has positioned linear perspective as the "natural" way of seeing the world. By questioning these rules of perspective, we can identify the assumptions that inform ableist societies. We automatically associate the ideal body with ability, but bodies that break with the norms of Whiteness, heteropatriarchy—those that don't conform to the golden ratio and do not function successfully within the demands of capitalism—are considered disabled and dehumanized and are discriminated against. Their needs for accessibility and mobility are ignored; they are considered *other* and are even seen as dangerous or savage. Ableist societies are organized around the able-bodied while the disabled are cast aside or monstrified, acts which become much more visible and obvious during periods of crisis or pandemic.

Under COVID-19, those with pre-existing conditions, such as asthma or diabetes, and the elderly are considered disabled precisely due to their age or medical condition. They don't have the same access to lifesaving ventilators as "healthier" patients. In triage, health care providers have been forced to choose between a patient who has none of these indicators and those that do.[5] The result is that the lives of those disqualified are valued less so that the younger, "healthier" subject can then survive to continue to work and consume in the neoliberal system for years to come. This ethical problem not only lays bare the workings of necropolitics but also signals the value system of ableist society.[6] The "perfect" body takes precedence over "wasted," "used," "queer," or not completely abled bodies.

According to Mitchell and Snyder's theory of "narrative prosthetics," horror cinema has always used disability to construct its narratives. This can take two forms: a monstrous and mutilated body that threatens and terrifies, or a disabled body that is to be read as morally superior. However, zombies complicate narrative prosthetics since, as Jamie McDaniel has pointed out, zombies themselves are metaphors for disabled subjects that express both cultural tensions such as race and contradictions between abled and disabled bodies. Therefore, zombies reveal the natural ableism of the horror genre.[7] Just as in the Russian icon paintings studied by Florensky, the film *Resident Zombie* presents a different vision of the human form in one of its vignettes.[8] Similar to the asymmetrical eyes of an icon, we see one eye infected by the zombie virus, while the other seems unchanged. The "Red-eye" virus, also known as the ID-7 virus, comes up in *Mayhem*: infected individuals look normal save for one blood-red eye.[9] They retain their humanity, but following the Freudian concept of the *id*, they show their aggressive instincts and lack of morality. Something similar happens in *Tokyo Ghoul*.[10] Ghouls look and act exactly like human beings but have one eye infected. As in *Mayhem*, they retain their cognitive capacities, but are different; they are monstrous cannibals. The suggested discrepancy in perspective between the two eyes necessary for depth perception, the identification of these subjects as *infected* yet *still human*, allows the viewer to visualize this liminal ambiguity embodied in the monster/zombie subject. While Florensky, through study of art history, helps us to grasp that our understanding of the perfect human form is a cultural construction reinforced through centuries of conditioning, Fiona Kumari Campbell, in her study of disabled bodies, informs us that ableist regimes have led to a devaluation of the disabled body, which is normalized as an aberration.[11] Both the ableist project that Campbell identifies and the golden ratio should be overturned. Applying Mirzoeff's theories, we can trace how linear perspective and ideas of the perfect human form imposed since the Renaissance evolved as *visuality*, which became the only correct way of seeing.[12] These have been the only accepted tools for understanding art for so long that it has transformed into the idea of the "natural." Any human form that varies in dimension or can be seen from a different angle is considered monstrous. *Countervisuality* as a response to what is not allowed to be seen demands the inclusion of other perspectives.[13] The figure of the zombie is an ideal strategy to first visualize these perceived aberrations of the disabled body and to then upend them to create a countervisuality that returns to us that "right to look" proposed by Mirzoeff. Through the realization of the zombie as metaphor for disability, we can dismantle ableist strategies and create a more inclusive future, an opening of time that encompasses the disabled body in its intersections with concepts of race, social class, and gender, as suggested by theories of queer temporality and crip theory and the notion of radical hope explained by ecofeminism.[14]

Zombies Overturn Christian Chrononormativity

Let's begin with the concept of *queer temporality*, which refers to a series of narratives that deal with "the practices, experiences, and sensations of gender and sex that enter into tension with socially legitimized social norms."[15] As explained by Marcela Solana, queer temporality unites three ideas that normally aren't studied together: the concepts of time, gender, and sexuality, and the norms to which they are expected to adhere. The question of who, exactly, experiences a queer temporality is complicated. On the one hand, queer temporality is associated with gay, lesbian, bisexual, and transgender subjectivity that does not conform to the sequences of heterosexual matrimony and reproduction. But this concept of time is also present in categories other than those of gender and sexual identity and practices. It is present in the way we experience time that diverges from the clocks imposed by various biopolitical markers. Biopolitics imposes a series of temporal limitations—for example, the age of consent, the age for marriage, the age to have children, the age to become independent, and so on. This regulation of time with respect to sexuality or any aspect that seeks to control the course of life is what Elizabeth Freeman calls *chrononormativity*.[16] Over the course of history there have been various ways in which time has become standardized. Calendars, diaries, and clocks impose a rhythm and schedule that *seems* natural: the eight-hour workday or the five-day workweek. As Freeman and David Harvey point out, this organization of time is tied to capitalist productivity. In fact, Western civilization has always married time to capital. In the Middle Ages, the Catholic Church believed that time belonged under its domain and that any bargaining of time would implicate the bargainer in a blasphemous form of usury. According to Jacques Le Goff, time, like eternity, was a theological concept, pertaining to God.[17] Zombies can be considered as subjects of queer temporality because they defy Christian chrononormativity. We can further say that zombies experience queer temporality from many different angles. First, with respect to sexuality, they are drawn to any living body, independent of gender or sex, therefore coinciding with the figure of the vampire: there is no distinction given whether the victim is straight, gay, bi, or trans, nor is there any preference as to age of the victim.[18] Zombies, as we have previously discussed, are also subjects of queer temporality because they resurrect before the Final Judgment, and therefore, disobey the Church's chrononormativity. In this way, they invalidate the Second Coming, rendering it meaningless.[19] In terms of their physical existence, zombies are again experiencing queer temporality: they have no need to align themselves to a daily routine regarding eating, sleeping, attending to their physical needs—they have only one requirement, and it is always time to eat. Zombies don't move like living humans; they either walk more slowly or with great speed, and with "unnatural" movements. They don't appear to have any cognitive capacity or ability to speak, laugh, cry, or show pleasure. Even the act of eating, as Mel Y. Chen affirms, is experienced by zombies in a way that can be considered "queer," since for zombies, "eating" does not seem to include what we usually consider to be the process of nutritional intake.[20] Eating is a process that doesn't include digestion, or the processing of waste. What is more, as Chen asserts, the viscera of a zombie are often visible, exposed to the eye, and other times, internal organs are simply missing.[21] Zombies don't gather at mealtime to give thanks for their food—the closest they get to that experience is the animalistic attack of a horde, appropriating the flesh of a victim into themselves.

According to heterolinear time, heterosexual reproduction is the only method to guarantee a human future. Zombies, however, parody this form of heteronormative reproduction. They replace the sexual penetration of penis and vagina and substitute for it another type of bodily penetration: the bite of zombie teeth into human flesh. This form of reproduction guarantees a *zombie* future that will survive the apocalyptic chaos of the outbreak. Following Chen, zombies don't reproduce themselves upon biting; they don't create a new being. Rather, they reproduce their disability, they destroy the concept of "life span," and they modify the idea of linearity in Western history.

Western Christian cultures divide history into a "before" and an "after," marked by the birth of Christ, and a "soon" that will be marked by the end times. The zombie revives and negates the Final Judgment. This queer temporality is a concept that resists linear history by changing the end of time in favor of zombie immortality. If in religious narratives, the end of the world is signaled by the Second Coming and the reward for the faithful on Judgment Day, zombies change that narrative by spreading virally and turning everyone into cannibals who seek to partake of the body and the blood. They break with chrononormative biopolitical edicts about death, and life after death. They decolonize the relationship between time and divine determination. All this is crucial to understanding the change proposed by z-narratives. Christian narrative tells us that God dies to save humankind, washing away original sin, and is resurrected owing to *felix culpa*.[22] The fall of man is validated by his eventual salvation, but zombies render this timeline irrelevant. Zombies neither require salvation nor endure judgment. Zombies break with the promise of eternal life (what they offer is eternal living death) and destroy religious icons in what Edelman calls "denial of teleology."[23] In *Zombie 2*, the corpses of the conquistadors resuscitate not with the trumpets of Judgment Day but with vodou drums.[24] In *Exit Humanity* (dir. John Geddes, Canada, 2012), a woman inadvertently causes the zombie plague after attempting to reanimate her dead sister with the aid of a found manuscript containing mysterious ancient rituals.[25] Magical and alternative beliefs have replaced Christianity and biblical knowledge, and vodou (or other "secret knowledge") raises the dead. In a comical denial of Christian knowledge, *Juan of the Dead*'s Lázaro accidentally (and casually) harpoons Preacher Jones, a savior-figure, complete with a large cross on his chest, who has promised to share his plan for salvation.[26]

There are many ways in which zombie movies rethink Christian myths in order to secularize history. *Saint Nick* (*Sint*) focuses on the evening of

December 5: the Feast of Saint Nicholas, which is also observed in Eastern Countries every December 19.[27] This movie attempts to rewrite the myth of Saint Nicholas by having this malevolent character expose the effects of chrononormativity in Christian culture. On this holiday, children are given some gifts, fruits, and chocolate that they find in hanging stockings. Also known as the Bishop of Myra, the patron of Russia and Greece, Saint Nicholas arrives with a horse carrying a crosier and wearing a red robe and a miter, and he is always accompanied by a freed slave called Black Peter or Zwarte Piet, who rewards the well-behaved children or punishes those who have not met expectations. According to the legend, "naughty" children are taken to Spain by the very same Zwarte Piet. *Saint Nick* does not contain typical zombies, but Saint Nicholas and his band of criminals resurrect after death as violent murderers, rapists, and kidnappers of children. Villagers manage to burn their ship and their belongings, but the sailor Saint Nicholas becomes a legend for he and his band return every time there is a full moon on December 5, killing hundreds of people.[28] The movie clearly criticizes capitalist consumerism during the Christmas season. But, most importantly, *Saint Nick* is also full of controversial images that question the benevolence of the historical Santa Claus (his face is in the form of a skull tinged with blood), as well as the role of the government in propping up a religious tradition denying cruel history and reality. The film emphasizes the way the government covers up these crimes so that people continue believing in Saint Nicholas and continue participating in consumerism. The movie destroys the myth of the saint and exposes racism (the Moor figure and the threat of taking children to Spain), pedophilia (numerous child abductions), sexual exploitation (prostitution in the red-light district), rapes and femicides (numerous murders of women), and violence in general that has been linked to the church.

The Spanish short film *Fist of Jesus* presents another biting satire of Christian narrative by imagining a scenario in which it goes horribly, comically wrong.[29] Christ completes his miracle, raising Lazarus from the dead (John 11:1–44). But in this version, Lazarus rises as a zombie and attacks all those around him. Soon the entire village is contaminated and zombified, including the Roman soldiers. In desperation and fear, Judas hangs himself. Christ attempts the resuscitation miracle once more to revive his disciple and gets it right this time, though, as he celebrates, Judas is still hanging and comically dies once more. Having re-resuscitated Judas, they are soon attacked by all the zombies. In a blasphemous satire of the miracle of the loaves and fishes, Christ takes the one fish and multiplies it, using the resulting fish as weapons (fortunately, they include swordfish and piranhas). In a comically low-budget but extremely gory scene, Christ fights the horde with a nasty sword made from the barbed bones of a fish. Apparently fighting near Calvary, in a Herculean feat of strength, Jesus heaves a cross from the ground and uses it to bludgeon the last of the zombies. This comic film not only questions religious narrative but explicitly turns Christian resurrection into zombification.

Bruce LaBruce's *L.A. Zombie* is much more explicit in the way zombies can radically change Christian narrative, introducing an extraterrestrial zombie that comes out of the sea, a sort of male Venus figure.[30] Changing his external appearance and shifting from a regular-looking guy to a tusked beast or even a corpse, our protagonist makes his way to Los Angeles. He manages to hitch a ride, but the driver dies in an accident. Our zombie survives and decides to help the corpse by penetrating the driver's bloody wound with his enlarged, monstrous penis. He ejaculates a dark red semen on the corpse, and the body resurrects. They then engage in oral sex. This pattern repeats through the film, and he resurrects and "saves" three other men. The biggest salvation comes with a group of men participating in an orgy, who are shot and killed by drug dealers. Our L.A. Zombie masturbates in front of the gory scene and splashes his red semen over all the corpses, resuscitating them. The scene is literally a bath of blood, as if the resurrected were washing themselves in the blood: "Are you washed in the blood / In the soul-cleansing blood of the Lamb?"[31] To "wash [oneself] in the blood" means to accept the act of salvation. When Christ died, his blood was spilled upon the earth to cleanse the sins of humanity. In this movie, the zombie literally spills his blood upon the dead, and people gratefully accept salvation. In an important passage, the zombie recalls all his corpses and short relationships and cries. His purpose for being has been for the salvation and resuscitation of the gay dead. Corpses resurrect thanks to erotic union with the zombie, not through the body of Christ or having to wait for the Final Judgment.

Not Your Sacrificial Lamb: Queer Temporality and Religious Sacrifice

In *The Girl with All the Gifts*, the sacrifice of Melanie, a juvenile "hungry" (zombie/human hybrid), seems inevitable and necessary for the salvation of humanity, at least from the point of view of Western medicine.[32] Doctor Caroline Caldwell leads a research team studying the "hungries," super-strong children who crave human flesh. In order to control these valuable but dangerous children, they use wheelchairs (symbolically linking them to disability) that have been adapted with straps and bars to immobilize them: these beings with superior ability are treated as disabled and studied as though suffering from illness. This film reveals the similarities between ableism and internalized racism as proposed by Campbell.[33] Melanie, the protagonist, is a child of African descent that is being treated as a violent and disabled subject who, along with the other hungries, is compelled to wear an orange sweatsuit reminiscent of a prison jumpsuit. As in racist and ableist regimes, racialization, along with disability, requires enclosure, control, and criminalization. Though Melanie comes to have feelings for and identify with some of the uninfected humans, she ultimately realizes that she and her kind are being targeted for eradication and refuses to sacrifice herself for a human future. Melanie rejects the role of sacrificial lamb and decides that her kind will own the future. She rejects human supremacy, and the future will have little room for human survivors, who will have to take precautions to live a contained and protected version of their old lives. There is no Christ-like sacrifice that will redeem humanity and neither the original sin nor the *felix culpa* have any meaning here: this z-narrative reforms the notion of salvation through sacrifice. This zombie future will be constructed upon new values that do not include the "natural" supremacy of humankind over all of creation.

The parental ties of the nuclear family often are the reason for self-sacrifice in these narratives. The last scenes of *Extinction* depict a father luring the infected toward himself so that his daughter Lu might survive.[34] The same familial sacrifice is observed in the third vignette of *Resident Zombie*, where a daughter selflessly mutilates herself, amputating one finger at a time to feed her zombie mother. Surrounded by photos of a happy childhood, her self-sacrifice transforms the zombie into a kind of monstrous god that must be appeased with human body and blood. This sacrifice doesn't have the noble objective of the salvation of mankind; it is simply required to perpetuate the existence of the mother. This self-amputation/tribute by the daughter repeats until a police officer comes looking for zombies and is quickly disarmed and captured by the daughter, who eventually decides to feed bits of the policeman to her zombie-mother instead.

Interestingly, the subtle announcement of queer temporality takes place via an alarm clock. The clock face, which fills the screen when the alarm sounds, has the image of Christ Pantocrator in Byzantine colors while the hands of the clock spin across his face, marking the passage of time and making the sign of the cross. The presence of Christ reminds us of the sacrifice of his body and blood, and the form of the alarm clock helps us to associate church-related chrononormativity with the feeding of the zombie. All of these connections are made manifest when the alarm sounds and the god/monster must be appeased with tribute. At one point, the clock face of Jesus fades into the face of the kidnapped officer, having a finger amputated by the daughter, marking the officer as sacrifice. Now humans will be sacrificed to save gods, instead of the other way around. Further, upon superimposing the images of the policeman and Christ on the clock, the officer releases Christ from that fixed position of his sacrificial role, at least temporarily, an act that reminds us of Heracles and Atlas and their struggle over who would bear the weight of the celestial spheres on his shoulders. It is also said of Christ that he bears the weight of the world's sin.

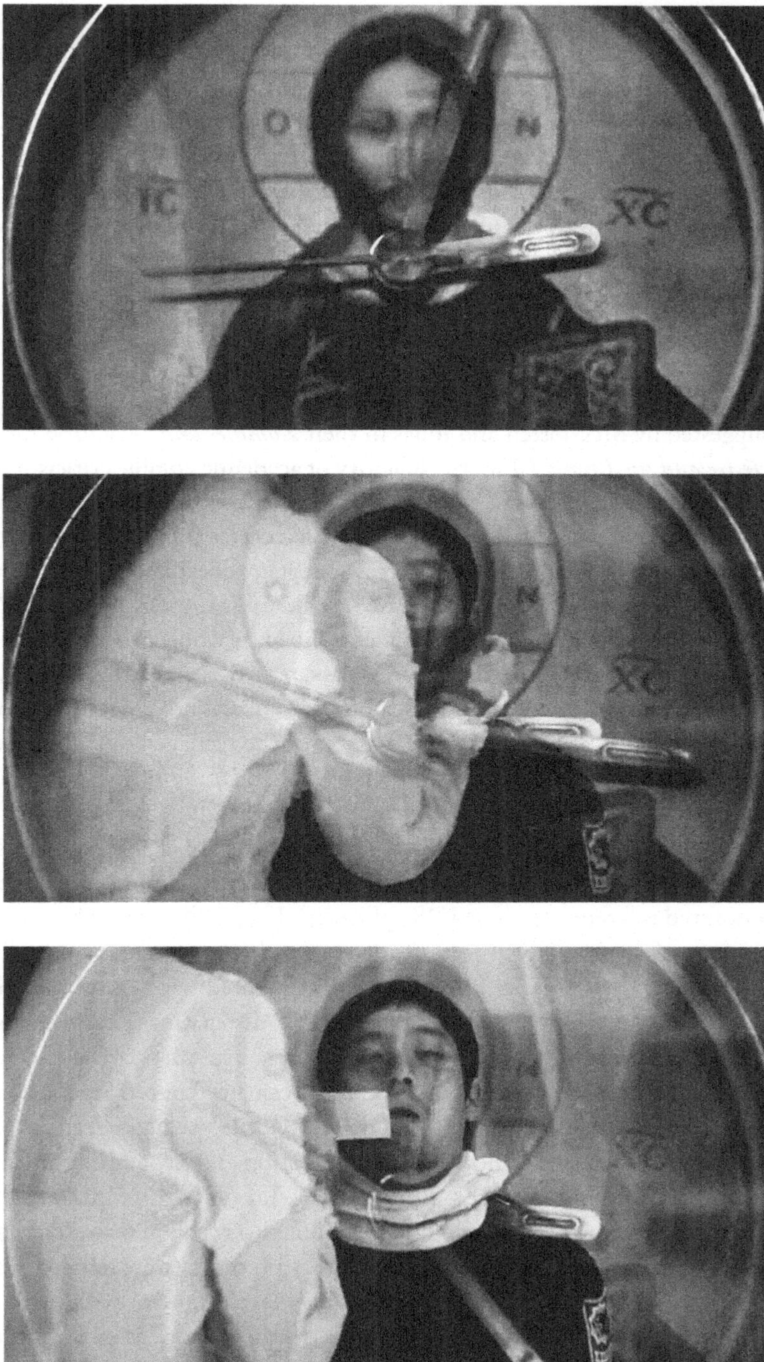

Resident Zombie. The clock face bearing the image of Christ fades to the image of the sacrificial victim. (Credit: Oh Young-doo, Ryu Hoon, Hong Young-geun, and Jang Youn-jung, *Resident Zombie* (aka *The Neighbor Zombie*, *Yieutjib jombi*), 2010.)

As Heracles is able, through trickery, to transfer the weight back to Atlas, Atlas will perform the task of holding up the heavens into eternity. Likewise, the police officer, having temporarily served the role of Christ-like sacrifice, eventually frees himself of both mother/zombie and daughter and can escape the confines of the sacrificial role. Though the face of the daughter is never seen on the clock, she serves as the model for a sacrificial paradigm based on affect and not on coercion. In theory, any uninfected human could become a paradigm of Christ, a sacrificial lamb to feed a new zombie sovereign.

Wounding the Patriarchy: Sexualizing Zombies, Emasculating Culture

As suggested by McGlotten and Jones in their *Zombies and Sexuality: Essays on Desire and the Living Dead*, the majority of academic zombie criticism has overlooked zombie sexuality.[35] Though, as we have asserted, the typical zombie doesn't show a gender preference for the flesh it craves and its preferred form of reproduction is through the bite, there is a subgenre of exploitation films that present the zombie as an object of desire or a desirous subject. In *Deadgirl*, a group of teenagers find an undead woman chained to a table in an abandoned psychiatric hospital and, over the next few days, return to rape her repeatedly.[36] Through a necrophilic impulse, the body of this zombie is heterosexualized and pornified as she becomes a chained sex slave for the teenage boys. We see an important twist on this trend in movies like *Otto; or, Up with Dead People*, the comic series *Lesbian Zombies from Outer Space*, or the film *Contracted*, which deal with lesbian and gay zombies.[37] In *Otto*, there is a wave of gay zombies who are perceived to be a plague on humanity in some form of divine punishment (in a pointed reference to the AIDS epidemic). In this film, there have been many waves of zombies infecting humanity, but as this last "generation" is identified as gay, it is thus hunted down and exterminated with even more violence. Zombies are referred to as "the Purple Peril," associating them with both political danger (reminiscent of the "Lavender Scare," a subpanic of the so-called Red Scare and McCarthyism in the twentieth-century United States) and a racialized threat (as the xenophobic fear of Asian cultures semanticized as "The Yellow Peril").[38] Otto denounces this discrimination and gay-bashing and justifies the film's storyline of rebellion and activism. Likewise, this film confronts theological condemnation of sodomy, and although gay zombies are described as a plague, their persistence and resistance are a protest against religious narrative. The inclusion of the song "Atrocities" invokes the presence of God as an observer of these crimes of bigotry, who mourns the damage as he takes it all in.[39] As God cries, humankind must accept and consume the tears of God. The film plays with identity on various levels: Otto believes he is a zombie, but those around him are unsure. To complicate matters, Otto also plays a zombie in the political zombie film within the film being directed by the character Medea. At one point, Otto stands outside a bar called Flesh, tempted by the name. He meets a man and goes to his apartment to have sex. The young lover is torn open by Otto, who feasts on his flesh, and the blood-soaked bedroom becomes a space where eroticism and violence coexist. Otto criticizes the conception and normalization of homosexuality as a death impulse because these zombies don't adhere to heterosexual "reproductive futurism."[40] In this film there is a gay/zombie futurism involving the passing of information to future generations, evolution of zombies, and recruitment of zombies to the cause. The film ends with a gay orgy, and erotic pleasure is generalized and pointedly questions the association of homosexuality and the death drive. *Otto* is the revolution to come, the inclusive future for which the gay zombies are fighting.

Contracted uses the rape of a lesbian by a man as the act of virus transmission. From the perspective of the woman's mother and the mother's priest friend, the disease that the victim, Samantha, suffers from after the rape is the consequence of being a drug-using lesbian—they believe it is something that can be "cured." Samantha's lesbian identity is problematic: she desires her ex-girlfriend Nikki, who rejects her. Samantha, Nikki, and another friend, Alice, are all subject to constant harassment from the heterocentric society. Samantha eventually kills Nikki and Alice (both Samantha's romantic interests) in a rage, even before she has fully transformed into her zombie state. At the end of the movie, fully zombified, she attacks her mother, Samantha's third female casualty. Samantha is a victim of heteronormative society and masculine violence, and in this film, she continues to inflict violence on the women closest to her.

Lesbian Zombies from Outer Space, a graphic novel with a rather self-explanatory title, presents a Freudian vision of lesbianism based on the concept of penis envy. In this horror/comedy comic, lesbians invade from outer space and begin to hunt down men and devour their sex organs. This literal and symbolic act of emasculation, while potentially misogynistic (or at least gynophobic), does suggest a violent method of doing away with heteronormativity in patriarchal societies. Emasculation is an act that is also present in *Halley* and *Blood Quantum*.[41] In *Halley* it is the protagonist himself who, in a postmasturbatory act, removes his own member in an attempt to excise desire and avoid possible reproduction. Meanwhile, in *Blood Quantum*, Lysol picks up a White girl at a party right before she is about to turn zombie, and before long he is attacked when she rips his penis off to devour it. Though Lysol is immune to the virus, he becomes much more violent and unpredictable after this grave injury. He even tries to kill his brother, along with many other members of his community, apparently driven mad by the trauma. *Juan of the Dead*, on the other hand, depicts homosexuality in a different way. Given the strong homophobic discourse in the movie, Juan and the viewers are surprised to hear Lázaro's last request when he believes he is about to die: Lázaro confesses his love to Juan and expresses his desire to give him a blow job. When Juan is about to reluctantly acquiesce, Lázaro jokingly laughs at Juan's gullibility, proving once more that the two characters hold a perjorative view of gay people. For Juan and Lázaro, oral sex between two men would mean losing their male power within a patriarchal society.

Freud asserted that penis envy was an important characteristic of female identity. However, it is these literally emasculated figures, who lose their cisgender identity and become self-rejecting male subjects, who suffer due to the absence of a penis. Either by their own choice or not, they have lost the physical marker of masculinity that makes them representatives of patriarchy. Interestingly, there exists the theoretical possibility that even after suffering the terror and pain of this mutilation, the wounded man could achieve immortality precisely due to his zombification. Kimberly J. Lau, in her study on vampires, asserts that what is interesting about this kind of monstrous immortality is what it says about our future, our mortality, and what the zombie can do as an immortal subject: "to queer mortality by trying to think beyond a 'meaningful' or (re)productive life . . . is thus to open ourselves to the possibility of living in the face of death in dramatically different ways."[42] The queer zombie can be conceived as a subject that projects itself as eternally queer if nonzombie humans disappear, leaving a zombie/queer future. The future then becomes a performative act in which the zombification of the world is created. In terms of what Elizabeth Freeman calls "temporal drag" (the pull toward the past that compels us to look backward but that also affects our present), the zombie can be read as an example of queer performativity. The zombie's present carries with it shreds of the past that have become anachronistic. Its physical traits no longer serve to differentiate it in terms of history or gender. The zombie embodies the coexistence of different chronologies and temporalities like a Benjaminian ruin in which the past life, violent demise, and eternal decay are all simultaneously present.[43] The zombie becomes a queer performer of new identities and futurities, though not necessarily cognizant of its past. It does not experience time in a chrononormative way. Nonetheless, it drags its corpse along, wearing traces of its lived past that only the spectator can recognize.

Compulsory Able-bodiedness and Gendered Disability

In *Halley*, the body of the zombie-protagonist, Beto, is slowly decomposing as he works as a security guard at a gym. Beto is a special case, a (literally) dead man walking who has managed to retain his cognitive capacity but whose physical body is decaying. As part of his daily routine, Beto injects himself with embalming fluid to keep his condition at bay. He regularly removes maggots from his flesh with tweezers and stuffs holes with cotton balls. *Halley* breaks with linear time in a very peculiar fashion—Beto refuses to die, though his body is dead, and he insists on maintaining a chrononormative schedule and incorporating himself into the capitalist system, continuing to work despite his frailty. Hofmann uses multiple shots that compare the exercising bodies of the gym clients, breathing heavily, with the breathless and decaying body of Beto. This underscores what McRuer has called "compulsory able-bodiedness," which is linked to heteronormativity. He contends that "compulsory able-bodiedness, which in a sense produces disability, is thoroughly interwoven with the system of compulsory heterosexuality that produces queerness."[44] When he finally decides to leave his job due to his disability, the female manager befriends him, and they develop a personal relationship. Beto strives to control his desire and avoid sexual contact to the extent that he mutilates himself in a particularly gruesome manner, thus entering a queer temporality. The act of ripping off his penis is his rejection of compulsory able-bodiedness and acceptance of disability. But as a zombie with a memory and consciousness, he feels that temporal drag, going through the motions of daily routine, sitting to "dine" off of empty plates that he later washes, compulsively unable to completely relinquish the signs of chrononormativity, while fighting against it by trying to slow the natural decomposition of his body and declining the reproduction of it. However, in a Frankensteinian act, after dying and resuscitating several times, Beto seeks out an icy resting place where he can stop the decay of his body. This move to avoid further decomposition is unusual in zombie narratives but reminiscent of the vampire who, as Hakola asserts, also struggles against signs of aging in favor of representing fantasies of immortality.[45]

Decolonizing "Women's Work": Disability and Confinement

In the Japanese film *Miss Zombie*, we can clearly see the intersection between gender and disability.[46] Shara, a female zombie, is trafficked and purchased by a wealthy couple as a domestic slave, arriving with both strict instructions not to feed her meat and a pistol to shoot her in case of trouble. From the very beginning, she is seen as a sexual object by the employees of the household. The head of the household, Dr. Teramoto, leaves the care of Shara to his wife, Shizuko, who dresses the zombie in her own used clothing and shoes (in a significant gesture that introduces the symbolic equivalence between these two characters) and assigns her daily work. Shara is ordered to wash the patio, which she does on her hands and knees and which the two male laborers on the property find provocative, and they assault her. Dr. Teramoto happens upon the laborers raping Shara and, instead of intervening, watches voyeuristically and eventually gets the idea to do the same. The director's shooting of this black-and-white film helps to blur the line between the mistress and the servant (played by two actresses of similar build). The film takes on the routine of the household and begins with the same establishing shots at the start of each day: the wife, the zombie, and the laborers pursue their daily routines. Kenichi, the son, runs out every day and takes Polaroid photos of household objects, his mother, and the zombie—even his childish gaze is beginning to objectify the two women. Shizuko stands to sweep, Shara crouches down and is awkward and very slow in her movements, but they are both doing very similar domestic work that shares a certain sonic similarity, a repetitive scraping sound that also reminds us of the zombie's slow shuffle. This reliable routine continues for several days until Kenichi has an accident at a pond and drowns. The desperate Shizuko demands that Shara bite him so he can be resuscitated, after which he will require blood to survive. Shara appears to revive a bit in her own way after this incident. She takes the initiative to suddenly attack local youths, collecting their blood to feed Kenichi, introducing a vampiric element while also maternalizing herself. Shara also begins to drink some of the blood, and as a result, her physical condition appears to improve, and her walk becomes less stumbling. She begins to have memories of life before she was a zombie, of her pregnancy and the zombie attack that ended it. In an inversion of the religious narrative, here the sacrificial blood of humans saves zombies: Kenichi can be nourished, Shara recovers her cognition and memories, and Shizuko can be resuscitated to become a zombified mother to Kenichi.

The interchangeability between Shara and Shizuko is built upon throughout the film, especially as Shara begins to replace the living woman as a sexual object for her husband and caregiver to her son. This realization has a terrible effect on Shizuko, and her ease of movement and ability to speak deteriorate. There are shots that focus only on parts of the women's bodies—feet, legs, hands—as they do their domestic chores, purposely confusing the viewer as to their identities. Shizuko chops meat with slow, rhythmic motions that mimic the zombie servant, and she loses control of her body as though she's lost the ability to walk. Likewise, the discovery of a box of her son's photos of the women's unidentifiable legs confuses the spectator as well. These examples perfectly illustrate the concept of the "material metaphor" first explained by Katherine Hayles and applied in the zombie context by Jamie McDaniel. According to him, a material metaphor is produced when an image or idea related to disability presents and critiques the values of an ableist society: in this case, the intersection between gender and disability.[47] Within this patriarchal society, gender automatically turns women into disabled subjects, as shown through the interchangeability of the wife and the zombie slave. Gender dictates the kind of work they are assigned: food preparation, domestic chores, sex work, and servitude. Just as Aníbal Quijano studies coloniality of power and concludes that race is a cultural invention resulting from colonization working alongside the capitalist spirit, María Lugones has formulated the concept of the coloniality of gender. For Lugones, before colonization, indigenous societies were not organized on the basis of gender. Power and authority were centered in other factors, such as age, but never gender.[48] Therefore, gender can be defined as a European cultural construction that begins to spread globally with colonization.[49] According to Breny Mendoza, Lugones's theory would explain the violence implicit in contemporary trafficking of women, femicides, and other aggressions toward non-European women.[50] In her 2010 article "Toward a Decolonial Feminism," Lugones compares the gender system imposed by the colonizers on both European and indigenous women.[51] If European women were marginalized and deprived of power within a heteronormative system, indigenous women were treated as savage beasts precisely because of their absence of gender. Therefore, they were categorized within a hierarchy that put them at the bottom; they were used for extremely grueling work; they were enslaved, exploited, and massacred. At the same time, they were perceived as a threat to patriarchal culture. The coloniality of gender has come to affect gender relations across the globe. Shara in *Miss Zombie* is exploited in a similar manner and perceived to be a potential threat to be dispatched with violence. Shara and Shizuko perform a paradigmatic function within the heteropatriarchal system they inhabit because they both suffer the consequences of coloniality of gender. And when we filter this context through the lens of disability, we see that this category is also applicable to both women. Shara is not shown to have any defined sexuality, yet from the moment she enters the household she is sexualized and she becomes a paradigm of the body of Shizuko, the wife. When Shara finally exchanges places with Shizuko, reviving her after death, the film briefly changes from black and white to color, signaling that Shara, having recovered the memories of her pre-zombie self, now is able to see the world from a "human" perspective, before she commits suicide.

White Slavery and the (Dead) Flesh Trade

Miss Zombie follows a tradition of White slavery we have observed in early films such as *White Zombie*, *I Walked with a Zombie*, *Night of the Living Dead*, and even in later films like *28 Days Later*, *Deadgirl*, the Portuguese short film *I'll See You in My Dreams*,[52] and *Attack of the Soviet Zombies*.[53] Though in the United States the notion of slavery is linked to African descendants and their exploitation beginning with the colonies, slavery has existed since antiquity, and many societies enslaved people regardless of the color of their skin. Because the first slaves in zombie movies are connected to sugar production, it is important to mention that slavery in the European sugar trade can be observed already in the year 1000 in the context of the Venetian market and its colonies in Crete and Cyprus.[54]

During the fourteenth-century plague, labor was dependent on the enslavement of the peoples of the Balkan Peninsula and the Slavic coast of Europe.

Nell Irvin Painter explains that the word "slave" derives from "slav."[55] However, with the transatlantic slave trade in the fifteenth century, enslavement became racialized. Portuguese and Spaniards trafficked people and goods all over the world. They valued people and distributed work in the colonies according to skin color. Indigenous populations were sent to the mines, while Blacks in the North were forced to work at cotton plantations.

By the nineteenth century, according to Painter, the concept of slavery was reduced to two types: the forced labor of Africans and Tartars, and the forced sexual slavery of women, principally from the region of the Black Sea, since they were thought to epitomize feminine beauty.[56] These women from Circassia, the Caucasus region, and Georgia represented the ideal of the odalisque based in the eroticism of Jean Baptiste Chardin (1643–1713), a traveler who had visited the region and identified them as the most beautiful he had ever seen.

Representations of White female beauty, such as the Circassian Beauty exhibition at P. T. Barnum's freak shows, always depicted women with some racialized features, meaning that they were not completely White, not blond or blue-eyed, and usually displayed kinky hair. These women often presented nude or in minimal clothing. In a letter from Barnum to John Greenwood (1864), he states that any beautiful woman can "pass for Circassian slaves." For the editor of the Lost Museum Archive, this letter shows the manipulation of public perception. These women were made "to appear exotic, regardless of [their] actual origins."[57] White women in early zombie movies are clearly White. However, they are racialized not in their own embodiment like in the freak shows but in the stigmatized space they inhabit. It is as if their bodies were marked and disabled through the physical space, their surroundings, and the people that they shared the space with, including its history of racialized slavery. Their racialization/zombification could even be understood as a kind of punishment for their choice of being in a stigmatized space.

In *White Zombie*, Madeleine Short, the White woman who arrives in Haiti and is zombified in order to be controlled by a man who desires her, represents very precisely this prototype of White slavery.[58] So does the Jessica Holland character in *I Walked with a Zombie*, who is turned into a zombie by her White mother-in-law for starting an affair with her other son.[59] Both are styled in the tradition of the beauty ideal of the Caucasian woman but are located in the Caribbean. It is important to point out that these two early notable Hollywood zombie offerings show a White woman turned zombie through a form of Haitian vodou practices, exoticizing these traditions in a way that could be made palatable to a White American audience looking for an orientalized view of women. Both women are disabled by their zombification. While Madeleine survives her zombie trance, Jessica dies at the hands of her erstwhile lover. Meanwhile, Barbra, in the later *Night of the Living Dead*, does retain some characteristics in common with the first two heroines.[60] Barbra not only carries the tradition of the same physical prototype but is also characterized as dependent upon men, fragile, and too incapacitated by her own gender and beauty to resist a zombie attack. Barbra's trauma is directly associated not only with her brother's death but also with the presence of Ben, the Black protagonist of the film. The fear of miscegenation haunts the film. The murder of fourteen-year-old Emmet Till, lynched after being accused of offending a White woman, occurred just over a decade before the filming of *Night of the Living Dead*, and the *Loving v. Virginia* decision, which finally made it legal for Black and White Americans to marry, was delivered just one year before the film was released.[61] The enclosure of a White woman, Barbra, in a house with a Black man against her will would have carried an extra load of racial tension and would in fact endanger Ben more than anyone. Violence toward White women during the late nineteenth and early twentieth centuries, loaded with the cultural effects of White slavery, was frequently used to justify violence toward Black men: according to the Equal Justice Initiative, some 25 percent of lynching victims were accused of sexual assault.[62] Many lynching spectacles of Black men were justified as for the "protection" of White women. The myth of the Black male beast and the sexually innocent White lady was used throughout the South during the late 1800s and first decades of the twentieth century and so anyone watching the film would have been familiar with this White anxiety about Black men.[63]

Regarding the z-genre, Kintra D. Brooks correctly states that there is a "violent erasure of black womanhood."[64] In *I Walked with a Zombie*, Black women are limited to serving and pleasing White women; they are completely inconsequential and yet visible. Black women in zombie narratives only start showing empowerment in movies such as *The Girl with All the Gifts*, *Atlantics* (*Atlantique*), and *Zombi Child*, where the perspective of Black women is centered, for they not only become protagonists but also are agents of their own future and the earth's.[65] The literal absence of Black women (worldwide, but especially in American productions) can be attributed to what Wilderson calls *Afropessimism*, according to which Black people are considered to always be in a state of social death (borrowing from Orlando Patterson), seen as perpetual corpses within twentieth-century humanism.[66] Their absence proves once more that Black bodies were never part of the humanist project and were, by definition, always fungible objects of pain.

Miss Zombie contains scenes that refer to trafficking of women in Asia. The Global Slavery Index (2014) indicates that almost two-thirds of a total 36 million trafficked women come from that continent.[67] Trafficked zombies are not only treated as domestic and sexual slaves but are also considered disposable in a world dominated by masculine hegemony.[68] We find a similar situation in the Korean animated film *Seoul Station*.[69] For protagonist Hye-sun, the life of an impoverished woman in a capitalist system offers no escape. She has run away from her pimp and seemingly found solace living with her boyfriend, who has betrayed her trust by creating a sex worker profile for her online. This allows her violent and vengeful pimp to track her down. In this film, fighting off a crowd of zombies is not the end of her worries; she will need to defend herself from the men for whom her worth is reduced to the commodity of her body. In the end, she kills the pimp, but only after she has become a zombie herself.

Attack of the Soviet Zombies presents us two distinct visions of the trafficking of women: one metaphorical and the other literal. While the first part is about a brigade of zombified soldiers led by a former general who controls zombies by wearing a mask of a dead person, the second part is the story of an emigrant to Russia called Georgina Spelvin who cannot get back to her country and is looking for help from the government. Both parts of the movie criticize government corruption. But the second part is also clearly about White slavery. Following government instructions, Georgina is led to a mysterious masked person who uses her as his sex slave. We do not know exactly who he is, but he is wearing a mask. All we can identify are some black and red gloves. Parallels with the general in the first part are clear. The general is not zombified, but he uses a mask to "help" women who want to get out of the building, leveraging this power to force himself on the captive women, who, like Georgina, have no other option but to comply. Actually, he never helps anyone to escape. We can only assume that this masked person in the second part, like the general, must also work for the government.

The 2019 *Trafficking in Persons Report* from the U.S. Department of State indicates that Russia does not meet the minimum standards for the elimination of trafficking of women.[70] The government has not done enough to protect immigrants who were deported after they were accused of prostitution without any investigation of exploitation. No wonder that exploitation of young immigrants who cannot return to their countries is part of a movie within a zombie movie. While Georgina is looking for the person she must meet, we do not see any interlocutor, and yet she is speaking aloud. It is as if she were addressing the spectator. It is a plea for help that needs to be heard. In reality, Georgina Spelvin is the artistic name of the American porn star Shelley Bob Graham (b. 1936). In this fictive movie within a movie called *The Unfortunate Life of Georgina Spelvin*, she is murdered and left to bleed out. Georgina becomes a paradigm of women who work in the sex industry or are forced into prostitution, are trafficked, and sexually exploited and/or murdered all over the world.

Liminality: Horrorizing Female Bodies

In most zombie films, the moment of resurrection is a moment of loss: loss of cognitive ability and memory, all that constitutes "soul."[71] The zombie returns to an animal state, driven only to reproduce and attack without selective criteria. Disturbingly for the spectator, he or she observes this transition from person to zombie. The viewer does experience horror at the transformation, even as the zombie does not. Though there is a process of change and decay in zombification, it is a slow process—fresh zombies look like the people they once were, making it difficult for those who previously knew them to easily kill them or destroy their brains.

For example, the little girl in the basement in *Night of the Living Dead* kills her mother, due to the parents' denial of her infection and their reluctance to destroy her. Barbra, in the same film, recognizes her brother Johnny as a zombie, attempts to reach out to him, and is seized by the mass of zombies as a result. In *Juan of the Dead*, it is the trans character "La China" who calls the viewer's attention even after she has become a zombie. That body, which does matter, survives until nearly the end of the film when Juan must destroy it in a gory scene that ironically earns the admiration of the failed *salvator mundi* American character. Even in *I Am a Hero*, the zombie Kyouko recognizes her ex-husband affectionately when he says her name.[72] Her momentary acknowledgment disarms him, allowing her to bite him. In *Resident Zombie*, love and care, as well as a moment of recognition in slow motion, do not stop the zombified mother from biting her daughter.

Some movies present the liminal state of zombies more clearly.[73] Across the genre, and depicted in steps, we see their bodies and minds in the process of transforming. This is what Anna Powell, following Gilles Deleuze, calls "becoming," or the liminal state of the transforming person that produces an effect of horror in "bodies and minds" of the spectators.[74] *Aaah! Zombies!!* (*Wasting Away*) plays with black-and-white and color footage to show us how important perception is when observing the process of changing from a human to a zombie state.[75] On the one hand, we have humans/spectators who see the group of four protagonists as black-and-white zombies, but the group itself cannot detect any major exterior changes among themselves. Their point of view is shown to us in full color. Kohen's technique allows us to visually perceive zombies as cognitive and sensitive human beings. It is only when Nick is shown a mirror that he can see how he really looks. Zombies in this movie fight to achieve a different future, which viewers perceive in black and white. The apocalyptic Australian movie *Cargo* follows Andy's metamorphosis from a concerned husband and father to a zombie, and we see him struggle to achieve his only goal, which is to provide a chance for survival for his infant daughter.[76] Andy prepares himself for his transformation: first he places a guard in his mouth and zip-ties his wrists so he cannot harm anyone. He works to prolong his liminal state as long as he can, so he can walk his daughter to safety.

As we have seen, since the very first Hollywood zombie films, the act of zombification has been explored through its effects on the female body in a way that not only exposes the traditional vulnerability of women in patriarchal systems but also highlights the ways that women are perceived to be monstrous. Mabel Moraña, following Rosi Braidotti, explains that "the monster and the woman represent difference because they are situated outside normality, as lack or as excess in relation to the parameters of a (phal)logocentrically defined normality."[77] This allows us to reject and devalue both women and the monstrous as things that are less than human.

In the Mexican film *Ladronas de almas* (whose title can be translated as "Soul Thieves"), the Cordero sisters, orphaned and isolated, adopt Haitian rituals to create zombies out of the men that would steal from them and abuse them as property.[78] It is the sisters' refusal to submit to the cruelties of the imperialist system and the coloniality of gender that marks them as uncontrollable women, and therefore unnatural. María (the eldest) is constantly warned by her servants that she is turning her sisters into "beasts" by involving them in her revenge. They learn to take advantage of a society in upheaval, the chaos of the revolution, and the absence of a paternal figure in their home to create and control monstrified men. Moraña explains that if, since antiquity, woman is seen as a "simultaneously mutilated body prone to the madness of flows, bodily deformation, and hysteria, the monster is also the site of irrationality, obsession, and the proliferation of matter."[79] We can recall Foucault's concept of biopolitics, which seeks to regulate the biological processes, the reproduction of bodies, and the effects of power on those bodies. The Corderos change reproduction by making creatures that are in thrall to them to take control of the biopolitical power within their reach.

Of course, within a biopolitical approach to the zombie genre, there is plenty of room to explore the female body as it makes its transformation to the living dead. *Pretty Dead* tells us the story of Regina, a medical student who suspects she has been infected by a parasitic fungus.[80] She decides to record her transformation step by step, sometimes filming herself, other times allowing other people to record events. The documentary style draws the viewer in and invites suspension of disbelief as we see the beginnings of her metamorphosis. Though doctors believe that she is suffering from schizophrenia and Cotard's syndrome, which makes her believe that she is dead, Regina is convinced she is becoming a zombie. While being interviewed by a doctor, she describes an incident in a bathroom when she felt so overwhelmingly attracted to the smell of blood that she opened the wastebasket and started sucking a used tampon as if it were a popsicle. Slowly, the fungus begins to have an impact on her brain, and Regina must increase the amount of blood and tissues she consumes in order to survive. This need leads her to kill at least three people, including her fiancé, Ryan. Regina dies and revives, but she is still able to distinguish between herself and what is inside her body. As Jones states, "Sociality impacts directly on how we position ourselves in the world, how we relate to others, how we assess ourselves, and so forth. . . . As she undergoes her transition into zom-being, Regina is torn between two incompatible modes of existence."[81] It becomes more and more difficult for her to justify her own actions within society, for she is sure that something inside her behaves like a beast.

Another important movie in this regard is the Japanese horror production titled *Splatter: Naked Blood*.[82] Although we do not encounter resurrected bodies in this production, we believe that it is a good example of the splattering violence imposed on women's bodies to make them appear cannibalistic and monstrous. Three women participate in a trial to receive a more permanent contraceptive solution. Instead, they are secretly given a substance called "My Son" that is supposed to be the ultimate painkiller because it turns pain into pleasure. The drug produces an excess of endorphins and affects each of the three subjects differently. The first woman becomes very hungry and devours all kinds of foods. In a grotesque and unexpected scene, she submerges her own hand in tempura sauce, fries it, and eats it. Slowly, she consumes parts of her own body, including her labia and an eye. Instead of pain, she appears to be experiencing erotic pleasure. The second woman decides to try body piercing. She begins by using pins to pierce her ears but ends up stabbing herself with an awl and other sharp tools all over her body, until she dies from her injuries. The third woman, Rika, is apparently not damaging her body, but we learn that she begins deriving pleasure from violence against others and ends up killing people she knows.

In *Contracted*, the filmmaker plays on body horror to detail Samantha's slow but inexorable transformation into a zombie. We feel her horror as she begins to literally fall apart. It is full of gory images of decay: she bleeds heavily as though menstruating, her eyes bleed, and her skin becomes pallid and rots; we are shown her decay in detail, organ by organ, including her hair, her teeth, and her fingernails. As in *Pretty Dead*, we get graphic details of the zombie transformation that culminates in her monstrous killings. All three movies, *Pretty Dead*, *Splatter: Naked Blood*, and *Contracted*, represent women as monstrous by focusing on female body productions or body parts that our culture has constructed as evil, damaging, or repulsive. In a scene in *Contracted*, reminiscent of the myth of the *vagina dentata*, Riley is afraid to penetrate Samantha's vagina because he perceives it as abhorrent: there are maggots coming out of it. This depiction of this orifice as the source of putridity is a reference to the body part usually associated with the uncleanliness of menstruation.

Though the man who infected Samantha displays abhorrent behavior in raping her, he is immune, clean, and handsome. Samantha is perceived as abominable for having been raped by an infected male, placing the blame for the unwanted sexual contact on the woman. In *Splatter: Naked Blood*, Rika's doctor has determined that part of her problem is based on a psychological trauma brought on by her first menstruation in fifth grade, for which she had not been prepared. Menstruation is to blame, and women are made the source of impurity. According to Kristeva, menstruation is the abject in the female body that needs to be expelled; it is the "death infecting life" that allows the in-between of a subject and an object.[83] Thomas Lacqueur explains that physicians in the Renaissance believed that menstruation was linked to an economy of excess: unlike male bodies, female bodies would not burn all the heat produced by nourishment, so residues were transformed into menstruation. Pregnant women, on the other hand, would transform menstrual fluid into breast milk to feed the fetus.[84] In *Splatter*, menstrual excess manifests itself as too many endorphins, the element of *jouissance* (in the Lacanian sense) that allows so much pleasure that it is painful to bear.

Horror movies, even in the twenty-first century, still use a focus on the supposed filthy quality of menstrual blood, which has always been linked to impurity and sin.[85] Regina, in *Pretty Dead*, helps us visualize that female monstrosity when she describes a tampon as a "fucking popsicle" that she really enjoys. In a way, she is redefining menstruation. Regina craves that blood; it is no longer a taboo, but satisfying and pleasurable. In *It Stains the Sands Red*, a zombie follows Molly through the desert.[86] In order to evade the creature, she throws a dripping bloody tampon into the distance to lure the zombie away so that she can escape. However, the zombie feels attracted to the smell of blood running down her legs and tracks her down. Even zombies seem to enjoy this newly resemanticized blood. As in Thomas Lacqueur's theories, menstruation is linked to nutritional excess, but a positive and gratifying one for zombies.

Beyond the Anthropocene: Toward a Crip Futurity

One way to think of female bodies in these zombie films is that there is something already crippling about inhabiting femininity. Whether they become zombies themselves or are simply added to the number of worldwide femicides, women in zombie films are bodies that are leaky, messy, and always vulnerable. Women in zombie films exist as dis-abled. Alison Kafer explores the connection between disability and "crip time." *Cripping* can be defined as the conceptualization of disability in temporal terms. If ableist society conceives of disability as temporary, looking for a future "cure" for any deviations from what is considered "normal," subjects with permanent disabilities will never see an optimistic future. However, cripping zombies means modifying our conception of able bodies. According to Kafer, we all, at some point in our lives, have had or will have a disability. Therefore, the state of being able-bodied is what should be seen as temporary, not permanent. This cripping suggests that we do away with our vision of an ableist society and break with the so-called ableist project implicit in the perspective culturally imposed upon us since the Renaissance, as described by Florensky.[87]

The Year of the Apocalypse (*El año del apocalipsis*) presents twelve vignettes, corresponding to the months of a zombie apocalypse year.[88] In one of them, the adults leave the very young and the very old in a secure location protected by teenagers and younger adults while they go searching for help and supplies. Upon realizing that the adults are unlikely to return, the teens decide to modify their own temporality and revise their concept of past and future. For this generation, the future is the present moment, and only by eliminating the children (of the future) and the elderly (of the past) will they be able to survive. For these young people, the end of the past and of the performative future constitutes their present, and their new beginning. They decide that, due to their respective ages, the elderly and the children are disabled, and so they poison them to control their present moment. The notion of the future is eliminated, and time shrinks down to what they can do in the present apocalyptic moment. Longevity is irrelevant. To a degree, this scene recalls the concept of "strange temporalities" proposed by Judith Halberstam referring to the AIDS-era reaction by some in the gay community to pursue a life that revolved around "risk, illness, infection and death."[89] The AIDS emergency brought the focus on the present moment as opposed to a long future life. This "strange temporality" is reflected in the teens in Arévalos's film since, confronting the risk of death and the zombie epidemic, they are forced to consider the supremacy of the present over the future or the past. They are anticipating a zombie (queer, crip) temporality that rejects future heterosexual reproduction and the durability of old age. But the horrific part is that they do so as humans, before becoming zombies (and in fact attempting to avoid that fate). In other words, what we are discussing on a figurative level with the metaphor of the zombie, they are enacting *literally*. The uninfected youths (with only a few exceptions) do not hesitate to reject the past as well as futurity. These actions leave the viewer with a question. Which is crueler: a mindless zombie attack or an orchestrated murder of children and elderly people within a safe harbor? Who are the true monsters? On the other hand, we were able to observe these same cruel considerations as to the value of young and old life during the COVID-19 pandemic. There was pressure to leave the elderly to die and to send the children to crowded schools because they are more likely to be asymptomatic, therefore endangering the lives of all those to whom they might spread the virus, including those family members with pre-existing conditions.[90] And all this, just for the sake of the economy.

Kafer suggests other methods of approaching the future that reject a notion of heterosexual reproduction in which only White, privileged children can be the recipients of a curative imaginary. The "queer, children of color, and street kids" have never been the basis for the imagined future.[91] These children are considered sick, degenerate, contagious; their mothers are sterilized in an attempt at extermination. The statistics of child casualties of COVID-19 show us that although the percentage of children with fatal cases is low, 85 percent of children who have died have been Black and Latinx children.[92] Kafer, for her part, proposes a union of queer temporality and crip time to create an intersectional vision that includes gender, disability, race, and class. For Kim Hall, too much criticism aligns with global capitalism and focuses on a privileged and classist reproductive future, ignoring marginalized communities. Hence, the opportunity to incorporate resistance movements into these unbalanced systems is lost. On the other hand, Hall opposes rejecting the future openly since any discussion of the future should include our relationship to the planet, sustainability, and climate change.[93] As we will see in the next chapter, we are invited to consider a vision that does not revolve around man and that considers, following Braidotti, a posthumanism that helps raise awareness of the nonhuman, therefore imagining a future that is inclusive and responsible.[94] The "radical hope" that Hall proposes for a queer, feminist, crip, and ecological future implies a compromise with alternative ways of life and incorporates organic and inorganic beings, even when this implies a context of uncertainty.[95] For example, the porous borders between the human and the nonhuman can create a future with beings of a *transcorporeal* identity—something that already in itself reveals the interdependence of man and nature.[96] It is indispensable to rethink the future in nonanthropocentric forms because only in this way can we achieve sustainability.

5

Of Matter, Dust, and Earth

Zombies and the Environment

The popularity of catastrophe films signals contemporary visual culture's fixation on the apocalyptic end to humanity and what that end will mean for the planet. According to Eva Horn, our obsession with environmental catastrophes in contemporary narratives illustrates the future from the viewpoint of our present, while imagining the future as a possible past.[1] Through these stories, we project the moment in which we will be able to see the destruction produced by the Anthropocene era as a past that has already happened. These narratives that we can find not only in film but also in literature, gaming, and other cultural manifestations are not entirely new (though their recent proliferation is notable). In fact, the influence of the biblical Book of Revelation made itself known as early as the turn of the first century when images of "apocalyptic virgins" (e.g., Immaculate Conception, the Virgin of Guadalupe) became very popular due to fears of the end of the world.[2]

The Coming Catastrophe

In the Middle Ages, personal catastrophe was expressed in skull imagery or in *vanitas* paintings. Individual endings are visualized vis-à-vis the end of the world. During the Baroque period, *vanitas* art was enhanced with an ecclesiastical background. Behind the skull, images of Christ and the Final Judgment were added, as a reminder that divine vigilance was eternal and that deeds conducted in life would decide our future, a fate imagined in the present, but as "future perfect," a sealed fate that is paradoxically presented as a choice.[3] The still lifes of the Baroque period depicted even inanimate nature in decay, emphasizing ephemerality. These concepts were adapted to avant-garde ideology in the twentieth century.[4] Twenty-first-century still life paintings continue to depict the decay of flora and fauna, while they also include the objectification and destruction of the human body.[5]

All this to say that visual art depicting the transitory nature of life and consciousness of impending death is an ancient and persistent tradition. The twist that the zombie film adds to this long convention is that it allows us to visualize possible catastrophic global consequences that are rooted in the impact of human activity on the climate and environment during the Anthropocene era. Following Horn, modern imagined scenes of climate catastrophe illuminate the political, social, and epistemological dimensions of these future disasters and also give us a clear indication of the current state of science.[6] For Horn, the coming *metacrisis* will not be produced by a single event or in a single place but will be the product of "the sheer perpetuation of current policies, lifestyles, and modes of managing the future."[7] Therefore, the visualized disasters of our collective imaginary (in popular culture) give us space to contemplate disasters that are overwhelming in their totality and yet are necessary in order to navigate the future, examine the anxieties and expectations, and understand the ideologies that carry us forward.[8] In the most apocalyptic terms (where "apocalypse" refers to its original meaning of "revelation"), these narratives reveal to us the underlying frameworks, the most horrific expressions of what already exists in the present, the foreseeable looming catastrophe.[9]

Priscilla Wald has focused on the outbreak narratives that have become even more popular since the AIDS epidemic of the 1980s. According to Wald, outbreak narratives in scientific texts, news reports, and even in fiction contain a common pattern: identification of the infection, elaboration of the global networks that give rise to its spread, and description of the epidemiological work of containment. Wald highlights the consequences of these narratives: "As they disseminate information . . . they promote or mitigate the stigmatizing of individuals, groups, populations, locales (regional and global), behaviors, and lifestyles, and they change economies."[10] Thus, many times in outbreak narratives, many of which are also zombie narratives, the infected can be stigmatized as the carriers of disease. We saw this during the AIDS crisis, which was reduced, in homophobic terms, to a "gay plague." We have also seen the same kind of process during the COVID-19 epidemic, in which the xenophobic terms "Wuhan virus" or "Kung Flu" were used early on to stigmatize the place the disease was first identified, including by the president of the United States.[11] Cultural criticisms were also involved, with the "wet market" where the disease was believed to have originated being exoticized and scandalized as though local food culture were to blame.

Animality of the Other: Immigrants as a Force of Nature

On June 29, 2020, President Trump tweeted: "Democrats are the problem. They don't care about crime and want illegal immigrants, no matter how bad they may be, to pour into and infest our Country, like MS-13." This commentary highlights the way in which biopolitics are conceived by some in the United States. Immigrants are explicitly described as a danger to personal and national security (like the gang MS-13, which actually originated in the carceral subculture of the United States) and as an *infestation*. They are thus equivalent to an influx of insects or rodents, which in the popular imagination are considered to be filth-ridden carriers of disease.[12] This threat is articulated in zoological language that associates them with pestilence. Trump often read the poem "The Snake" at his rallies to describe his views on immigration, always with a wildly positive response from his supporters. The reading describes a generous woman who finds an ailing snake who begs to be taken in and helped. When she cares for the snake and takes him to her bosom, he bites her. She weeps, knowing that the snake's venom is poisonous, and asks him why he would do that after being treated with such kindness. At this point, Trump's dramatic reading becomes more exaggerated as he recites the snake's answer, "'Oh shut up, silly woman,' said the reptile with a grin / 'You knew damn well I was a snake before you took me in.'" At the 2018 Conservative Political Action Conference, Trump prefaced the poem with an explicit instruction to the crowd to think of the poem in terms of immigration, just in case his intent was unclear. In Trump's retelling, the woman is a lovely and generous personification of the United States, and the snake represents the ungrateful immigrant that will bite its host *because that is its nature*. To add insult to injury, Trump has never attributed the poem to its author, Oscar Brown Jr., an African American musician and activist who, his family members have said, would be horrified at this use of his work.[13] While Trump is not the first nationalist leader in history to characterize minority populations as animals, it would be difficult to hammer the point home with less subtlety than he: "These aren't people. These are animals," he said on May 16, 2018. His discourse also repeatedly includes water imagery, as in how immigrants "pour into" the country. He has used "floods," "flow," and "overflow" many times to describe the movement of immigrants (and the dangers he insists they bring). This confers upon the already "animalized" immigrants the qualities of an unstoppable tidal wave—they *flow* like a torrent and *flood* our country that is *overflowing* with crime—framing many categories of would-be immigrants (migrant workers, asylum seekers, the undocumented, and those attempting to enter legally) in the terms of natural disaster.

Campesi states that the discourse of biopolitics, and especially securitization discourse,[14] classifies immigrants as threatening transnational agents; as the embodiment of a dangerous potential for cultural, ethnic, or social imbalance; or as economic rivals that only wish to take advantage of an existing system.[15] The above examples of Trump's rhetoric place immigrants at the intersection of these three factors. Trump's use of the "infestation" of immigrants, about "invading caravans" that threaten our national security, intends to justify a crisis created at the southern U.S. border, to institute a *state of exception* in which to suppress asylum requests, separate families, and keep immigrants in cages as though they are infected animals, depriving them of medical attention, thereby murdering them.[16]

The parallel between immigrant and minority groups and zombie hordes is obvious in this kind of rhetoric, and it turns the incarcerated immigrant from political refugee to caged beast who deserves its fate. *Infection* (*Infección*) is a Venezuelan film that was banned by Nicolás Maduro for containing social and political commentary that equates *Chavismo* with pandemic disease.[17] When impoverished, starving Venezuelan survivors leave national territory (after the credits); they are seen as infected immigrants, literally as zombies (though they are not), who put the national security of other Latin American countries at risk. Pedota shows 5 million people fleeing misery and violence in their country, only to receive the same treatment Trumpist rhetoric deals to Central American migrants. Salazar in *Savageland*, a movie that takes place at the border between the United States and Mexico, experiences a similar fate.[18] While the border, according to Gloria Anzaldúa, might be perceived by Whites as a way to protect themselves from mixing with "savages,"[19] Sayak Valencia describes it as a liminal space where anything can happen.[20] Priscilla Wald certainly cautions against stigmatizing spaces with characterizations of "the primitive."[21] To ascribe savagery to a space and its people is to ignore the structural racism and extreme poverty that contribute to our perceptions and to impose qualitative judgments on cultural difference.

Human Exceptionalism: Who Is Nature "For"?

In this section we will study the reductionist development of the term "nature," in both its metaphysical meaning and accessibility to bodies considered disabled. Part of the reason for the rhetorical use of animalizing, naturalizing, and essentializing language is to allow the speaker to feel hierarchically and morally superior to the targeted population. It sets up an opposition between the "civilized" and the "savage," the "human" and the "animal": man versus nature. Those higher on the hierarchical structure therefore can use or exploit that which falls lower on the scale, which includes nature and the animal world. Zombie narratives explore this opposition. Zombies are stripped of their identity and reduced to their biological matter; they are violent, brain-dead, bloodthirsty. They are us, only lacking what we feel makes us human. They are disastrous and catastrophic and often arise from tragic human error. They thus embody that uncontrollable element that evokes horror in nature, while simultaneously being explicitly *un*-natural, rising when they should rest. The opposition between humanity and nature, however, does not include all humans. Atypical or disabled bodies also fall outside of this hierarchy and can therefore be denied access to nature. It will be helpful then to examine how attitudes toward nature have changed over the centuries and how we have arrived in the Anthropocene era, in which human activity is the dominant force affecting the environment. How do we define the concept of *nature* today?

What do we mean by "the natural world"? Who should have access to it? The poem "On the Nature of Things" (*De rerum natura*) by the philosopher Lucretius (99 B.C.–55 B.C.) includes a reflection on the philosophy of Epicurus, his interest in *atomism* and thoughts on immortality and the materialism of the soul.[22] This didactic poem also imparts a clear understanding of the concept of nature as it was known in antiquity. While in postindustrial society nature has come to signify untouched wilderness and natural resources, nature for Lucretius was a vast concept that included a secular view of metaphysics, ontology, theology, and physics. The poem is directed at Venus, the mother of nature: "I will disclose / the first principles of matter, the ones / nature uses to produce, increase, sustain / all things, and into which she changes them / once more, when they disintegrate . . ."[23] The relationship between nature and humanity in Lucretius can be seen in his vision of the effect of the plague on the human body.[24] During the Peloponnesian War between Athens and Sparta a plague fell, covering parts of the Greek world.[25] Lucretius notes that the body of a survivor of the plague would be visibly marked. And it is exactly this visibility on the human body that unites man and nature. Before the development of modern science, nature was considered in terms of philosophical union with the universe. Natural philosophy aimed to explain the universe, and so it delved into areas such as astrology, cosmology, the nature of matter, and infinity. But beginning with the nineteenth century, modern science separated natural philosophy into the disciplines of biology and physics, and "nature" was eventually reduced to physical matter, to exploitable (or nonexploitable) resources that were only accessible to a very few.

Who can reach the mountain peak, or walk along beaches, or go to the desert dunes? Who can freely use the forest routes and mountain passes? Which bodies have access to rivers and oceans? Who can dig gold from the mines? Alison Kafer notes that modern architecture has limited this access to only able bodies. It is assumed that the pathways, streets, and bridges between the civilized world and untouched wilderness will only be "walked" by the able-bodied who can appreciate contact with "nature."[26] In this way, the experience of

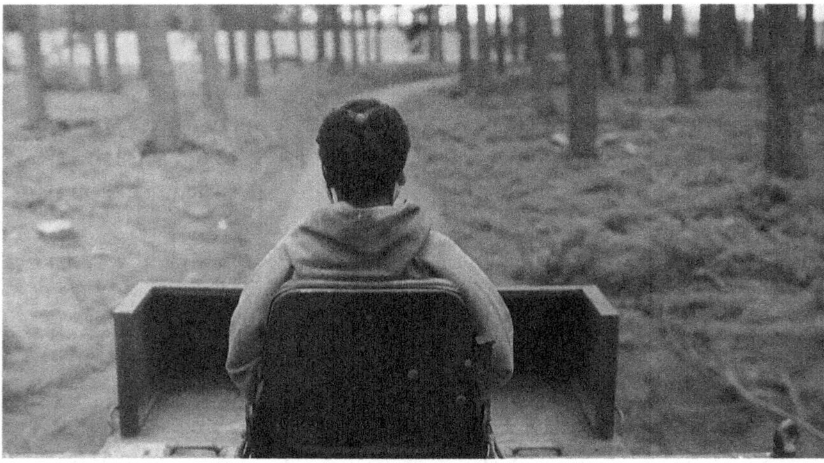

Melanie, in *The Girl with All the Gifts*, experiences nature while strapped to the roof of a vehicle. (Credit: Colm McCarthy, *The Girl with All the Gifts*, 2016.)

illness and disability must be considered to change the way we conceive of spaces for human use. *The Girl with All the Gifts* contains a crip view that allows us to understand the temporal element of what we consider "ability" and the inversion of the idea of "disability" as the film progresses.[27] The young "hungries" (the children born of infected mothers but who, unlike infected adults, retain their ability to think and speak) possess a mutation that makes them superior to humans in many respects: they are more intelligent, faster, and have more finely tuned senses. This mutation also makes them cannibals. They are treated as disabled: though they have better reflexes and physical ability than uninfected humans, they are restrained in wheelchairs that immobilize them at all times. Even their heads are held immobile with restraints. Their cannibalism—the thing that makes them monsters—must be forcefully disabled and locked up. Since Melanie, the protagonist of the film, is played by an actress of African descent, the relationship between race and disability plays a role here. Her race disables her, and her disability racializes her. The young "hungries" are dressed in sweatsuits reminiscent of prison garb, which also has a racializing effect, since in the United Kingdom the proportion of racial minorities in prisons is at 25 percent, although this group only comprises 14 percent of the total population. Disability, united with racial difference, is presented as monstrous. When the army base where they are contained is attacked by mindless adult "hungries," the research team escapes, taking Melanie along because of her value as a research subject that may embody the only solution to save humanity. She is not allowed within the vehicle, however—she is fixed to the roof of the truck, immobilized, and muzzled in her chair. The first time she is allowed to interact with nature, she does so from her perspective as a disabled body. However, over the course of the film, as Melanie realizes that she is more in tune with the modified nature of the post-outbreak planet, it is the one surviving uninfected member of the research team who is jailed, restrained in a protective bubble. As Melanie's understanding of her categorization as "monster" is shattered, the tables turn. Now the previously "healthy" human is "disabled" by the changing environment and the world that will be inherited by the "hungries."

Imagined Immunities: Natural and Acquired

To understand the concept of infection, we should examine its relationship to immunity. As Roberto Esposito proposes, in a sovereign state, control of the population is based on immunization against racial and cultural viruses.[28] If medical immunization is achieved via a vaccine containing small doses of the pathogen, in political life, immigrants slowly trespass into national territory and have gradual effects on the culture, language, and racial composition of a nation. Here is the model of the immigrant as pathogen with immunological potential, contributing to the general health of the population in small doses, but a "cure" that can hurt or kill if taken to extremes. Immunization is paradigmatic of migratory politics and thus, as explained by P. B. Preciado, Esposito ties the biopolitical notion of *community* with the epidemiological notion of *immunity*. The common root of the two terms, *munus*, implies a gift, a bribe, or a tribute that must be paid to participate in a given community. In sovereign states, again according to Esposito, *immunity* refers to the state of being protected from certain communal (political, legal) obligations—a state that is enjoyed by only some of the members of a community. Others are de-munized, deprived of privileges, having been deemed a threat to a community, which automatically creates a hierarchy that places the immunized above the less privileged. Preciado reminds us of the way that the Nazi government de-munized Jews, gays, and the disabled, among others, and symbolically turned them into a threat that endangered the Aryan race. This immunitary ethos did not end with the Nazis—it is the very same ethos that informs the actions of Immigration and Customs Enforcement at the U.S.-Mexico border.[29] The treatment of migrants at the border is informed by the belief that they are like an infectious pathogen; they are de-munized as a destabilizing physical and cultural threat.

During a real pandemic, such as AIDS or COVID-19, it is easy to see which bodies matter, which are the sovereign bodies: the able bodies, the AIDS-free bodies, heteronormative bodies, White bodies, young bodies, and socially and economically privileged bodies from which labor and profit can be extracted. These are the immunized bodies that can work from home, continue to receive paychecks, and proceed with online purchases. On the other hand, the elderly, the disabled, the criminalized and incarcerated all are housed in institutions that have been the center of the worst outbreaks. Those considered essential workers (wage laborers that are disproportionately migrants and minorities) are de-munized to the extent that they are obligated to continue to expose themselves to the virus in dangerous circumstances. Preciado asserts that COVID-19, unlike other pandemics, has exposed a very different type of biopolitics since the borders we must protect are the borders of our physical bodies: our masks and sanitized skin are the liminal spaces that we must control and defend. Our houses are the "soft prisons" of the future and the site of surveillance and discipline.[30] In film, the zombie body is not only a body bereft of soul or consciousness but also the embodiment of the pathogen we must protect ourselves against, a pathogen that has acquired a series of nuances of meaning: undocumented migrants, people of color, the homeless, the poor, sex workers, and so on. These de-munized bodies are seen as the cause of the infection. Even in films where there is a cure that will reverse the effects of a zombie disease, the cured survivors sometimes continue to be de-munized in society (as they are paradoxically immunized from the virus). In *Resident Zombie*, cured subjects commiserate in their poverty, unable to find jobs or be accepted in society. In the Irish film *The Cured*, traumatized former zombies are trying to reintegrate into a general population that no longer considers them human.[31] They form a Cured Alliance that sometimes takes drastic and violent measures to make their cause known, which in the Irish context resonates with the historical Troubles of the end of the twentieth century. In both of these films, having been once infected and then cured is no antidote for the perception of the once-zombie subject as an eternal Other, and therefore not acceptable in large doses. In our own current context, as welcome news of vaccines for COVID-19 spreads, we are left with an ethical question: Which populations have been used to test vaccines during all of their stages? It is said that nations with high infections have benefited, but it turns out that many pharmaceutical companies exclusively used Latin American populations for experimentation.[32] In other words, in this case we see how the process of immunization (here in the medical sense) de-munizes some populations. Their bodies are experimental spaces where potential immunization from the virus is being created.

As introduced above, there has been a turn toward not only vaccinating against zombification but curing those already infected, and we have noticed a variety of approaches to the concept of a cure. For example, *Warm Bodies* depicts how a consumption of affect in neoliberal societies manages to neutralize and even reverse the effects of zombification.[33] Affect has been commodified, and simply seeing images of love and affection has the ability to "cure" the afflicted. The zombie is seen as morally inferior precisely because of its lack of affect. In the Disney film *Z-O-M-B-I-E-S*, the zombies' integration into society is all thanks to a "disneyfied" romance in which two teens from opposite sides of the tracks—or in this case, the Zombie Wall—are able to bring their communities together, and the audience is encouraged to believe that societal problems, including racism, can be solved through the love of a White girl and excellence in football. These two examples, both falling under the description of a zombie romantic comedy (zom-rom-com?) express a type of wish-fulfillment fantasy, in which any horror can be overcome, if we just love one another. What kind of love is capable of such miracles? Heterosexual romantic love, of course! On the other hand, *Pontypool* suggests that viral spread can be halted by a refusal to understand language—that is to say, by the examination of what lies behind the meaning. The virus in this Canadian film is spread through a contagion of language, its emptiness of meaning: for example, the rhetoric of "fake news" and the false and commercialized sentiment of Hallmark cards is partially spread via a news broadcast on Valentine's Day. As opposed to *Warm Bodies*, which relies upon the cliches of the romantic comedy genre, *Pontypool* questions the possibility of conveying affect through terms of endearment. In a critique of colonialism and patriarchal hegemony, only English words carry the virus in a semiotic game between signified and signifier within the colonial Canadian context. By removing meaning and affect from linguistic games, *Pontypool* underscores one way humanity separates itself from its natural environment by attempting to have control over reality itself through manipulation of representation. In this way, the affect associated with a traditional happy ending can be implemented to distract from impending environmental catastrophe.

The 2019 South Korean film *The Odd Family: Zombie on Sale* explores the ideas of immunities, cures, and their effects.[34] This comedy begins when an idiosyncratic family of grifters (an odd family, as the title suggests) finds a zombie that was created as a result of illegal experimentation by a company called HumanBio that was pursuing a cure for diabetes. The irony of creating a deadly virus while hoping to cure another human ailment is, in itself, a commentary on human attempts to control nature.[35] When the zombie escapes his storage pod and stumbles upon Man-duk, the patriarch of the family, and bites him on the head, Man-duk eventually realizes that the bite has endowed him with enhanced virility and a youthful vitality. Soon the elders of the village are all clamoring to be bitten by the zombie and Man-duk (a gambler and a cheater who is keen to make a profit) promises them all a bite for cash.

The zombie Jjong-bi himself is at the family's mercy, ready to be kidnapped, manipulated, and chained. Luckily, the pop-star-handsome zombie is not simply carnivorous. He is able to content himself by eating cabbage, when necessary, especially under the care of the lovestruck daughter, Hae-gul. In fact, he appears to become more and more passive under her influence. He not only seems to benefit from the same type of affective cure we saw in *Warm Bodies* but becomes the source of a revitalization of village life. After he has bitten dozens of old men, conferring on them some of his masculine vigor, the patriarch takes the money and absconds to Hawaii. However, at the wedding of one of these old men to a new young bride, all the formerly old men start to turn violent, exposing their zombie state. They turn the celebration into a bloodbath, infecting all the villagers and turning them into traditional, undead, flesh-tearing zombies. As the family escapes, the father returns from Hawaii, and it becomes clear that he alone is immune to the zombie infection and so must become the source of the vaccine.

The notion of a natural immunity to the zombie plague has been explored in various films of the genre, and very often in terms of a younger generation, emphasizing the possibility of a post-zombie futurity. The immune character appears in many films, *28 Weeks Later* and *I Am Legend* among them.[36] In *Infection*, director Pedota includes a character with a natural immunity, a young boy who is treasured and protected for the genetic secret he carries within him, which will be used to eradicate the pandemic and save the nation and humanity. In *Blood Quantum*, the indigenous population of Canada is immune to the virus suffered by White, colonizing society. This presents an alternative to the reality of the historical, White-borne diseases that killed so many indigenous peoples across the Americas. At the end of the film, the surviving mixed-race daughter of Charlie and Joseph represents future hope, having been an immune infant born of an infected mother. Unlike the narrative of this film, however, COVID-19 has had a disproportionate effect on native populations for multiple societal and economic reasons.

Descendents (*Solos*), directed by the Chilean Jorge Olguín, presents us a post-humanist alternative for the future. Camille wanders through a dystopian landscape in which the adults have been turned into cannibals or destroyed by a violent military. The children are revealed to be mutants, as they develop something akin to gills, and feel themselves drawn to the sea. Once there, Camille finds a weird sea-creature that has been calling to the children, indicating that they represent a step toward amphibious evolution that will improve upon humanity. *Descendents* suggests the possibility of going beyond the anthropocentric idea of what "survival" should look like.

The Philippine film *Block Z* follows a zombie outbreak at a university medical school and centers on the character of P. J., a student, and her father, Mario.[37] The immunity factor here is due to random luck: Mario and his daughter have some kind of genetic immunity. As the victims continue to fall due to the spread of the virus, the film changes gears and incorporates a natural catastrophe into the narrative: a typhoon lays waste to the island and destroys the zombies, who are vulnerable to water. This event recalls the deadly Typhoon Haiyan (aka Yolanda) that devastated the Philippines in 2013. But this Great Flood narrative ends with apocalyptic salvation: though the zombie virus is a cataclysmic event that was probably caused by humanity, the typhoon is a second apocalyptic event that intervenes to negate the first and cleanses the island of its pestilence. Mario, the source of the DNA immunity, becomes a paradigm of the biblical Noah, or even flood heroes of earlier myths, like Atrahasis.[38] Both the Bible and Ovid's *Metamorphoses* contain Great Flood narratives; both events are the result of divine punishment for human sinfulness, and both have a hero chosen by the gods. This unilateral decision that chooses the victims and survivors of a catastrophe in advance aligns with the premise of ecofascism. Though speaking of ecofascism in ancient texts is certainly an anachronism, part of the intention of these mythical floods, including in the epic poem *Gilgamesh*, is to control bad behavior and overpopulation. In *Block Z*, the typhoon eliminates the undesirable zombies. The film ends with the news that P. J.'s boyfriend also survived the zombies and the flood, which opens the possibility of a heterosexual future as commanded in Genesis: "Be fruitful and multiply and fill the earth." (Genesis 9:1). This film, then, presents a much more traditional apocalypse, where some will die horribly, but the chosen few will continue on to ensure the survival of humanity.

"It will be best if we open up and flood the zone," wrote science advisor Paul Alexander to President Trump, referring to a herd immunity strategy that was supposed to give natural exposure/immunity to young Americans: "We want them infected." The message was clear, the COVID-19 virus should inundate the population like the flood because only the weak and infirm will be lost. As Dan Diamond states, these intentional "natural" immunity plans "deliberately expos[ed] less vulnerable populations in hopes of re-opening the economy."[39] However, we all know that as children get infected, they bring the virus home and spread it to other family members. And thus, more vulnerable people are exposed due to limited access to health care: Blacks, Latinx, indigenous, the disabled, the elderly, the poor—in general, all those who would be sacrificed in ecofascist necropolitics.

Along with the notion of a natural immunity, the trope of a "patient zero" as a possible source for answers and solutions to the virus recurs frequently in the genre. For example, in the film *Battle of the Undead*, a squad of Israeli soldiers is sent on a secret mission to Lebanon with the objective of capturing Manzur, who they are told is an important person in Hezbollah and is suspected of creating biological weapons.[40] When they arrive at his villa, they find his daughter, who reveals that Manzur had been making a biological weapon but was working for the Israeli general who sent the squad. She also tells them that her father had experimented on himself under pressure from the Israelis and in fact is the "patient zero" of the zombie outbreak. When the Israeli squad members obtain a sample of his blood, they eliminate him, hoping to develop a cure from the sample. As a zombie, he is no longer of value; the raw material of his blood becomes the mission target.

Likewise, in *Dead Trigger*, "patient zero" was once the original test subject in a trial for a cancer cure that went horribly wrong and started a violent outbreak.[41] Jjong-bi, "patient zero" in *The Odd Family*, is dealt a kinder fate, in a gentler tale, but he is also used and abused as an object until he eventually proves himself worthy of becoming part of the family. Priscilla Wald has explored the myth of "patient zero" in real historical scenarios such as Typhoid Mary and the man popularly identified as Patient Zero in the AIDS epidemic. She elaborates the ways that these fellow sufferers of the same disease have been turned into symbols of the foreign, the intrusive, and sometimes, the intentional spreader in order to serve a narrative that grants innocence to the healthy and levels judgment upon the sick.[42] In zombie films, the "patient zero" is often considered to be a means to a cure, but rarely as a human participant in his own fate. The immunity narratives and the "patient zero" narratives differ in that respect: the healthy are saviors; the afflicted are tools.

Return to the Garden: Ecofeminism, Ecofascism

The interdependence between humans and nature is implicit in the zombie genre. The many forms that zombification takes in global zombie films tend to affect the environment as well as the humans-turned-zombies. These forms include (but are not limited to) radiation from nuclear explosions, global spread of a virus, toxic pollution by transnational corporations, extractivist[43] exploitation of natural resources, mining, fracking, toxins from outer space, even necrophilia[44] and zoophilia.[45] An ecofeminist reading of zombies might help us to understand the relationship between zombies and nature and the kinds of futures they propose. The idea that a zombie apocalypse is equal to the cancellation or negation of the future is incorrect. From a queer, crip, *and* ecofeminist perspective, the zombie allows a break with ableist, heteronormative societies. Ecofeminism adds a feminist aspect to ecological concerns. Authors such as María Mies and Vandana Shiva explore how *biocidal* capitalist systems are based on the colonization of women, lands, and their resources.[46] Thus, we see that in the so-called Third World, women's health suffers most from the consequences of "modernization." For example, reproductive rights should be seen through the lens of demographic pressure on the planet; toxic materials used in construction should be examined in terms of the endocrine disruptors they produce that affect women's health, as should the use of xenoestrogens that have an impact on the number of cases of breast cancer.[47] But it is also important to understand that ecofeminism doesn't imply that "woman" should be identified with "nature" in an essentialist manner. Doing so gives rise to an extractivist mentality that harms nature as much as it harms women, exposing them both to exploitation and violent use. We cannot continue with what Alicia Puleo calls the *naturalization of women* and the *feminization of nature*.[48] She proposes an "enlightened ecofeminism," one that "inscribes itself into the tradition of the critique of oppression and the defense of equality."[49]

Ecofeminism studies intersectionality of gender, sex, race, class, North–South divisions, and environmental damage.[50]

Endzeit,[51] German for "the end of time" but known in English as *Ever After*,[52] is a feminist project directed by Swedish/German Carolina Hellsgård, based on a graphic novel by Olivia Vieweg. In this film, the territory that used to be East Germany is divided in two and consists of the only two cities with survivors of the zombie outbreak: Weimar, where the infected are executed immediately without exception, and Jena, where they are attempting to find a cure. In this zombie-infested landscape where the cities have strict rules about enclosure and security (these protected spaces and their barbed-wire fences, informed by the setting, recall the enclosures of Nazi concentration camps), two very different young women manage to escape Weimar, and they find themselves on a train bound for Jena. Vivi is depicted as weak, dependent on psychiatric drugs, and ill equipped to survive in a dystopian world. Eva, on the other hand, worked as a supervisor on the wall that keeps the zombies out. Eva forces Vivi to disregard her disability by throwing away her medication. After Vivi discovers that Eva is infected, the two are separated in a zombie attack. Vivi comes across a woman known as "the Gardener," a posthuman character who appears to be part woman, part plant: she has united with the earth, and roots of plants and trees spring from her veins. She cultivates apples, tomatoes, and strawberries in a greenhouse, and the food she grows appears to allow her union with nature and also protects her from the zombie virus. Meanwhile, Eva has survived the attack, and Vivi finds her as she is about to become a zombie. The Gardener gives Eva a "life extension" (in the form of food she has produced) but in return asks that Vivi remain with her. The Gardener character, whose function is to "open unexpected doors," is fairly problematic, for she assumes the divine power to morally judge humans. According to her, mortals have wasted their chance to live in Paradise (Eden). What is more, when asked by Vivi when the zombie outbreak will end, she answers, "When an angel comes accompanied by a beast." These apocalyptic images have the effect of a relapse to a religious narrative that accuses all Eves of original sin. *Ever After*'s Eva, however, insists that Vivi leave with her when she is recovered. The two women's future does seem to be promising in the moment that they decide to leave the Gardener, to strike out on their own, and not to continue to Jena. They know they can survive together and have no need to return to a restrictive society.

The fact that the Gardener justifies the death of humanity based on its fall from grace[53] implies an ecofascist spirit. In fact, the origins of ecofascism are tied to a reactionary political framework that joined naturalism to the nationalism of German Romanticism.[54] The twenty-first century has seen a revival of these themes in recent terrorist attacks, such as the one in Christchurch, New Zealand.[55] For Janet Biehl and Peter Staudenmaier, the term "ecology," coined by Ernst Haeckel in 1867, refers to the study of the interactions between

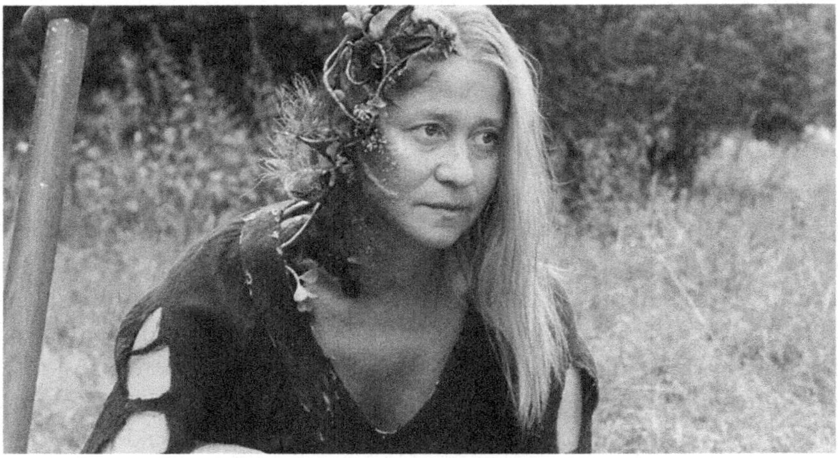

Ever After's Gardener. (Credit: Carolina Hellsgård, *Ever After* (*Endzeit*), 2019.)

organisms and the environment. Haeckel believed in the superiority of the Aryan race and his theories were foundational for the racial eugenics of National Socialism. And it was in Weimar where a youth movement arose, called Wandervögel (wandering birds/free spirits), whose adherents have been described as the hippies of the extreme right, who eventually turned their worship of nature into a reverence for Hitler. The slogan "Blut und Boden" (Blood and Soil), popularized by Richard Walther Darré in 1930, promoted the union of the people with the earth and fostered the institutionalization of organic farming.[56] *Ever After*'s Gardener not only naturalizes women and feminizes nature but also is representative of some of the ideas of the Nazi past, her blood being symbolically connected to the soil to the extent that her veins resemble roots. Her organic garden produces food that can save humanity because her fruits unite blood and soil. This fetishization of nature was used to formulate the antisemitic "racial purity" arguments that culminated with the Holocaust. Today, ecofascism is associated with a biopolitics that would sacrifice human lives in favor of conservation of the earth. That a German zombie film, set in Weimar, would literally unite "body" and "soil" and go on to justify the death of humanity implies, without any doubt, an allusion to the ecofascist generation that is rejected by Vivi and Eva. A. M. Stern notes that in the extreme-right version of "deep ecology" (ecology tied to the ethical conservation of the earth), only White men can achieve a profound connection with the earth.[57] In this sense, *Ever After* proposes to distance itself from ecofascism but is still rooted in it, since only the Gardener, like a version of the biblical Peter, possesses access to salvation. But Vivi and Eva have the potential to create a new, inclusive feminist future, transcorporal[58] and posthuman, in which disabled (here: infected) bodies can have access to radical hope.[59] They are headed toward an epicurean and posthuman future that is more inclusive and less moralistic than that of the Gardener.

The Global (and Glocal) Consequences of Ecological Mismanagement and Extractivism

The Nigerian film *Ojuju*, awarded the Best Nigerian Film Award at the African International Film Festival, takes place in a slum of Ikeja, Lagos.[60] From the beginning of the film, environmental pollution is highlighted: piles of garbage along the river are foregrounded in a zone that only has one entrance, and whose only source of water is contaminated by metals, petroleum, pesticides, and toxic chemicals. The virus is transmitted through the drinking of polluted water and then through the bites of the infected. Themes of the lack of potable water for 70 million Nigerians, poverty, lack of education for children, and the grotesque sexualization of women are all present. Three of the female leads are grossly monstrified: Iya Sikiru, an old and obese woman, is shown smoking while defecating in a Bachtinian grotesque feast. Alero consumes the flesh of her child's father.[61] Aisha, the town "slut," is depicted forcing herself sexually on a sick man. *Ojuju* denounces the sexualization of women and the view of women as monstrous, as well as the criminalization of the poor in a society whose only source of water is so polluted that it is the carrier of a deadly virus. When the virus spreads beyond the slum, it arrives next in a prison, which highlights the fact that the most marginalized are the first to become infected and suffer the consequences. Klemmer and McNamara correctly point out that it will not be possible to combat climate change without changing the ideology that values possessions and consumerism above all else, indicating that radical social change is in order.[62] Recently, it has been proposed that COVID-19 is less of a pandemic than a syndemic: societal inequality, along with preexisting conditions such as diabetes, obesity, cancer, and heart problems that are more widespread among less privileged minorities coincide with higher death rates.[63] Solving the problem of COVID-19 without radical social change will not cure the problems that made the virus so deadly.

In an interview for the Carthage Film Festival in 2019,[64] C. J. Obasi, the director of *Ojuju*, discusses how the film relates to the phenomenon known as "Nollywood."[65] Though Obasi uses several traditional tropes of the z-genre, he emphasizes the societal message of his film. Though he doesn't claim to reject Nollywood, he has made a "social horror film" that distinguishes itself from the commercial mainstream. By presenting the problem of pollution in the context of an isolated slum in Nigeria, *Ojuju* also comments on global interdependence as it relates to environmental issues. What one nation does with its water starts in isolation, but it soon affects all those around them as a zombie virus spreads across the world. In this sense, the zombie genre becomes part of the concept of *globality* proposed by Manfred B. Steger.[66] Globality explores a social condition marked by the global interconnections of economy, politics, culture, and the environment that mitigates the importance of borders, whether local (such as the borders of the slum in Lagos) or transnational. In the universe of this film, the walls that have been built to "contain" the poverty and pollution within and separate the source of the outbreak from the more privileged areas of Nigeria and the world become irrelevant as soon as the zombie contagion begins to break out. Environmental problems having an effect in one part of the world will have consequences for us all. These issues are not just global and cannot be strictly "localized." They are an example of the *glocal*, in which global and local considerations are exposed as inextricably connected.

Last Ones Out alludes to a similar problem of potable water in Liberia.[67] When Vincent drinks river water, the reflection of his face is superimposed over the face of a dead American in the water. It is a subtle detail that doesn't call attention to itself at first. When Vincent turns into a zombie, it is not clear what contaminated him: the water or a zombie attack. We recall that Vincent was asked to pull the dead American from the water and give his clothing to another American, Henry—establishing a clear transfer of meaning between these two characters. Though the film falls prey to some unfortunate clichés, it contains a subtle but clear critique of U.S. influence in that continent as well as the U.S. history of exploitation. This can be observed in the figure of Henry, as well as the film's locations. Harbel, the site where Henry is to meet with his rescuers, is named in honor of Harvey S. Firestone, founder of the Firestone Tire and Rubber Company in 1926. The colonial history of Liberia, which began as a settlement of freed and freeborn African Americans and Afro-Caribbeans, maintained the structures of colonialism well into its independence, refusing to offer citizenship to natives. The poverty of the region, which suffered an Ebola epidemic from 2014–2016, is due in great part to the extraction of rubber by Firestone. The phantom of Firestone is complicated by its involvement with Charles Taylor, who started the bloody First Liberian Civil War (1989–1996) to overthrow the government, using the Firestone factory as a base of operations and a source for equipment, while allowing it to keep producing rubber.[68] Another location charged with significance is the refugee camp Duazon, where Henry is instructed to find shelter and food. His African companions, however, would recognize the place as the ruins of the camp that was abandoned during the Civil War. That the United Nations doesn't know that the camp is no longer functioning is a commentary on the failures of international aid organizations.

As we have seen, zombie films critique international politics and extractivist interests of the so-called First World. Yet, the First World also suffers consequences from its own extractivism and misanthropic handling of basic resources such as clean and safe water. Let us take the case of Flint, Michigan, one of the most egregious examples of mismanagement, neglect, and damage to the public in recent American history.[69] City officials, attempting to cut corners economically and giving minimal thought to where poor and Black people were getting their water from, took actions that resulted in dangerous levels of lead in city tap water that poisoned 6,000–12,000 children in the area. *The Crazies* deals with the theme of water poisoning in an American context.[70] A remake of the 1973 film of the same name by George Romero (he is a producer of the remake) is set in the fictional small farming community of Ogden Marsh, Iowa. When a military plane carrying a secret bioweapon crashes into the town's water supply, formerly supportive neighbors become violent, indiscriminate killers, slowly taking on some of the physical corpse-like traits of zombies. The victims of this engineered virus can be traced to the water flow, and those closest to the source are the first to fall. This fact is covered up by the mayor, who chooses to ignore the problem to avoid economic disaster for the town: during planting season, cutting the water would bankrupt the whole county. When the sheriff manages to turn off the water, the military, attempting a national cover-up, must "initiate containment protocol," quarantining the town by force. As the townspeople become infected and murder each other, members of the military begin indiscriminately killing the uninfected in a necropolitical bid to cover the truth and contain the consequences of their mistake, eventually firebombing the whole town to incinerate and sterilize the area. Only the sheriff and his wife escape on foot to neighboring Cedar Rapids. The final shot is an aerial view of the couple, revealing that they have been picked up by satellite and that Cedar Rapids is next for undergoing "containment protocol." As in *Ojuju*, the water pollution that causes the breakdown of the community is ignored because the populace has no other option for drinking water. Like the Nigerian film where the slum in Lagos is mostly contained with only one controlled exit, Ogden Marsh has been sealed off from the outside world. Although one film deals with a rural American community and the other with a more urbanized African setting, they both imply that containment is impossible, and the effects of one small community's tragedy are bound to spread into the rest of the world. Viruses, whether engineered, caused by pollutants, or naturally occurring, don't respect boundaries and will go wherever humans do.

The Colombian *Zugar Zombie* exposes corruption and misappropriation of political funds, dealing with the ecological effects of extractivism and its consequences upon local communities.[71] To bribe voters and prove his generosity, mayor Mario Mendoza distributes donated provisions that were left in his care fifteen years earlier after a mudslide (probably caused by deforestation). Not only did he not distribute the goods when they were most needed, but he distributes them now with only political gain in mind. By bringing the spoiled food to cane field workers, the movie returns zombies to the fields where they began. But here it is not Haitian vodou that creates zombies and makes them into undead flesh-eaters: it is the corrupt government's poisoning of the people that causes it. With very little dialogue, this short film concentrates on the imagery of the cane fields, a trope that has become charged with the horror of Caribbean slavery.

During the conquest of the Americas, the indigenous population was reduced by 96 percent in the Andean region between 1519 and 1620. The causes of this genocide were many, from imported illnesses (the common flu, salmonella bacteria, smallpox, and measles) to forced mining labor to the general violence of the conquest.[72] In *Zombie Dawn*, the consequences of mining are dire.[73] The film takes place fifteen years after the Hamilton Company engaged in experiments in the Chilean Cerro Negro area. Though the zombie virus originates in the mine, scientists are not able to identify the exact cause. One young girl, apparently an asymptomatic survivor, appears to contain the answer, but she also represents a danger, since, as a carrier, she might infect a population that, until now, has been protected behind an armed and fortified border. The movie explores corruption in the military and the vulnerability of women who are raped and killed even when "safe" and uninfected. It is not surprising that a Chilean take on zombies would focus on mining, considering the country's history.[74] Since the colonial era, working conditions in the mines have been catastrophic. In 2010, thirty-three miners were trapped for sixty-nine days deep in the San José mine. More than ten years after the accident, the affected miners say they have been ignored by the Chilean government. The miners in *Zombie Dawn* are also abandoned by the state. Macarena Gómez-Barris studies the relationship between extractivism and Quijano's coloniality of power, suggesting extractive capitalism "violently reorganizes territories as well as continually perpetuates dramatic social and economic inequalities that delimit Indigenous sovereignty and national autonomy."[75] For Gómez-Barris, mining is one of those mega-extractive projects that require a huge investment in technology, creating a "developmentalist fallacy" (Enrique Dussel) that ends up destroying local industries in favor of global markets.[76] The abandonment of the miner population in *Zombie Dawn* is normalized within coloniality of power due to the indistinguishable economic interests of corporations and states.

What happens in a distant or isolated region in the Philippines, or in Lagos Liberia, or Tamil, cannot be fully understood without considering global interdependence in environmental terms. The ecological effects of globalization threaten life on the planet—no "local" problems are confined to having local effects. As Steger asserts, we are interconnected by the air that we breathe, the food we eat, the water we drink and the climate upon which everything depends.[77] And the effects of the Anthropocene are visible in the greatest problems facing the environment: the global population explosion of the last thirty years, along with the attendant reliance on fossil fuels, chemical pollution of agriculture, and the overall toxification of the planet. In the last millennium, at least 15 million people have died as a result of natural catastrophes such as volcanic eruptions, earthquakes, floods, and so on.[78] The year 2004 was one of the most lethal, being the year of the tsunami in the Indian Ocean, as well as a year of accumulated earthquakes and floods that amounted to a total of one-third of a million deaths.[79] The COVID-19 pandemic, by September 2021, had already reached a toll of more than 4.5 million dead. And as of this writing, the number of victims keeps climbing. The United States has a record infection rate, with an average of 215,000 new cases daily.[80]

Historian Dipesh Chakrabarty proposes that since at least as far back as the industrial revolution, mankind has become a subject with geological agency such that it is impossible to separate natural history from human history.[81] To recognize the geologic force of humans is to identify the idea of the Anthropocene within the process of globalization and the traces that humanity has left on the globe.[82] Only by understanding history as "the combined genetic and cultural changes that created humanity" can we arrive at a secular understanding of why climate change constitutes a crisis for humans.[83] Studying humans from the perspective of the Anthropocene helps us to understand that we are not the only important life on earth and that the world, in reality, could go on without us.[84] This is just what Kim Hall lays out with her concept of radical hope, a world where we might adapt our relationship to nature, a world that can adapt to disabled bodies. Consideration of the environment is key to that future.

If the majority of zombie films comment on the anthropogenic consequences that lead to the spread of the undead, a film like *The Dead Don't Die* attributes our zombie condition to specific technologies that enable exploitation of natural resources—in this case "polar fracking." The use of fracking is controversial since it has tremendously contributed to record levels of production in the gas and oil industries but has been plagued with risks.[85] Fracking is a technique of breaking up bedrock with pressurized liquid in order to let gas or oil flow more freely. Its effects on the environment can include methane leaks, water and air pollution, and disruption of the layers of the earth, triggering earthquakes.[86] In *The Dead Don't Die*, polar fracking destabilizes the earth's axis and causes severe consequences for the environment, allowing strange vibrations from outer space to overturn the natural order of things on Earth. The media, in the film, provides contradictory interpretations of what is happening. The secretary of energy lauds the industry that has contributed so much to the economy by creating jobs, money, and energy for the public[87] and attacks critics: "These alarmists are dangerous liars. . . . Let's not believe something because one so-called 'scientist' says it's true."[88] But in the town of Centerville, the effects of these changes are evident: the days are unnaturally long, electricity is unpredictable, and animals start to act strangely aggressive. That's how sage, observant Hermit Bob interprets it when he comments on the strange lunar vibrations and sees ant colonies that are "all jacked up like it's the end of the world." Centerville is full of contradictions between the "official version," and what the characters (and the audience) perceive. The setting is established with a sign that proclaims, "Centerville, A Real Nice Place." But what we are shown are places of potential and future violence: the funeral home, the youth detention center, a gas station, a police station, a diner (where the first shocking attack takes place), and a motel (thanks to *Psycho*, a horror-movie trope).[89] It is this discrepancy between what we are told (signifier) and what we perceive (signified) that adds to the creeping suspense of the otherwise comedic film.

Decentering Anthropos: Posthumanist Tendencies

Interaction between animals and people is another key element when considering humanity's relationship to the environment. Especially in the case of animals that are part of our food chain, have been domesticated, or have medical or psychological use, humanity has formed close relationships with the zoological world.[90] These relationships have exposed all to the transmission of bacteria, viruses, fungi, parasites, and so on. According to the Centers for Disease Control and Prevention, we can't be sure of the exact source of COVID-19, but it is assumed that it originated in bats.[91] By April 2020, the lions and tigers in the Bronx Zoo had contracted the virus and by December of the same year four lions in the Barcelona Zoo had as well.[92] Some domesticated animals were also infected, including dogs and cats living in European mink farms. In November 2020, Denmark destroyed 17 million minks for fear that a mutated version of the virus could be passed back to humans and reduce the efficacy of a potential vaccine. The precipitous and deadly action, which may not have been necessary or legal, has had a dire consequence: horribly, but interesting for our purposes, the bodies of the minks appear to have been rising from their graves (due to swelling of the corpses and too-shallow burial), giving rise to the clickbait headline appearance of the *zombiemink*.[93]

The role of animals in zombie films is becoming more evident in the way it explores possible anthropogenic consequences that go beyond the human species. In *Train to Busan*, animals are the first to show the deadly effects of a factory chemical spill. There is talk of contaminated fish, and then we see a deer hit by a truck. The camera stays with the dead animal long enough to see it revive, indicating the interspecies nature of this contamination. Similarly, *Blood Quantum* opens with an old man cleaning his day's catch of fish, when he is surprised that the dead and gutted fish begin to revive and flop around. *Zombeavers* begins with a similar incident.[94] When a deer is hit by a truck, toxic chemicals are leaked into the river where a large population of beavers live, who will in turn come to attack humans. *Black Sheep* deals with genetic experimentation to transform sheep into bloodthirsty carnivorous monsters, which has the effect of turning the victims of their bites into sheep.[95] The mutation between man and sheep, without a doubt, is a parody of transubstantiation. In fact, many of the animals discussed here—fish, deer, sheep—have been associated with Christianity. We might read the moment the deer in *Train to Busan* resuscitates as a Second Coming of sorts and as a harbinger of the apocalypse. Another film that begins with this human-caused animal to human contamination (in a kind of nature's revenge), is *28 Days Later* in which chimpanzees are tortured in a lab with images of violence and experimented on in hopes of finding a way to treat human rage—a study that goes badly, to say the least. The ensuing "rage virus" is loosed upon the population when a well-meaning animal rights group frees the chimps. As the title indicates, twenty-eight days after the incident, a coma patient awakens to an empty and partially destroyed London. India's *Zombie* (*Miruthan*), whose title in Hindi title means "half-animal, half-man," reminds us of the animal nature of man and hints at the extension of the virus beyond the realm of mankind.[96] Again, the contamination in this film is caused by human error. In this case, the city of Ooty in Tamil Nadu suffers a poisonous spill near a chemical factory. The animality suggested by the title and by the monstrous transformation of the infected is also reflected in the political corruption of the officials who receive bribes and engage in violent revenge for imagined slights.

We have referred to the term "posthuman" several times throughout this book to describe a postapocalyptic future that has been shaped by a zombie catastrophe and the changes that it brings about for humanity. The term is fluid and applies to a range of theoretical studies. We turn to Rosi Braidotti who observes that "the posthuman condition encourages us to move beyond the Eurocentric humanistic representational habits and the philosophical anthropocentrism they entail."[97] This movement that we propose to make in the reading of zombies is intended to distance us from the heteronormative, patriarchal, ableist, Eurocentric humanism that would insist on mastery over nature and would privilege humanity over every other form of life, viewing animals as mere resources to be used or cared for by human masters and nature to be commodified, colonized, and used up. Posthumanism accepts the blurring of the lines between the human and the animal, nature and technology, allowing an alliance of "non-human agents, technologically-mediated elements, earth-others (land, waters, plants, animals) and non-human inorganic agents (plastic, wires, information highways, algorithms, etc.)."[98] It breaks from traditional Enlightenment humanism. It rejects the Cartesian dualism that separates the mind and body in favor of a new kind of materialism in which the nonhuman can participate. The zombie provides the perfect problematic for this, being, in theory, a body without a mind, though we have seen the ways depictions of zombies are changing. We would not be talking about posthumanism in a zombie context without seeing the zombie's development: from the Haitian victim of vodou, through the Romero-influenced rotting cannibal, to the twenty-first century where it becomes faster, more conscious, and eventually embodies the multifarious presentations we have discussed in this chapter, or what Sarah Juliet Lauro calls a zombie (r)evolution: "For one of the things that we see happening is the zombie's claim to a kind of post-identity—appropriately, since the zombie, in its most basic definition, is post(mortem)."[99]

The broadening of the zombie genre has given us many approximations to posthumanism. Melanie, *The Girl with All the Gifts*, who decides her kind should not be sacrificed for the sake of humanity, is posthuman. As is Camille in *The Descendents*, whose generation will be able to live in an ever-rising ocean. As are *Ever After*'s Eva and Vivi, rejecting both human "civilization" and the ecofascism of the Gardener. All of these characters, either as zombies who have developed special abilities, as zombie by-products, or as zombie survivors, are posthuman in that they have been introduced to new ways of being that will carry them beyond the initial catastrophe of the zombie condition, which in itself is a kind of an end to the human(ist) condition—a condition that was always just a vector of becoming.[100] From a crip and feminist perspective, it is important to note here that all these characters that will lead the way to a post-human future are young women. In this sense, "apocalypse" stops being a stand-in for "end times" and reverts to its original meaning. Apocalypse becomes a *revelation* of a new relation to the world and each other through a reconsideration of old humanist categories.

The same may be said of the many, sometimes shocking, ways of being in the raucous Portuguese film *Mutant Blast*.[101] In it, a government experiment results in hundreds of zombie-like by-products of experimentation and a couple of truly terrible super-soldiers. María, an incredibly fearless member of the resistance to this government, and Pedro, a slacker, try to get to safety on the island headquarters of the resistance. The government, meaning to drop conventional bombs, accidentally nukes the whole countryside. Everyone suffers from all kinds of mutations: extra limbs or eyes, partial conversion into animals, horns, scales, and so on. At one point, the pair befriend a group of welcoming mutants, one of whom, Jean-Pierre, is a six-foot French-speaking lobster. When María asks him why he became a lobster after the blast (was he near a lobster?), Jean-Pierre is indignant. "I've always been a lobster! The human blast made me grow to your size!" Why, then, does he speak French? Because he is French, obviously. This absurdist dialogue is the nucleus of wisdom in the film.

The posthumanism that *Mutant Blast* suggests is also post-lobster and post-animal—every classification is upended. All are affected and on equal footing (especially after the bumbling government blows itself up in a postcredit scene). So, what of the zombies? Throughout, the word "zombie" is censored in the dialog—it is bleeped out whenever mentioned. In the subtitles, it appears as a series of asterisks (z*****s). María insists on correcting everyone: they are not z*****s; they are the result of human experimentation. As one character sarcastically says, "Forgive me for thinking they are z*****s: they have rotten skin, they eat people, they walk slowly." María insists on labeling them as the necropolitical by-product of the military-industrial complex. That is, until a horde including some children menace them, and Pedro asks her how she can shoot them, they're just children. She takes aim and says, "They are not children, they are *zombies*." When it is time to ruthlessly eliminate them, regardless of their outward appearance, she can no longer avoid the characterization. Alle, the film's director, says, "I became disinterested in doing a zombie movie, so it's a zombie movie but it turns into something else." It is as though we are seeing the zombie genre becoming Other during the movie.

Further Traces of the Anthropocene: Invasive Species

One major side effect of globalization is the movement of people. This movement results in animal and plant species appearing in areas that are not their natural habitats. What are the effects of invasive species on the environment? There are many studies that focus on the relationship between biotic invaders, the environment, and the decline of biodiversity in ecological systems.[102] Invasive alien plants species also alter the ecosystem and socioeconomic conditions. These types of effects are clearly demonstrated in the Galapagos Islands.[103] While most of these invading species are transplanted to a new environment through the movement and influence of humanity, they are echoed by the post–Cold War anxiety of unknown extraterrestrial invaders and their possible effect on mankind's place in the earthly order. As humans invade and unwittingly destroy environments with our all-consuming, extractivist ways, we also sense the decentering possibility that the same could be done to us. We see this anxiety reflected in the subcategory of the zombie outbreak caused by influence from outer space. In *L.A. Zombie*, a creature comes from space and can mutate into a normal, attractive man, a zombie, or a monstrous beast with fangs. This zombie creates other zombies not by sinking its teeth into humans but through sexual penetration into a mortal wound. Two Peruvian independent films imagine the way other, more powerful species may interact with humanity if such an encounter ever were to occur, and the possibilities are harrowing. *Inner Trip* (*Entonces Ruth*) presents a future in which humanity lives alongside androids.[104] When extraterrestrials invade Earth, an attempted peace agreement with the aliens fails when the human delegation is eaten by the invaders in a gruesome zombie-like attack. Like zombies, they approach humans as food, which draws a sharp parallel to the voracious way humans have consumed animals. It is even implied through the biblical figure of Ruth that this fate is a punishment for our sins. In the short film *A Prequel to Chaos* (*La precuela del caos*), post–World War III mutants, who have lost their sexual organs in their mutations, require the DNA of the unmutated humans in order to reproduce.[105] They hope to create a superior race that will dominate the universe, indicating that humanity had its chance and failed again and again. All these films enunciate fears of being used as breeding stock, or flesh for the consumption of a more "advanced" species—just the way humans have used nonhuman species for millennia.

Last Call for the Apocalypse . . . and What Comes After

The Dead Don't Die takes a more subtle approach to the use of extraterrestrial dangers. In this film, the mortician at the funeral home is perceived as odd, with a foreign accent and strange habits. As it turns out, she has alien connections. After managing to send messages to space, she goes out to meet a UFO and is lifted in a beam of light. This scene, anomalous to the plot of the film, is an echo of apocalyptic narratives of the Rapture, in which faithful Christians will be transported from the earth to heaven while the remainder of humanity is left to suffer with the Antichrist.[106] The fact that Zelda is "raptured" up to her vessel can be read as a reference to dispensationalism, and the fact that she is carried off by an alien UFO instead of some divine power is a parody of the rapture narrative. Interestingly, there is even a reference in the film to a future history written in advance of the events. When police chief Robertson and officer Peterson are in the cemetery surrounded by zombies and about to meet their violent ends, Peterson confesses that he always knew things would end badly because Jim (Jarmusch, the director) had let him read the whole script in a metafilmic nod to the true author of the piece. There is a parallel drawn between the cinematic fiction and the biblical prophecies in the sense that both are apocalyptic—the final battle with the zombies in the cemetery in Centerville is a kind of battle of Armageddon. The only discrepancy is that the moment when Zelda is lifted to the UFO was not in the script that Peterson had read, and as such, this "improvised" scene questions the truth of the prophecies in Revelation. The film, as a catastrophe narrative, is an imagining of a possible dystopian future (as Eva Horn might say), just as Revelation is an imagining of a utopian future (for believers), but the film posits a scenario in which everyone will suffer the same fate.

What does this have to do with environmental catastrophe? Plenty. Over the centuries, various theological thinkers and movements have interpreted the Book of Revelation to herald the coming of an Antichrist who will bring on the end of times. Throughout history there has been much speculation about who will be that change agent and how the Second Coming can be hastened. The iconoclastic elements of the Trump regime, such as his insistence on declaring Jerusalem as the capital of Israel and moving the U.S. embassy there has been acknowledged to be an appeasement to the Christian right in the United States who wish to bring on the return of Christ.[107] The elimination of environmental protections and international agreements geared toward slowing global warming are a manifestation of the iconoclastic and destructive tendencies, along with the will to power, of the Trump period. What is being conserved with these moves is not the planet but the neoliberal system, and this is an example of apocalyptic rhetoric.

In a talk at Colóquio Terraterra, Déborah Danowski observed that while we are presented with a vast number of narratives about the end of the world in film, literature, and gaming, there is a paradoxical tendency of denialism.[108] We can accept a world-ending narrative when it refers to antiquity, or to the decline of *other* cultures and states, or stories of *nonhuman* decline.[109] But Danowski sees a tendency to reject the reality of humans' influence in the biophysical processes on our ecological system as well as the refusal to accept that we are in imminent danger with respect to climate change. Therefore, it is not surprising that neoliberalism rejects the implications of climate change or even that the dangers of the COVID-19 virus are denied by those who would ridicule science and scientists.[110] But beyond this first level of denialism may reside what Braidotti terms "the scholarship of anxiety" that expresses a moral panic about our humanist legacy in these rapidly changing times.[111] Some of the refusal to accept the reality of end-of-the-world narratives may be based in a reluctance to let go of humanism (and the entitlements and privileges it implies) in favor of whatever comes next. Humanity feels fear inspired by Paul Virilio's "bombs": the ecological bomb, the informational bomb, and the genetic bomb. These elements—environmental "apocalypse," speed and ubiquity of information, and scientific interventions in human biology and development—along with their acceleration, create the "feeling that something essential is being definitely lost," and we dive headfirst into that acceleration, paradoxically propelling ourselves forward to find a remedy.[112]

Zombies, in their refusal to follow "natural" law, their material decay, and their ravenous violence, have been avatars of the worst-case scenario and have been used to represent the horror of "surviving" possible extinctions caused by Cold War fears, accelerated technologies, and the commodification of life. Twenty-first-century zombies, with their mutations that confound expectations, and most importantly, their stubborn refusal to go away, invite us to reimagine the heretofore unimaginable.

Conclusion

Throughout this book, we have argued that zombies represent the Other, those that we consider monstrous. The humanist tradition has always left a large portion of the population in the realm of the nonhuman, centering Christian, European, White, heteronormative, and able bodies in a patriarchal and capitalist system. This denied participation in the human domain to anyone not conforming to the visuality that was imposed upon us in the Renaissance with the Vitruvian Man.[1] We see the figure of the global zombie questioning the value of the humanist project and its hierarchical valuation of man over all other life on earth, as well as its definition of progress as the result of divine providence.

As soulless subjects, zombies expose the colonial Christian mentality (rooted in a long Greek philosophical tradition) that separates the body from the soul just as it separates populations into "humans" and "nonhumans."[2] Zombies, though they may seem incomplete, are actually building multitudes in themselves by feeding on other bodies and defining themselves as new political subjects. Following Hardt and Negri, a multitude is a consequence of globalization, a reaction to power. The multitude is like a counternetwork in which different voices can be heard. As a political subject, zombies become agents of *necroactivism* who resist, react to, and protest political and economic injustices. As Steven Shaviro puts it, they "serve to awaken a passion for otherness and for vertiginous disidentification that is already latent within ourselves."[3] But let us be clear, while on the one hand zombies represent victims of slavery, colonization, and necropolitics in the embodiment of the Other, zombies also can stand for the colonizing and destructive force of White supremacy. In some cases (e.g., *Blood Quantum*) they represent the last dying gasp of the toxicity of late-stage capitalism and coloniality. In both cases, zombies express our anxiety about the tensions that result from these imposed hierarchies.

Zombies are descendants of the omnipresent skulls of the Medieval and the Baroque eras that, along with apocalyptic virgins, were used to channel fears of the end of the world. As spectacles of the other, they can also be considered the continuation of the freak shows that proliferated beginning in the eighteenth century. In the Benjaminian sense, zombies can be seen as allegorical subjects through whom we can perceive the end of history from a secular perspective: they are a ruin, a cadaver whose embodiment tells us about the past, the present, and the future.

The embodiment of the undead helps us visualize the hidden conflicts that underlie societies by inviting viewers to question their own gaze and see that which was not previously permitted. By allowing countervisuality, they give us back the "right to look"[4] so that nonconforming bodies may take part in a posthumanist world, which makes room for all races, genders, and conditions of ability. In this way, those previously considered "less human" are resemanticized from objects of horror to subjects that have the right to participate fully in an inclusive crip futurity.

If we consider the zombie as an empty signifier, the meaning we assign to it is most often related to our understanding of humanity, both how we see ourselves and others. The walking corpse is a human shape, reduced to its biological materiality, and as such is primed as a receptacle of human meaning, while also embodying a shocking reminder of our own abjection. Being confronted with our understanding of the Other (be it the slave, the poor, racialized peoples, or the disabled) gives us an opportunity to achieve self-knowledge in a masocritical act of giving the self over to the other.[5] This is the case in *Zombiology* in which the central zombie-creating monster confronts the young protagonist, Lone, and removes its costume to reveal that it is identical to Lone—they are the very same person: "Wherever there are superheroes, there are also monsters."[6] Monsters live inside of our own minds, and it is up to us to confront them. Broadly defined, zombies are seen as the cultural logic of fear and can be used to face our own monstrosity. The genre, therefore, reflects upon the anxieties of twenty-first-century society when faced with alterity and otherness.

At the same time, if we follow the evolutionary trend in horror theory (e.g., Arme Öhman, Mathias Clasen) knowledge about zombie movies can also help us for survival purposes.[7] According to this line of thought, we react with fear and anxiety, and we sometimes overreact to danger that threatens our existence. Following Classen, "the reaction elicited by an effective horror story is qualitatively similar to that elicited by a real threat from a predator." What happens in the zombie world has a clear parallel in our twenty-first-century COVID-19-infected society. We conceive of zombies as Other; we mistreat them, incarcerate them, or kill them for our own security. This is the way we treat the Other: people of color, the poor, the elderly, female bodies, and the differently abled. Ableist societies give preference to bodies they consider "non-disabled" when choosing for whom to provide lifesaving treatment. Law enforcement reacts differently toward the protestors in the Black Lives Matter movement than to the White supremacists invading the U.S. Capitol.[8]

We have studied the way zombie films have altered the presentation of the ghouls they exploit, changing the accepted "zombie rules" along the way. This sort of zombie "development" can be read as a mirror of the sociopolitical concerns of the cultures that have produced it over the decades of its popularity as a cinematic genre. First, they were the creation of slave culture in Haiti, a country founded on a revolution of rebellious ex-slaves. They were promptly appropriated and exoticized by Hollywood. They returned to U.S. cultural production in the late 1960s, during a time of extreme social unrest at home and the Vietnam War abroad and were used to criticize capitalism and to express Cold War fears. Their continued popularity and development in the twenty-first century reflects anxieties about looming catastrophes and is an exploration of what we are becoming. Rosi Braidotti, discussing Deleuze and Guattari's notion of the present, notes that the "force of the present . . . is that it does not coincide completely with the here and now." She explains that this also affects our conception of ourselves, giving us "the sharp awareness of *what we are ceasing to be* (the end of the actual) and on the other hand, the perception . . . of *what we are in the process of becoming*."[9] Zombie narratives help us to experiment with the possibilities of action in the worst-case scenario and how these possible future events may change (post)human existence.

Self-Referential Zombies

The growing self-referentiality of recent zombie films is, in a way, typical of genre cinema. Theories of intertextuality (e.g., Bahktin, Kristeva, Barthes, Genette, Hutcheon) have always emphasized the basic idea that intertextual repetition aids the definition of writing per se (vis-à-vis the *hypotext*) and allows readers/spectators to make connections between the past, the present, and the worldview presented in the work of art. It could even be conceived as an act of rebellion by bringing the political aspects of history into the *hypertext*.[10] Postmodernist theory has also focused on the interdependence among all texts and the impossibility of originality. Intertextual statements can therefore be seen as an attempt to provide definitions for the genre itself, revitalize it, or manifest signs of exhaustion.

Throughout history, there are self-referential repetitions that can be explained within a specific episteme. Rewriting secular works of art into the "divine mode," or as religious parody, was a trend typical of the European

Renaissance and Baroque. In the twentieth to twenty-first centuries, we see an effort to re-create classic works into specific genres such as pornography and z-narratives.[11] We approach self-referentiality in z-films as proof that zombies have become entrenched in popular culture, emphasizing the importance of the genre and the knowledge that can be extracted from it. As we have mentioned in previous chapters, z-narratives question Christian chrononormativity, heteropatriarchy, capitalism, neoliberalism, and an imposed visuality that is based on Whiteness and abledness. In this way, they are working toward the decolonization of our societal values. Quests for knowledge are a common trope in horror narratives (e.g., the conflict between good and evil, the fantastic, and the search for forbidden knowledge), and they help us, spectators, to examine our own attitude toward knowledge. The experience of watching horror movies intensifies feelings of suspense and affects our relationship to what we are watching. Steven Shaviro writes about Romero's genre-defining trilogy, specifically the experience of watching a character waiting for a dead person to horribly revive, or for the shuffling undead to inevitably appear, as a kind of waiting for death. Time seems to slow. We watch as nothing happens, waiting along with the protagonist for what we know will come. As moviegoers, we experience the "unfulfilled threats" of the zombie presence turn into "seductive promises" of a form of entertainment that is laden with affect and the taboo of violence. Shaviro says this is "the zombie state *par excellence*: an abject vacancy, a passive emptying of the self . . . a kind of mimetic transference that exceeds and destroys all structures of representation."[12] We intuitively suspect what is going to happen, we feel it with the characters: a satisfaction when the moment arrives as expected, and a thrill if the moment defies our expectations. Part of this experience is understanding the nature of the genre. What knowledge can be absorbed from watching zombie movies?

At the level of character, specific knowledge of zombie classics can be lifesaving. In *Anna and the Apocalypse*, as in any number of similarly satirical zombie films, characters know how to deal with zombies because of knowledge gleaned from all the movies they have watched.[13] When dealing with attacks, in *Corona Zombies* one of the characters asks, "Have you not watched Romero? You gotta shoot them in their heads."[14] We also see an important meta-emphasis in *The Dead Don't Die*, in which some of the characters seem to be aware that they are in a zombie film and discuss the script and the theme music.[15] While working on this book, we ourselves have experienced some of this self-referentiality. Completing a zombie project during the global pandemic has influenced the way we see films and the way we see current events.

The vignettes in the anthology film *Resident Zombie* (aka *The Neighbor Zombie*) explore the power and consequences of creating the metaphor of a zombie.[16] The first vignette, titled "Crack," is about a young hipster nerd obsessed with action figures. His apartment is packed with all kinds of cultural references to superheroes, anime, and manga comics. While he is completing a figure on his worktable, he cuts himself, and his blood falling upon the figurine brings it to life. If Pygmalion fell in love with the sculpture of the beautiful Galatea and brought it to life, Prometheus was punished for stealing fire from the Gods. Similarly, our comic-book nerd is punished for stealing gods' wisdom and using his own blood to produce human life. But in this case, his passion for the superheroes creates something evil: the soldier figure is infected and attacks his own creator. As a consequence, he becomes a hungry zombie whose first victim is himself: he shockingly eats his own foot before attacking a hapless delivery man. Bringing a piece of art to life is an old strategy that makes spectators aware of the artificiality of art and the potential dangers of obsessive creation. The final vignette of *Resident Zombie* (entitled "Pain Killer") occurs during the closing credits and explores the process of writing the movie itself. A frantic man at a computer is writing against a deadline. Bits of dialogue from the film scroll by on his screen. Zombies enter his room while he works, and he defeats them by deleting them from the script. When the credits are over, and the deadline alarm sounds, the writer himself has become a zombie, entering his own fiction.

In other films, the metafilmic element is used to comment on the production of meaning. *Otto; or, Up with Dead People*[17] describes zombies as "just a metaphor," explored through many examples of metalepsis (sometimes made with changes from color to black and white, involving techniques of silent film, documentary, etc.).[18] *Dead Trigger*, on the other hand, plays with virtual reality, but the spectator does not know it until the very end of the movie, when we discover that we have been watching players in a virtual reality game, a game that instructs (characters and spectators) how to behave in real life.[19] Other metafilmic approaches include found-footage techniques, which have become a staple in horror films (especially since 1999's *The Blair Witch Project*) and have been used to great effect in this genre.[20] In the Spanish *REC*, "found footage" greatly adds to the suspense, urgency, and claustrophobia of the events of that film.[21] The pseudo-documentary *Savageland* uses "found" elements of Salazar's photographs of the attack, providing proof of filmic events.[22] The film also ends with more found footage suggesting his z-transformation. The trio of protagonists in *What's Left of Us* (*El desierto*) decide to make video recordings to leave as proof of their isolated existence as the apocalypse grinds on, but they end up using the video messages to communicate with each other furtively, questioning the limits of interpersonal communication itself.[23] These narrative techniques reveal the role of documentation, which has become democratized (sometimes to the point of virality) with the availability of the smartphone, changing the way we produce our own countervisuality by promoting visual texts that upend establishment imagery.

The horror comedy *One Cut of the Dead* (*Kamera Wo Tomeruna!*) is metafilmic on several levels.[24] We watch the production of a zombie film, which is invaded by "real" zombies in the first half. In the second half, we explore the making of the film we have just watched and observe the process of assigning meaning to a one-cut production, thus revealing the complexity of the creation of zombies: it is a calculated product of gore that uses a profitable metaphor, reflecting on the commodification of affects, both real and fake. It entertains the audience with suspense, gore, and humor while shining a light on the manufactured nature of what we are watching. There is no doubt that any metareferential statement within a movie validates the genre: it is not only about making its own definition more precise but also about allowing spectators to participate in that process of creation. We can connect cultural manifestations we encounter in contemporary society to the films we watch and realize that the zombie imaginary has become an artistic narrative based on a monster that we ourselves have created. The genre has become so pervasive that even those who do not watch zombie films understand the basics of what zombies are, how they function, and what an invasion looks like, allowing zombie tropes to be used in other genres.

Documenting Zombies

Some European filmmakers, such as Portugal's Pedro Costa or France's Sylvain George and Nicolas Klotz, make references to zombie cinema in productions that are outside of the z-genre. Real immigrants (not professional actors) are the protagonists of these movies, which use documentary and *cinéma vérité* techniques. These films explore the suffering of recent immigrants in trying to reach the promised land of Europe and in attempting to build a life there. Though the films are extremely realist in style, references to zombie tropes underscore the immigrants' experiences as a sort of living death.[25] Pedro Costa's *Down to Earth* (*Casa de lava*) subtly retells the story of *I Walked with a Zombie*.[26] If Halperin's *White Zombie* forces former slaves back into the mills, Costa's 2014 *Horse Money* (*Cavalho Dinheiro*) shows us that the life of Ventura, a Cape Verdean in Lisbon, is similar to a zombie's.[27] He lives in the destroyed neighborhood of Fontainhas. According to Fillol, Salvadó-Corretger, and Bou i Sala, he personifies Carrefour, the eerie figure from *I Walked with a Zombie*.[28] Ventura is portrayed as a passive necroactivist who goes back to his workplace to wait to be paid. Ventura sleeps under the construction site which owes him money and patiently waits for justice that never arrives. When he asks about the possibility of being murdered, the answer we hear is, "You have already died one thousand deaths, why do you care about one more?" Costa's cinematography creates his own aesthetics of immigrants' misery. When Cape Verdeans

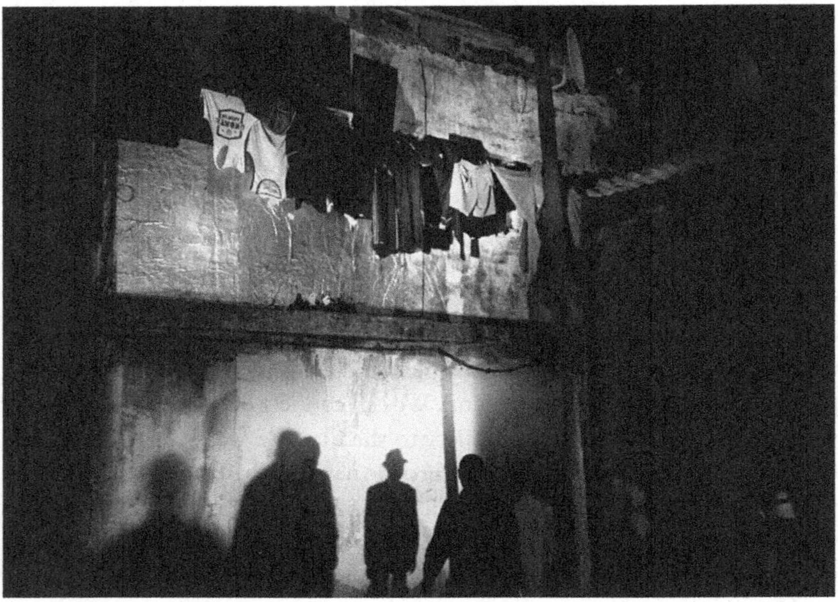

In Pedro Costas's *Vitalina Varela*, the shadows of immigrants pass through the streets. (Credit: Pedro Costas, *Vitalina Varela*, 2019.)

walk on the wet streets of Lisbon, their images are projected as shadows, defining their presence as a sort of absence.

Sylvain George's immigrants must go through extreme pain in order to arrive in England: they burn their fingertips in order not to get recognized by authorities, erasing their identities and their pasts. In Klotz's *Low Life*, a rejection-for-asylum letter is sent to the "Rue Carrefour" where the student immigrant Hussein lives, in an homage to Jacques Tourneur's film.[29] In these movies, zombies are not cannibals; they do not produce gore violence for movie spectators, but the real, lived violence they go through is gore. They are fed with garbage, they are treated like animals, and they are perceived as dangerous and contagious. A product of contemporary Brazilian cinema, *Seven Years in May* (*Sete Anos em Maio*) uses strategies similar to Costa's and Klotz's movies to depict how hard it is to survive neoliberalism within a corrupt and violent state.[30] Using shots alternating between very bright and almost no light that depict the struggles that members of the working class go through if they want to stay alive, *Seven Years in May* presents citizens as always fluctuating between life and death. As in the aforementioned European films, Affonso Uchoa's characters have almost zombie-like identities and are forced to play a sort of Simon Says game in which participants are either left "alive" (*vivo*—standing) or "dead" (*morto*—crouching). The border between life and death, light and dark, standing or on the ground is a constant motif.

Iconoclastic Zombies

Self-referential apocalyptic movies also make us reconsider the meaning of the word "catastrophe." The word's etymology indicates that it comes from Old Greek; it was used as a *terminus technicus* to refer to the last part of a play. Although Aristotle and Horace had their own prescribed sequence of drama, Euanthius (in the first half of the fourth century) proposed four parts: the "*prologus, protasis, epitasis* and *catastrophe*." In addition to the poetological meaning, the word "catastrophe" also referred to a change in the direction of fortune (either for the worse or for the better) and to an intentional reception of that change of state in spectators. According to Briese and Günther, the word most commonly meant a turn toward a state of happiness and stillness until the eighteenth century. It was only at the beginning of the nineteenth century that definitions of "catastrophe" included an unexpected, sudden, and negative change, such as death. The connection with nature also came at the beginning of the nineteenth century when German Romantic discourse introduced a catastrophe of nature.[31] Slowly, the use of the term expanded to other fields such as politics, technology, and so on until it was systematically applied to all fields of knowledge. The fact that "catastrophe" was read as a poetological structure coincides with self-referentiality in zombie cinema. Metapoetic statements in zombie movies also aim at presenting us with a change in potential outcome that can captivate spectators. And depending on how we conceive of the future, "catastrophe" can mean a negative destruction or a positive change for a different futurity.

"Iconoclasm" (image-breaking) can be defined as the belief in the necessity of the destruction of images for political or religious reasons. Within Christianity, some opposed divine images because they were prohibited in the Ten Commandments. Iconoclasts rejected them because they were presumed to contain some sort of divine presence that would command worship, contrary to biblical law. Iconophiles, on the other hand, or those who defended images, insisted upon the absence of God in those images; they reasoned that icons only *represented* divinity but did not *embody* it. We believe that zombie cinema is iconoclast because it destroys religious narratives as well as cultural icons and concepts (death, capitalism, compulsory heterosexuality, chrononormativity, White supremacy, visuality, disability, walls and borders, utopias, etc.). Zombies also decolonize our constructed views of perspective, the way we usually see, for example, allowing us to accept disability as the norm and abledness as a temporary condition. Zombies also destroy humanity: humans die, but zombies continue on in living death. Zombie iconoclastic cinema can therefore be understood as religious and cultural violence.

Zombies also make us aware of the death of utopia, question our understanding of millennialism in religious and secular narratives, and change our concept of history. A zombie future is the destruction of not only religious utopian dreams but also socially constructed utopias, from neoliberal to socialist. For Ignacio Padilla, the notion of "the end of the world" has become an industry that we have been fueling with panic throughout centuries. And this horrific affect is linked to one of the most iconoclastic books of Western civilization: the Bible's Book of Revelation. Padilla's *La industria del fin del mundo*, as well as John Gray's *Black Mass*, reflects on the meaning and the consequences of millennialism, which can be broadly understood as the belief that the Second Coming of Christ will occur in the near future and will result in a thousand years of peace on earth for the faithful and just punishment for those who persecute them.[32] The exact timing of His arrival, the destruction that it would bring to the sinful, and the utopian period to come after has long been the subject of speculation by some religious groups and used as a tool by political regimes to further their own ends through manipulation of their citizens.[33] As specific dates for the so-called end times have come and gone, disappointment has not cooled the ardor of those waiting for their reward. The problem, as outlined by Padilla, is that the millennialist utopia is more a look back to a paradise lost than a vision of a tenable future, since there can be no progress, and no humanity, without conflict: "Insofar that it does not recognize the fallibility and misery of man, utopia is a fiction . . . the promise of an imminent reign of happiness has always come hand-in-hand with an abandonment of the world."[34] Our world, and the terror of change that it contains, would have to be transcended, putting us in the double bind of fearing change as we long for it. Moreover, as Gray asserts, the supposedly secular idea of revolution and human-created utopias are just as unreliable as religious narratives, and indeed replace religious rhetoric with their own, but "theories of progress are not scientific hypotheses. They are myths, which answer the human need for meaning."[35] Though utopia (be it Christian, Marxist, Andean, or any other) seems impossible, we perversely yearn for the destruction that would supposedly bring it about.[36] And, paradoxically, we see examples of humanity barreling toward destruction, in the form of international and domestic terrorism, climate disaster, wars, and financial crises. What zombies provide, with their iconoclastic destructive tendencies and their impulse to eat the world whole, is the sense of an ending without any soothing utopia to follow, in a context that trivializes and satirizes the religious narratives of resurrection, eternal life, and blissful peace.

The End?

The destruction of these traditional narratives upon which humanism is based can be the source of violent anxiety. The right-wing, fascist nationalist movements that look back in history for inspiration—and are sweeping the United

States and most of the world—function in parallel to this fear of change and the dilution of national identities based on exclusion of the Other and resistance to change. However, considering the alternative, positive, meaning of "catastrophe," this can open the way for a new futurity. Our world will definitely change: there is no other way than posthumanism to move beyond humanism. The figure of the zombie, therefore, reveals itself as the epitome of the new inclusive and uncertain futurity.

A humanism that considers the Anthropocene the center of the universe is gone and will not be able to regain its power. Zombies already embody posthumanism and have revolutionized reproduction. But we know that, while humanity may end, the world will persist, though it may not look anything like what we recognize as ours. Zombies destroy our civilization but also create more permeable, leaky spaces in which a new world can be built; they destroy us in order to save us. Zombies are preparing us to work out narratives of change in the face of imminent future scenarios that terrify us, and, as avatars of popular culture and metaphors for humanity, are changing the possibilities for reading the world. The end may indeed be nigh, but the zombie horde will rise.

Acknowledgments

First, we would like to express our gratitude to our tireless readers, Laurie Essig, Catharine Wright, and Glenn Gamblin, whose help and input have been crucial in this project.

We also thank students from Middlebury College and the Middlebury Spanish Language School who participated in the Decolonizing Zombie course. Their comments and enthusiasm for the subject were inspirational. Special recognition goes to Mireille Becerra for her many hours spent helping with bibliographical work. To friends and colleagues including Enrique García, Irina Feldman, Roberto Pareja, Nicolas Poppe, and Jonathan Risner: our discussions in the planning stages of this project helped us immensely. As soon as we shared that we were writing about zombies, we received a number of suggestions from friends and family members from all over the world. Thanks to every single one of you. We would like to acknowledge Fernanda Rodrigues for her help with Portuguese language and navigating European access to film. Participation in a number of workshops through Middlebury College and reading and writing working groups with dedicated and amazing colleagues from different departments was instrumental in further developing our intersectional and global approach. Many thanks as well to the anonymous readers whose comments and suggestions were always useful and to the point.

We are also very grateful to all the filmmakers, actors, and writers who have created the movies we work with. Many special thanks to Alexis Díaz de Villegas for his insight and kindness in agreeing to speak with our group from Middlebury. We are very grateful to Rafael Arévalo for his generosity in sharing his films and suggestions. Our reading of zombies would not be the same without previous books and articles on the subject. We are pleased to be joining their ranks. We are delighted to work with Rutgers University Press, especially Frederick Aldama and Nicole Solano.

Last but never least, we would like to thank our families, especially Glenn and David, for their unflagging support as we devoted so much of our lives to the undead. Our love for you is undying.

Notes

Introduction

1 Don Gonyea and Lorenzo Sierra, "Arizona Lawmaker Reflects on Surviving COVID-19," NPR.org, December 26, 2020, https://www.npr.org/2020/12/26/950476637/arizona-lawmaker-reflects-on-surviving-covid-19.

2 Martha Bebinger, "Another COVID-19 Medical Mystery: Patients Come Off Ventilator But Linger in a Coma," NPR.org, August 24, 2020, https://www.npr.org/sections/health-shots/2020/08/24/904347130/another-covid-19-medical-mystery-patients-come-off-ventilator-but-linger-in-a-co.

3 "Circle of Confusion," pilot episode, *The Walking Dead* (American Movie Classics [AMC], Valhalla Motion Pictures, 2010).

4 Danny Boyle, dir., *28 Days Later* (London: DNA Films, British Film Council, 2002).

5 Other reasons one might sleep through the end of the world include a severe hangover (*Mutant Blast*), or maybe just a nap (*The Night Eats the World*).

6 Coltan Scrivner, John Anthony Johnson, Jens Kjeldgaard-Christiansen, and Mathias Clasen, "Pandemic Practice: Horror Fans and Morbidly Curious Individuals Are More Psychologically Resilient During the COVID-19 Pandemic," preprint, PsyArXiv, June 30, 2020, https://doi.org/10.31234/osf.io/4c7af.

7 Eva Horn, *The Future as Catastrophe: Imagining Disaster in the Modern Age*, trans. Valentine Pakis (New York: Columbia University Press, 2018), 4.

8 Horn, *Future as Catastrophe*, 11.

9 See Dahlia Schweitzer's work on outbreak narratives and how they interact with real-world rhetoric of fear: Schweitzer, *Going Viral: Zombies, Viruses, and the End of the World* (New Brunswick, NJ: Rutgers University Press, 2018).

10 Horn, *Future as Catastrophe*, 231.

11 Michael Hardt and Antonio Negri, *Empire* (Cambridge, MA: Harvard University Press, 2000), xii–xiii.

12 Hardt and Negri, *Empire*, xv.

13 As proposed by decolonial theorists such as Aníbal Quijano, Walter Mignolo, and Nelson Torres-Maldonado, among many others.

14 Nelson Maldonado-Torres, "On the Coloniality of Being: Contributions to the Development of a Concept," *Cultural Studies* 21, no. 2–3 (2007): 243.
15 Ariadna Estévez, "Biopolítica y necropolítica. ¿Constitutivos u opuestos?," *Espiral. Estudios sobre Estado y Sociedad* 25, no. 3 (September–December 2018): 9–43.
16 Noël Carroll, *The Philosophy of Horror: Or, Paradoxes of the Heart* (New York: Routledge, 1990), 18.
17 Carroll, *Philosophy of Horror*, 43.
18 Anna Powell, *Deleuze and Horror Film* (Edinburgh: Edinburgh University Press, 2005), 62.
19 Powell, *Deleuze and Horror Film*, 63.
20 Marco Abel, *Violent Affect: Literature, Cinema, and Critique after Representation* (Lincoln: University of Nebraska Press, 2007), 25.

Chapter 1

1 Gary Hatfield, "René Descartes," in *Stanford Encyclopedia of Philosophy*, ed. Edward N. Zalta, Summer 2018, https://plato.stanford.edu/archives/sum2018/entries/descartes/.
2 Benedictus Spinoza, *Ethics* (Cambridge: Cambridge University Press, 1996); Roberto Esposito, *Persons and Things*, trans. Zakiya Hanafi (Cambridge: Polity Press, 2015).
3 William Seabrook, *The Magic Island*, illustrations by Alexander King (New York: Harcourt, Brace, 1929).
4 Victor Halperin, dir., *White Zombie* (Victor & Edward Halperin Productions, 1932).
5 Seabrook, *Magic Island*, 93.
6 In this context, cf. Guillermo Serés's *La historia del alma: Antigüedad, Edad Media, Siglo de Oro* (Barcelona: Galaxia Gutenberg SL, 2019).
7 Bonar L. Hernandez, "The Las Casas–Sepúlveda Controversy: 1550–1551," *Ex Post Facto* 10 (2001): 95–105, https://history.sfsu.edu/sites/default/files/images/2001_Bonar%20Ludwig%20Hernandez.pdf.
8 René Descartes, *Meditations on First Philosophy: With Selection from the Objections and Replies*, trans. and ed. John Cottingham (Cambridge: Cambridge University Press, 2017).
9 For further information about Descartes's *Meditations*, see Gary Hatfield, "The Senses and the Fleshless Eye: The *Meditations* as Cognitive Exercises," in *Essays on Descartes' Meditations*, ed. Amèlie Rorty (Berkeley: University of California Press, 1986), 45–79.
10 Saul Fisher, "Pierre Gassendi," in *The Stanford Encyclopedia of Philosophy*, ed. Edward N. Zalta, Spring 2014, https://plato.stanford.edu/archives/spr2014/entries/gassendi/, section 3.
11 James Warren, ed., "Removing Fear," in *The Cambridge Companion to Epicureanism* (Cambridge: Cambridge University Press, 2009), 234–248.
12 Benedictus de Spinoza, *Ethics* (Cambridge: Cambridge University Press, 1996), Preposition XIV.
13 Steven Nadler, "Eternity and Immortality in Spinoza's Ethics," *Midwest Studies in Philosophy* 26 (2002): 231.
14 Esposito, *Persons and Things*, 1–15.
15 Esposito, *Persons and Things*, 108–117.

16 Esposito, *Persons and Things*, 14–15.
17 Titus Livius, *Ab urbe condita*, ed. John Briscoe (Oxford: Oxford University Press, 2016).
18 Zondervan Bibles, *NIV Study Bible* (Grand Rapids, MI: Zondervan, 2011). All further citations from the Bible are from this edition.
19 George A. Romero, dir., *Dawn of the Dead* (U.S.: Dawn Associates, Laurel Group, 1978).
20 George A. Romero, dir., *Land of the Dead* (U.S.: Universal Pictures, Atmosphere Entertainment MM, Romero-Grunwald Productions, 2005).
21 Ryûhei Kitamura, dir., *Versus* (Japan: WEVCO Produce Company, napalm FiLMS, KSS, 2000).
22 Shinsuke Sato, dir., *I Am a Hero* (Japan: Avex Pictures, Dentsu, East Japan Marketing & Communications, 2015).
23 Due to the countless films in the genre, we are aware that there are some exceptions, such as *The Unliving* (Sweden, 2014), and *Ravenous* (Canada, 2017), in which zombies appear to express some pain, anger, and even sadness.
24 Jonathan Levine, *Warm Bodies* (U.S.: Summit Entertainment, Make Movies, Mandeville Films, 2013).
25 Esposito, *Persons and Things*, 108–117.
26 Esposito, *Persons and Things*, 108–117.
27 Mel Y. Chen, "Lurching for the Cure? On Zombies and the Reproduction of Disability," *GLQ: A Journal of Lesbian and Gay Studies* 21, no. 1 (January 2015): 25.
28 Michael Hardt and Antonio Negri, *Empire* (Cambridge, MA: Harvard University Press, 2000); Michael Hardt, *Multitude: War and Democracy in the Age of Empire* (New York: Penguin Press, 2004).
29 Hardt, *Multitude*, xiv.
30 Sayak Valencia, *Gore Capitalism*, trans. John Pluecker (South Pasadena, CA: Semiotext(e), 2018). See chapter 3 in this volume for further discussion of gore capitalism.
31 Chen, "Lurching for the Cure?," 26.
32 Julia Kristeva, *Powers of Horror: An Essay on Abjection*, trans. Leon S. Roudiez (New York: Columbia University Press, 1982), 53.
33 Michael Bakhtin. *Rabelais and His World* (Bloomington: Indiana University Press, 1984).
34 Sebastián Hofmann, dir., *Halley* (Mexico: Mantarraya Producciones, Piano/Simplemente, 2013).
35 Esposito, *Persons and Things*, 99–107.
36 Walter Benjamin, *Ursprung des deutschen Trauerspiels* (Frankfurt am Main: Suhrkamp Taschenbuch Wissenschaft, 1996).
37 Refer to chapter 4 in this volume for more on this subject.
38 Romero, *Day of the Dead*.
39 Benjamin, *Ursprung des deutschen Trauerspiels*.
40 Alejandro Brugués, dir., *Juan of the Dead* (*Juan de los muertos*) (Spain/Cuba: La Zanfoña Producciones, Producciones de la 5ta Avenida, Soundchef Studios, 2012).
41 Christoph Behl, dir., *What's Left of Us* (*El desierto*) (Argentina: Duermevela, Instituto Nacional de Cine y Artes Audiovisuales [INCAA], Subterránea Films, 2015).
42 Benjamin, *Ursprung des deutschen Trauerspiels*, 156; Graeme Gilloch, *Myth and Metropolis: Walter Benjamin and the City* (Cambridge: Polity Press, 1997).

43 Heinz Bude and Jessica Spengler, *Society of Fear* (Malden, MA: Polity Press, 2018).
44 Bude and Spengler, *Society of Fear*, 17.
45 Paul Virilio and Bertrand Richard, *The Administration of Fear*, trans. Ames Hodges (Los Angeles: Semiotext(e), 2012), 30.
46 Priscilla Wald, *Contagious: Cultures, Carriers, and the Outbreak Narrative* (Durham, NC: Duke University Press, 2008), 2–3.
47 Sang-ho Yeon, dir., *Seoul Station (Seoulyeok)* (South Korea: Studio Dadashow, 2016).
48 Amparo Cano Esteban and Miguel A. V. Ferreira, "Pero . . . ¿Qué es un zombi? ¿Todos somos zombies?," *Nómadas: Critical Journal of Social and Juridical Sciences* 51, no. 2 (2017); Lana Wachowski and Lilly Wachowski, dirs., *The Matrix* (U.S.: Warner Bros., Village Roadshow Pictures, Groucho Film Partnership, 1999); James Cameron, dir., *Avatar* (U.S.: 20th Century Fox, Dune Entertainment, Lightstorm Entertainment, 2009). Transhumanism is defined as an intermediate state between human and posthuman.
49 George Orwell, *1984* (New York: Penguin Books, 1949), 269–273.
50 Mainly *Die Protestantische Ethik und der Geist des Kapitalismus* by Max Weber (1905; reprint, Tübingen: Mohr, 1934).
51 Bolívar Echeverría, ed., *Modernidad, mestizaje cultural y ethos barroco* (Mexico City: UNAM- EI Equilibrista, 1994).
52 Julio Díaz and Carolina Meloni, "La noche del capitalismo viviente," in *Abecedario zombi: La noche del capitalismo viviente* (Madrid: El salmón contracorriente, 2016), 179–180.
53 Juan José Patón, dir., *Zombie World* (Spain: Menos es Más Producciones, 2013).
54 Alison Kafer, *Feminist, Queer, Crip* (Bloomington: Indiana University Press, 2013); see also chapter 4 in this volume.
55 Chen, "Lurching for the Cure?," 25.
56 See chapter 4 for explanations regarding queer and crip temporality.
57 See chapter 5 in this volume.
58 George A. Romero, dir., *Night of the Living Dead* (U.S.: Image Ten, 1968).
59 Carlos Jáuregui, *Canibalia: Canibalismo, calibanismo, antropofagia cultural y consumo en América Latina* (Madrid: Iberoamericana/Vervuert, 2008), 14.
60 Jáuregui, *Canibalia*, 34.
61 Jáuregui, *Canibalia*, 52.
62 Aimé Césaire, *Discourse on Colonialism*, trans. Joan Pinkham (New York: Monthly Review Press, 2000).
63 Ignacio Sánchez Prado, "La utopía apocalíptica del México neoliberal," *Alter-Texto* 10, no. 5 (2007): 9–15.
64 Bruce McDonald, dir., *Pontypool* (Canada: Ponty Up Pictures, Shadow Shows, 2008).
65 Sharon J. Kirsch and Michael Stancliff, "How Do You Not Understand a Word? Language as Contagion and Cure in Pontypool," *Journal of Narrative Theory* (2018): 256.
66 Georges Bataille, *Lo que entiendo por soberanía*, trans. Pilar Sánchez Orozco and Antonio Campillo (Barcelona: Paidós, 1996), 86.
67 Achille Mbembe, "Necropolitics," trans. Libby Meintjes, *Public Culture* 15, no. 1 (2003): 16.
68 Giorgio Agamben, *State of Exception* (Chicago: University of Chicago Press, 2004).
69 Mbembe, "Necropolitics," 21.

70 Agamben, *State of Exception*, 30.
71 Agamben, *State of Exception*, 40.
72 Office of the Chairman of the Joint Chiefs of Staff, *DOD Dictionary of Military and Associated Terms* (Washington, DC: The Joint Staff, August 2021), https://www.jcs.mil/Portals/36/Documents/Doctrine/pubs/dictionary.pdf.
73 Robert A. Goldwin, "Is There an American Right of Revolution?," *AEI* (January 1990): 1.
74 George Bataille, *The Accursed Share: An Essay on General Economy* (New York: Zone Books, 1988).
75 Antonio Negri, "El monstruo político: Vida desnuda y potencia," in *Ensayos sobre biopolítica: Excesos de vida*, comp. Gabriel Giorgi and Fermín Rodríguez (Buenos Aires: Paidós, 2007), 93–140.
76 Negri, "El monstruo político," 96–97.
77 Agamben, *State of Exception*.
78 Rosemarie Garland Thomson, ed., *Freakery: Cultural Spectacles of the Extraordinary Body* (New York: New York University Press, 1996), 3.
79 Rachel Adams, *Sideshow U.S.A.: Freaks and the American Cultural Imagination* (Chicago: University of Chicago Press, 2001), 11.
80 Adams, *Sideshow U.S.A.*, 165.
81 Adams, *Sideshow U.S.A.*, 167.
82 Garland Thomson, *Freakery*, 11.
83 Adams, *Sideshow U.S.A.*, 13.
84 Edward L. Schwarzschild, "Death-Defying/Defining Spectacles: Charles Willson Peale as Early American Freak Showman," in Thomson, *Freakery*, 82–96.
85 Roger Bartra, *Historias de salvajes* (Mexico City: Siglo XXI, 2017), 14.
86 Bartra, *Historias de salvajes*, 18.
87 In *Crossed*, the infected openly express their sexual urges and engage in sex and rape; infected women can even become pregnant. A living girl who is raped by her father sees that rape exists among zombies as well, and she wonders which version of existence is preferable.
88 Bertrand Bonello, dir., *Zombi Child* (France: My New Pictures, Les Films du Bal, Arte France Cinéma, 2019).
89 Jaume Balagueró and Paco Plaza, dirs., *REC* (Spain: Castelao Producciones, Filmax, Instituto de la Cinematografía y de las Artes Audiovisuales [ICAA)], 2007).
90 Hong-jin Na, dir., *The Wailing* (*Gokseong*), (South Korea: 20th Century Fox, Fox International Production, Ivanhoe Pictures, 2016).
91 Mati Diop, dir., *Atlantics* (*Atlantique*) (France/Belgium: Ad Vitam Production, Arte France Cinéma, Canal Plus, 2019).
92 Phil Guidry, Simon Herbert, and David Whelan, dirs., *Savageland* (U.S.: Massive Film Company, 2017).
93 In general terms, queer temporality could be understood as a queer, rule-breaking, disruptive approach to time. See chapter 4 for further discussion.
94 See chapter 4.
95 Esposito, *Persons and Things*, 10.
96 Connections between posthumanism and the environment will be developed in chapter 5.
97 Jorge Olguín, *Descendents* (*Solos*) (Chile/Spain/Venezuela: Chile Films S.A., Olguin Films, Sleeping Giant Entertainment, 2007).

98 Colm McCarthy, dir., *The Girl with All the Gifts* (U.K.: BFI Film Fund, Creative Entertainment, Altitude Film Entertainment, 2016).

Chapter 2

1 Vodou practitioner.

2 Anibal Quijano, "Coloniality of Power, Eurocentrism, and Latin America," ed. Michael Ennis, *Nepantla: Views from South* 1, no. 3 (2000): 534.

3 Sarah Juliet Lauro, *The Transatlantic Zombie: Slavery, Rebellion, and Living Death* (New Brunswick, NJ: Rutgers University Press, 2015), 8.

4 Lauro, *Transatlantic Zombie*, 31.

5 Michel Foucault, *The History of Sexuality: An Introduction*, vol. 1, trans. Robert Hurley (New York: Pantheon Books, 1978), 138.

6 Achille Mbembe, "Necropolitics," trans. Libby Meintjes, *Public Culture* 15, no. 1 (2003): 1.

7 Mbembe, "Necropolitics," 22.

8 Jennifer Rutherford, *Zombies* (New York: Routledge, 2013).

9 William Seabrook, *The Magic Island* (New York: Harcourt, Brace, 1929), 93.

10 "Why, so often do you see a tomb or grave set close beside a busy road or footpath where people are always passing? It is to assure the poor unhappy dead such protection as we can." Seabrook, *Magic Island*, 94.

11 Jacques Tourneur, dir., *I Walked with a Zombie* (U.S.: RKO Radio Pictures, 1943).

12 Mbembe, "Necropolitics," 17.

13 Juan Antonio de la Riva, dir., *Ladronas de almas* (Mexico: Eficine, 2015).

14 Mbembe, "Necropolitics," 34.

15 Mbembe, "Necropolitics," 35.

16 Marc Forster, dir., *World War Z* (U.S.: Paramount Pictures, Skydance Media, Hemisphere Media Capital, 2013).

17 Mbembe, "Necropolitics," 27.

18 Tell Meggido, a mount in northern Israel, is considered by many millennialist and dispensationalist groups to be the future site of the battle of Armageddon. More recently, the Trump administration's decision to move the U.S. embassy to Jerusalem and to recognize it as the capital of Israel has been read by evangelical Christians in the United States as a prophetic element that will signal the Second Coming. See, for example, Edward Wong, "The Rapture and the Real World: Mike Pompeo Blends Beliefs and Policy," *New York Times,* March 30, 2019, https://www.nytimes.com/2019/03/30/us/politics/pompeo-christian-policy.html; Stephanie Mencimer, "Evangelicals Love Donald Trump for Many Reasons, but One of Them Is Especially Terrifying: End Times." *Mother Jones*, January 23, 2020, https://www.motherjones.com/politics/2020/01/evangelicals-are-anticipating-the-end-of-the-world-and-trump-is-listening/.

19 Adam Lowenstein, *Shocking Representation: Historical, Trauma, National Cinema, and the Modern Horror Film* (New York: Columbia University Press, 2005), 2.

20 Mbembe, "Necropolitics," 40.

21 Michael Hardt and Antonio Negri. *Multitude: War and Democracy in the Age of Empire* (New York: Penguin, 2004), 4.

22 Hardt and Negri, *Multitude*, 5.

23 Alejandro Brugués, dir., *Juan of the Dead* (*Juan de los muertos*) (Spain/Cuba: La Zanfoña Producciones, Producciones de la 5ta Avenida, Soundchef Studios, 2012).
24 Robert Rodriguez, dir., *Planet Terror* (U.S./Mexico: Dimension Films, Troublemaker Studios, Rodriguez International Pictures, 2007).
25 One of the most infamous centers of interrogation and torture in Chile under Augusto Pinochet, it was operational approximately from 1974 to 1978.
26 Mikhail Red, dir., *Block Z* (Philippines: Star Cinema, Keep Filming, PelikulaRed, 2020).
27 Sang-ho Yeon, dir., *Seoul Station* (*Seoulyeok*) (South Korea: Studio Dadashow, 2016).
28 Travis Linnemann, Tyler Wall, and Edward Green, "The Walking Dead and Killing State: Zombification and the Normalization of Police Violence," *Theoretical Criminology* 18, no. 4 (April 7, 2014): 520, https://doi.org/10.1177/1362480614529455.
29 Linnemann, Wall, and Green, "Walking Dead and Killing State," 510.
30 A frighteningly similar case, also in Florida, occurred in 2016. In this case the perpetrator was a White teenager and the victim was a homeowner, found in the driveway of his own house. Here, the teenager was not shot and survived to face the justice system. Peter Holley, "Police Killed the Black 'Miami Zombie.' So Why Did a Terrifying, Face-Eating White Teen Live?," *Washington Post*, August 24, 2016, https://www.washingtonpost.com/news/post-nation/wp/2016/08/24/police-killed-a-black-face-eater-heres-why-they-say-a-white-guy-turned-zombie-lived/.
31 Linnemann, Wall, and Green, "Walking Dead and Killing State," 518.
32 Paul Hoen, dir., *Z-O-M-B-I-E-S* (U.S.: Disney Channel, 2018).
33 William Seabrook, we recall, wrote *The Magic Island*, interpreting the Haitian zombie legend from Haiti for popular consumption in the United States.
34 Mel Y. Chen, "Agitation," *Wildness (South Atlantic Quarterly)* 117, no. 3 (July 2018): 556.
35 Chen, "Agitation," 553.
36 Chen, "Agitation," 554.
37 Jack Halberstam and Tavia Nyong'o, "Introduction: Theory in the Wild," *South Atlantic Quarterly* 117, no. 3 (July 1, 2018): 454.
38 Frantz Fanon, *The Wretched of the Earth*, trans. Richard Philcox (New York: Grove Press, 2005), 164.
39 Suvendrini Perera and Joseph Pugliese, "Introduction: Combat Breathing: State Violence and the Body in Question." *Somatechnics* 1, no. 1 (March 2011): 1–14, https://doi.org/10.3366/soma.2011.0002.
40 Hardt and Negri, *Multitude*, 8.
41 Hardt and Negri, *Multitude*, xiv.
42 Hisup Shin, "Monstrous National Allegory: The Making of Monstrous Otherness in Na Hong-jin's *The Wailing*," *Journal of Film and Video* 72, no. 3–4 (Fall/Winter 2020): 92, https://doi.org/10.5406/jfilmvideo.72.3-4.0090.
43 Hardt and Negri, *Multitude*, 192.
44 For discussion of Marx's fixation on the vampire as a metaphor for capitalism, see chapter 3 in this volume.
45 Hardt and Negri, "Empire, Twenty Years On." *New Left Review* 120 (November–December 2019): 67, https://newleftreview.org/issues/ii120/articles/empire-twenty-years-on.
46 See chapter 3 in this volume.
47 Quijano, "Coloniality of Power," 533.

48 Quijano, "Coloniality of Power," 541.

49 Walter D. Mignolo, "I Am Where I Think: Epistemology and the Colonial Difference," *Journal of Latin American Cultural Studies* 8, no. 2 (1999): 237.

50 This is also the name of a real, historical Haitian man who claimed to have been turned into a zombie.

51 A priestess.

52 Colm McCarthy, dir., *The Girl with All the Gifts* (U.K.: BFI Film Fund, Creative England, Altitude Film Entertainment, 2016).

53 Chris Osmond, "Time to Die: Zombie as Educational Evolution in *The Girl with All the Gifts*," *Journal of Curriculum Theorizing* 34, no. 5 (October 31, 2019): 67.

54 Jeff Barnaby, dir., *Blood Quantum* (Canada: Prospector Films, 2019).

55 Suzan Shown Harjo, "Vampire Policy Is Bleeding Us Dry—Blood Quantums, Be Gone!," in *The Great Vanishing Act: Blood Quantum and the Future of Native Nations*, ed. Kathleen Ratteree and Norbert Hill (Golden, CO: Fulcrum Publishing, 2017), 79.

56 Breny Mendoza, "Decolonial Theories in Comparison," *Journal of World Philosophies* 5, no. 1 (2020): 51, https://scholarworks.iu.edu/iupjournals/index.php/jwp/article/view/3600.

57 Canadian Broadcasting Corporation, "Jeff Barnaby Recalls the Incident at Restigouche," *George Stroumboulopoulos Tonight*, accessed January 7, 2021, https://www.cbc.ca/strombo/videos/web-exclusive/jeff-barnaby-the-incident-at-restigouche.

58 Ben Howling and Yolanda Ramke, dirs., *Cargo* (Australia: Addictive Pictures, Causeway Films, Head Gear Films, 2018).

59 Nell Irvin Painter, "What Whiteness Means in the Trump Era," *New York Times*, November 12, 2016, https://www.nytimes.com/2016/11/13/opinion/what-whiteness-means-in-the-trump-era.html.

60 Here we cannot fail to point out that a character in Jim Jarmusch's 2019 zombie film *The Dead Don't Die*, played by Steve Buscemi, sports a red baseball hat like the iconic hats sold by the Trump campaign, except that the slogan has been changed to "Keep America White Again."

61 "US Capitol Riot: 'It was Like a Zombie Movie,'" *BBC News*, January 8, 2021, https://www.bbc.com/news/av/world-us-canada-55581269.

62 Wendy Grossman Kantor, "Witness to Rioters Jumping through Capitol Building Window Says 'It Was Like Out of a Zombie Movie,'" *People*, January 9, 2021, https://people.com/politics/witness-to-rioters-jumping-through-capitol-window-like-out-of-zombie-movie/.

63 Cortlynn Stark and Bryan Lowry, "Robocalls Sent by GOP Attorneys General Group Pushed March to Capitol, NBC Reports," *Kansas City Star*, January 9, 2021, https://www.kansascity.com/news/local/article248392700.html.

Chapter 3

1 Mabel Moraña and Andrew Ascherl, *The Monster as War Machine* (Amherst, NY: Cambria Press, 2018), 139.

2 John William Polidori, *The Vampyre and Other Tales of the Macabre*, ed. Robert Morrison and Chris Baldick (Oxford: Oxford University Press, 2008); Bram Stoker, *Dracula* (1897; repr., New York: Oxford University Press, 1990).

3 Karl Marx and Friedrich Engels, *Capital: A Critique of Political Economy* (New York: International Publishers, 1967).

4 Sarah Burns, "'Better for Haunts': Victorian Houses and the Modern Imagination," *American Art* 26, no. 3 (Fall 2012): 2–25.

5 "Opulence," YouTube, uploaded by Contrapoints, October 12, 2019, https://www.youtube.com/watch?v=jD-PbF3ywGo.

6 See John Taggart and Kevin Granville, "From 'Zombie Malls' to Bonobos: What America's Retail Transformation Looks Like," *New York Times*, April 15, 2017, https://www.nytimes.com/2017/04/15/business/from-zombie-malls-to-bonobos-americas-retail-transformation.html; Mary Hanbury, "50 Haunting Photos of Abandoned Shopping Malls across America," *Business Insider*, updated November 8, 2019, https://www.businessinsider.com/american-retail-apocalypse-in-photos-2018-1.

7 Steven Shaviro, "Contagious Allegories: George Romero," in *Zombie Theory: A Reader*, ed. Sarah Juliet Lauro (Minneapolis: University of Minnesota Press, 2017), 7–19.

8 Steven Shaviro, "Capitalist Monsters," *Historical Materialism* 10, no. 4 (2002): 281–290.

9 Such as in *iZombie* (the CW television series, 2015–2019) when an energy drink creates a population of hidden zombies that, in turn, create a black market of healthy brains for their own subsistence.

10 *Bio-Zombie* and *Planet Terror*, to cite two examples.

11 Oh Young-doo, Ryu Hoon, Hong Young-geun, and Jang Youn-jung, dirs., *Resident Zombie* (aka *The Neighbor Zombie, Yieutjib jombi*) (South Korea: Kino Mangosteen, 2010).

12 Jim Jarmusch, dir., *The Dead Don't Die* (U.S./Sweden/South Africa: Animal Kingdom, Film iVäst, 2019).

13 Nicolás Goldbart, dir., *Phase 7* (*Fase 7*) (Argentina: Aeroplano Cine, Instituto Nacional de Cine y Artes Audiovisuales [INCAA], Televisión Federal [Telefe], 2011).

14 Wilson Yip, dir., *Bio-Zombie* (*Sang Faa Sau See*) (Hong Kong: Toho Company, Brilliant Idea Group [BIG], Cameron Entertainment Ltd., 1998); Shinsuke Sato, dir., *I Am a Hero* (Japan: Avex Pictures, Dentsu, East Japan Marketing & Communications, 2015).

15 Jonathan Levine, dir., *Warm Bodies* (U.S./Canada: Summit Entertainment, Make Movies, Mandeville Films, 2013).

16 Aarón Rodríguez Serrano, "Spaces of Contemporary Horror: Poverty and Social Exclusion as 21st Century Spectres," *Home Cultures* 16, no. 3 (2019): 195.

17 *The Walking Dead* (series) (U.S.: Valhalla Motion Pictures, 2010); *Black Summer* (series) (Canada/U.S.: The Asylum, Go2 Digital Media, Alberta Film Projects, 2019).

18 Dominique Rocher, dir., *The Night Eats the World* (*La nuit a dévoré le monde*) (France: Haut Et Court, Canal+, Ciné+, 2018).

19 John Edgar Browning, "Survival Horrors, Survival Spaces: Tracing the Modern Zombie (Cine)Myth through to the Post-Millennium," in *Zombie Talk: Culture, History, Politics*, ed. David R. Castillo, David Schmid, David A. Reilly, and John Edgar Browning (New York: Palgrave Macmillan, 2016), 34.

20 Robin Aubert, dir., *Ravenous* (*Les affamés*) (Canada: La Maison de Prod, Christal Films Distribution, Téléfilm Canada, 2018).

21 Peter Schwenger, *The Tears of Things: Melancholy and Physical Objects* (Minneapolis: University of Minnesota Press, 2006), 75.

22 Schwenger, *Tears of Things*, 76.

23 See Graeme Gilloch, *Myth and Metropolis: Walter Benjamin and the City* (Cambridge: Polity Press, 1996), 165, referring to Walter Benjamin's *The Arcades Project*, trans. Howard Eiland and Kevin McLaughlin (Cambridge, MA: Belknap Press of Harvard University Press, 2002). See also Frederik Le Roy, "Ragpickers and Leftover Performances: Walter Benjamin's Philosophy of the Historical Leftover," *Performance Research* 22, no. 8 (2017): 127–134.

24 Roberto Esposito, *Persons and Things*, trans. Zakiya Hanafi (Cambridge: Polity Press, 2015).

25 Dawn Keetley, "Zombie Republic: Property and the Propertyless Multitude in Romero's Dead Films and Kirkman's *The Walking Dead*," *Journal of the Fantastic in the Arts* 25, no. 2–3 (2014): 295–313. She cites Hardt and Negri's *Commonwealth*, and she cites Butler and Athanasiou in *Dispossession*.

26 Keetley, "Zombie Republic," 326.

27 Sang-ho Yeon, dir., *Seoul Station* (*Seoulyeok*) (South Korea: Studio Dadashow, 2016); Sang-ho Yeon, dir., *Train to Busan* (*Busanhaeng*) (South Korea: Next Entertainment World, 2016). *Seoul Station* is the prequel to *Train to Busan*.

28 See chapters 2 and 4 in this volume.

29 George A. Romero, dir., *Land of the Dead* (U.S.: Universal Pictures, Atmosphere Entertainment MM, Romero-Grunwald Productions, 2005).

30 Edgar Wright, dir., *Shaun of the Dead* (U.K.: Universal Pictures, StudioCanal, Working Title Films, 2004).

31 SABU, dir., *Miss Zombie* (Japan: Amuse Soft Entertainment, Dub, 2013).

32 Andrew Currie, dir., *Fido* (Canada: Lionsgate Films, Anagram Pictures, Astral Media, 2006).

33 Hugo Lilja, dir., *The Unliving* (*Återfödelsen*) (Sweden: Dramatiska Institutet, 2010).

34 Karl Marx and Friedrich Engels, *Capital: A Critique of Political Economy*, vol. 1 (New York: International Publishers, 1967), 108.

35 Marx and Engels, *Capital*, 1:127.

36 James Tyner, *Dead Labor: Toward a Political Economy of Premature Death* (Minneapolis: University of Minnesota Press, 2019), xiii.

37 Tyner, *Dead Labor*, xi.

38 Best Horror Short in First Glance Film Festival, Phoenix International Horror & Sci-Fi Film Festival, and Rhode Island International Horror Film Festival.

39 Matthew Van Vorst, dir., *Zombied* (short) (U.S.: Chiron Films, Chiron Films, Little Nap Productions, 2019).

40 As an example, Texas lieutenant governor Dan Patrick suggested that saving the economy was more important than the lives of the elderly. "As a senior citizen, are you willing to take a chance on your survival in exchange for keeping the America that all America loves for your children and grandchildren?" Abby Livingston, "Texas Lt. Gov. Dan Patrick Says a Failing Economy Is Worse than Coronavirus," *Texas Tribune*, March 24, 2020, https://www.texastribune.org/2020/03/23/texas-lt-gov-dan-patrick-says-bad-economy-worse-coronavirus/.

41 David McNally, *Monsters of the Market: Zombies, Vampires and Global Capitalism* (Chicago: Haymarket Books, 2011).

42 McNally, *Monsters of the Market*, 51–59.

43 John Gilling, dir., *The Plague of the Zombies* (U.K.: Hammer Films, Seven Arts Productions, 1966).

44 Tyner, *Dead Labor*, 16.

45 Sayak Valencia, *Gore Capitalism*, trans. John Pluecker (South Pasadena, CA: Semiotexte, 2018), 126.

46 Valencia, *Gore Capitalism*, 45.

47 We follow Valencia in using the terms "First World" and "Third World" in a critical way in the context of her theories (*Gore Capitalism*, 301n2).

48 Valencia, *Gore Capitalism*, 85.

49 Valencia, *Gore Capitalism*, 70, 37.

50 Alejandro Brugués, dir., *Juan of the Dead* (*Juan de los muertos*) (Spain/Cuba: La Zanfoña Producciones, Producciones de la 5ta Avenida, Soundchef Studios, 2012).

51 In an August 2020 video interview with Patricia Saldarriaga (et al.), the star of the film, Alexis Díaz de Villegas, was asked about the zombie metaphor. He replied, "Es una metáfora para alguien que quiere comer. Quiere comer carne. La carne escasea." / "It's a metaphor for someone who wants to eat meat, where meat is scarce."

52 "Juan of the dead, we kill your loved ones."

53 See chapter 2 in this volume.

54 Valencia, *Gore Capitalism*, 62–63.

55 *Juan of the Dead* is one example of many films (including *Warm Bodies*, *Fido*, *Shaun of the Dead*, *Zombie for Sale*, *Fists of Jesus*, and *Little Monsters*) that are mentioned in this book and are representative of a thriving subgenre of zombie comedies. While we are not addressing this subgenre specifically in this book, there is a great opportunity here for further study. For more on *Juan of the Dead* and satire, see Emy Manini and Patricia Saldarriaga, "Zombis nada más: *Juan de los muertos*, iconoclasta y antiimperialista," in *Nuevas miradas sobre el antiimperialismo y/o el antiamericanismo desde la historia, la literatura y el arte*, ed. Misael Arturo López Zapico, Aida Rodríguez Campesino, and Gonzalo Vitón (Madrid: Instituto de Estudios Internacionales y Europeos Francisco de Vitoria, 2019), 147–161.

56 Sang-ho Yeon, dir., *Train to Busan Presents: Peninsula* (South Korea: Next Entertainment World, RedPeter Films, New Movie, 2020).

57 Issa López, dir., *Tigers Are Not Afraid* (*Vuelven*) (Mexico: Filmadora Nacional, Peligrosa, 2017).

58 Valencia, *Gore Capitalism*, 26.

59 Valencia, *Gore Capitalism*, 20.

60 "El mensaje escrito en el cuerpo del otro es un mensaje para uno mismo, ¿no?," Síntesis TV, *El Capitalismo Gore con Dra. Sayak Valencia con José Oporto*, 2016, https://www.youtube.com/watch?v=_Ot2VJ45RRU&ab_channel=S%C3%ADntesisTV.

61 Phil Guidry, Simon Herbert, and David Whelan, dirs., *Savageland* (U.S.: Massive Film Company, 2017).

62 "Hauntology" being a term first coined by Jacques Derrida in *Specters of Marx: The State of the Debt, the Work of Mourning and the New International*, trans. Peggy Kamuf (New York: Routledge, 2006). It includes references to "haunting" and "ontology."

63 Avery Gordon, *Ghostly Matters: Haunting and the Sociological Imagination* (Minneapolis: University of Minnesota Press, 2008), 18.

64 Mati Diop, dir., *Atlantique* (*Atlantics*) (France/Belgium: Ad Vitam Production, Arte France Cinéma, Canal Plus, 2019).

65 Sarah Juliet Lauro, *The Transatlantic Zombie: Slavery, Rebellion, and Living Death* (New Brunswick, NJ: Rutgers University Press, 2015), 17.

66 Mandy Camara and Ruth Maclean, "Hundreds Die at Sea Off Senegal's Coast on a Perilous Route to Europe," *New York Times*, November 3, 2020, https://www.nytimes.com/2020/11/02/world/africa/senegal-migrants-drown.html.
67 Jason Motlagh, "Border Crisis: Arizona Desert Crossing Has Claimed Thousands of Lives," *Rolling Stone*, September 30, 2019, https://www.rollingstone.com/politics/politics-features/border-crisis-arizona-sonoran-desert-882613/; Jason De León, *The Land of Open Graves: Living and Dying on the Migrant Trail* (Oakland: University of California Press, 2015), 32.
68 Eunjung Kim, "Continuing Presence of Discarded Bodies: Occupational Harm, Necro-Activism, and Living Justice," *Catalyst: Feminism, Theory, Technoscience* 5, no. 1 (April 1, 2019): 8, 2.
69 Valencia, *Gore Capitalism*, 299–300.
70 Kiah Roache-Turner, dir., *Wyrmwood: Road of the Dead* (Australia: Guerilla Films, 2015).
71 Peter Orsi, "In Mexican Capital, Red Shoes to Protest Killings of Women," AP News, January 11, 2020, https://apnews.com/article/bbd6e02268849ee6d34cdd110865c041.
72 Amanda L. Petersen, "Breaking Silences and Revealing Ghosts: Spectral Moments of Gendered Violence in Mexico," *Interdisciplianry Mexico (iMex)* 16, no. 2 (2019): 33.
73 Matthew Schwartz, "In Selma, a 'Final Crossing' for John Lewis across the Edmund Pettus Bridge," NPR, July 26, 2020, https://www.npr.org/2020/07/26/895149942/in-selma-a-final-crossing-for-john-lewis-across-the-edmund-pettus-bridge.
74 Paul Blest, "Teachers Are Making Their Own Gravestones and Coffins to Protest Going Back to School," Vice, August 4, 2020, https://www.vice.com/en/article/y3zxp5/teachers-are-making-their-own-gravestones-and-coffins-to-protest-going-back-to-school.
75 Bruce LaBruce, dir., *Otto; or, Up with Dead People* (Germany/Canada: Jürgen Brüning Filmproduktion, Existential Crisis Productions, New Real Films, 2008).
76 Kimberly Kindy, "More than 200 Meat Plant Workers in the U.S. Have Died of Covid-19. Federal Regulators Just Issued Two Modest Fines," *Washington Post*, September 13, 2020, https://www.washingtonpost.com/national/osha-covid-meat-plant-fines/2020/09/13/1dca3e14-f395-11ea-bc45-e5d48ab44b9f_story.html; Michelle A. Waltenburg et al., "Update: COVID-19 among Workers in Meat and Poultry Processing Facilities—United States, April–May 2020," Centers for Disease Control and Prevention, *MMWR: Morbidity and Mortality Weekly Report* 69(27) (2020): 887–892, https://doi.org/10.15585/mmwr.mm6927e2.
77 Adnan Ahmed, dir., *Altered Skin* (Canada/Pakistan: Federgreen Entertainment, Indiecan Entertainment, 2018).
78 Jean Comaroff and John Comaroff, "Alien-Nation: Zombies, Immigrants, and Millennial Capitalism," reproduced in *Zombie Theory: A Reader*, ed. Sarah Juliet Lauro (Minneapolis: University of Minnesota Press, 2017), 139.
79 In *The Social Dilemma*, a 2020 Netflix-produced documentary, Tristan Harris, formerly of Google, reminds us, "If the product is free, *you're* the product."
80 Slavoj Žižek, "Coronavirus Is 'Kill Bill'–esque Blow to Capitalism and Could Lead to Reinvention of Communism," Íkaro, March 19, 2020, http://www.revistaikaro.com/slavoj-zizek-coronavirus-is-kill-bill-esque-blow-to-capitalism-and-could-lead-to-reinvention-of-communism/.

Chapter 4

1 Pável Florenski, *La perspectiva invertida*, ed. Felipe Pereda, trans. Xenia Egórova (Madrid: Siruela, 2005).

2 It is assumed that linear perspective was created by Filippo Brunelleschi (1377–1446). The goal was to achieve the illusion of a three-dimensional space on a two-dimensional surface.

3 Da Vinci's *Vitruvian Man* was made following Marcus Vitruvius Pollio's *De architectura*, a first-century multivolume work that discussed perfect proportion in bodies and architecture.

4 Also called the golden mean, golden section, or divine proportion. Ancient Greek mathematicians had already studied it in geometry. Luca Pacioli's *Divina proportione* (1509) explains its main principles, and yet, it was only in a 1597 letter to Johannes Kepler by Michael Maestlin that the golden ratio was attributed the decimal value of 1.618034 (phi).

5 For information about ethics surrounding triage and ventilators, see Mike Baker and Sheri Fink, "At the Top of the Covid-19 Curve, How Do Hospitals Decide Who Gets Treatment?," *New York Times*, March 31, 2020, https://www.nytimes.com/2020/03/31/us/coronavirus-covid-triage-rationing-ventilators.html. Cf. Joseph Shapiro, "As Hospitals Fear Being Overwhelmed by COVID-19, Do the Disabled Get the Same Access?," NPR, December 14, 2020, https://www.npr.org/2020/12/14/945056176/as-hospitals-fear-being-overwhelmed-by-covid-19-do-the-disabled-get-the-same-acc. See also Shapiro, "Oregon Hospitals Didn't Have Shortages. So Why Were Disabled People Denied Care?," NPR, December 21, 2020, https://www.npr.org/2020/12/21/946292119/oregon-hospitals-didnt-have-shortages-so-why-were-disabled-people-denied-care.

6 See chapter 3 in this volume.

7 Jamie McDaniel, "'You Can Point a Finger at a Zombie. Sometimes They Fall Off': Contemporary Zombie Films, Embedded Ableism, and Disability as Metaphor," *Midwest Quarterly* 57, no. 4 (Summer 2016): 425.

8 Oh Young-doo, Ryu Hoon, Hong Young-geun, and Jang Youn-jung, dirs., *Resident Zombie* (aka *The Neighbor Zombie, Yieutjib jombi*) (South Korea: Kino Mangosteen, 2010).

9 Joe Lynch, dir., *Mayhem* (U.S.: Circle of Confusion, Royal Viking Entertainment, 2017).

10 Kentarô Hagiwara, dir., *Tokyo Ghoul* (*Tôkyô Gûru*) (Japan: Geek Sight, Shochiku, 2017).

11 Fiona Kumari Campbell, *Contours of Ableism: The Projection of Disability and Abledness* (London: Palgrave Macmillan, 2009), 166.

12 By 1435, Leon Battista Alberti had already written his masterpiece *De pictura* (*On Paintings*), explicitly delineating how to apply linear perspective.

13 As proposed by Nicholas Mirzoeff in *The Right to Look: A Counterhistory of Visuality* (Durham, NC: Duke University Press, 2011).

14 See Robert McRuer, *Crip Theory: Cultural Signs of Queerness and Disability* (New York: New York University Press, 2006); Kim Hall, "No Failure: Climate Change, Radical Hope, and Queer Crip Feminist Eco-Futures." *Radical Philosophy Review* 17, no. 1 (2014): 203–225.

15 Mariela Solana, "Asincronía y crononormatividad: Apuntes sobre la idea de temporalidad queer," *El banquete de los dioses: Revista de filosofía y teoría política contemporánea* 5, no. 7 (November 2016), 39; translation by the authors.

16 Elizabeth Freeman, *Time Binds: Queer Temporalities, Queer Histories* (Durham, NC: Duke University Press, 2010).

17 Jacques Le Goff, "Church Time and Merchant Time in the Middle Ages," *Social Science Information* 9, no. 4 (August 1970): 151–157.

18 Cf. Kimberly J. Lau, "The Vampire, the Queer, and the Girl: Reflections on the Politics and Ethics of Immortality's Gendering," *Signs: Journal of Women in Culture and Society* 44, no. 1 (August 13, 2018): 3–24. In some narratives, the vampire requires the blood of a female virgin.

19 *Zombie Church: Breathing Life Back into the Body of Christ* by Tyler Edwards (Grand Rapids, MI: Kregel Publications, 2011) characterizes people attending churches without really committing to the Christian principles as "zombies." Edwards's reading focuses exclusively on the negativity associated with the undead. In a similar rhetoric to the *conquistadors*, he sees these creatures as lacking the Holy Spirit, feeding on rules and rituals, and not on Jesus.

20 Mel Y. Chen, "Lurching for the Cure? On Zombies and the Reproduction of Disability," *GLQ: A Journal of Lesbian and Gay Studies* 21, no. 1 (January 2015): 25.

21 A clothing/art collection by the Belgian designer Caroline Bosmans was designed for children to look like zombies with their skin rotted off and their organs hanging out.

22 "Happy fault," as in the Catholic *Exultet* or Easter Proclamation.

23 Lee Edelman, *No Future: Queer Theory and the Death Drive* (Durham, NC: Duke University Press, 2004), 27.

24 Lucio Fulci, dir., *Zombi 2* (Italy: Variety Film, 1979).

25 John Geddes, dir., *Exit Humanity* (Canada: Eggplant Picture & Sound, Foresight Features, Optix Digital Pictures, 2011).

26 Alejandro Brugués, dir., *Juan of the Dead* (*Juan de los muertos*) (Spain/Cuba: La Zanfoña Producciones, Producciones de la 5ta Avenida, Soundchef Studios, 2012).

27 Dick Maas, dir., *Saint Nick* (*Sint*) (Netherlands: Parachute Pictures, 2010).

28 The song "Sankt Niklas war ein Seemann" is still very popular among children.

29 Adrián Cardona and David Muñoz, dir., *Fist of Jesus* (short) (Spain: Eskoria Films, Productions of The Universe, 2012).

30 Bruce LaBruce, dir., *L.A. Zombie* (U.S./Germany: PPV Networks, Dark Alley Media, Wurstfilm, 2010). There are two versions of the same movie: a "cut" version that was showcased in theaters and a longer version that includes graphic sex.

31 The hymn refers to Revelation 5:1–13, in which the lamb bleeding from the heart represents the suffering of Jesus Christ and the process of shedding his blood to save humanity from their sins. See also Revelation 7:14. The "Washed in the Lamb" hymn was written in 1878 by Elisha Albright Hoffman. See W. K. McNeil, ed., *Encyclopedia of American Gospel Music* (New York: Routledge, 2005), 188.

32 Colm McCarthy, dir., *The Girl with All the Gifts* (U.K.: BFI Film Fund, Creative England, Altitude Film Entertainment, 2016).

33 See chapter 2 in this volume.

34 Miguel Ángel Vivas, dir., *Extinction* (Spain/U.S./Hungary/France: La Ferme! Productions, Laokoon Filmgroup, Ombra Films, 2015).

35 Shaka McGlotten and Steve Jones, *Zombies and Sexuality: Essays on Desire and the Living Dead* (Jefferson, NC: McFarland, 2014).

36 Marcel Sarmiento and Gadi Harel, dirs., *Deadgirl* (U.S.: Hollywoodmade, 2013).

37 Bruce LaBruce, dir., *Otto; or, Up with Dead People* (Germany/Canada: Jürgen Brüning Filmproduktion, Existential Crisis Productions, New Real Films, 2008);

Jave Galt-Miller and Wayne A. Brown, *Lesbian Zombies from Outer Space*, vol. 1 (n.p.: Big Things Productions, 2016); Eric England, dir., *Contracted* (U.S.: Boulder-Light Pictures, Southern Fried Films, 2013).

38 Presented in the Lothrop Stoddard text titled *The Rising Tide of Color against White World-Supremacy* (New York: Charles Scribner's Sons, 1920).

39 Performed by Antony and the Johnsons, lyrics by Anohni.

40 Edelman, *No Future*, 27.

41 Sebastián Hofmann, dir., *Halley* (Mexico: Mantarraya Producciones, Piano/Simplemente, 2013); Jeff Barnaby, dir., *Blood Quantum* (Canada: Prospector Films, 2019).

42 Lau, "The Vampire, the Queer, and the Girl," 11.

43 See previous discussion of Benjamin and the *vanitas* paintings in chapter 1 of this volume.

44 McRuer, *Crip Theory*, 2.

45 Outi Hakola, "Zombies, Vampires and Frankenstein's Monster: Embodied Experiences of Illness in Living Dead Films," *Thanatos* 8, no. 1 (2019): 97.

46 SABU, dir., *Miss Zombie* (Japan: Amuse Soft Entertainment, Dub, 2013).

47 McDaniel, "You Can Point a Finger," 432–443.

48 This claim is in dispute, as some critics consider this statement as controversial.

49 Maria Lugones, "The Coloniality of Gender," *Worlds & Knowledges Otherwise* (Spring 2008): 1–17. This posits the construction of gender as a category as parallel to Quijano's conception of race.

50 Breny Mendoza, "Coloniality of Gender and Power: From Postcoloniality to Decoloniality," in *The Oxford Handbook of Feminist Theory*, ed. Lisa Disch and Mary Hawkesworth (Oxford: Oxford Handbooks Online, 2015), 18, https://www.escuelaformacionpolitica.com/uploads/6/6/7/0/66702859/003_breny_coloniality-gender-power.pdf.

51 María Lugones, "Toward a Decolonial Feminism," *Hypatia* 25, no. 4 (Fall 2010): 742–759.

52 Miguel Ángel Vivas, dir., *I'll See You in My Dreams* (short) (Portugal: Pato Profissional Limitada, 2003).

53 Andreas Marfori, dir., *Attack of the Soviet Zombies* (*Ataka Sovetskikh Zombi*) (Russia/Italy: Victor Boulankin, 2016).

54 Nell Irvin Painter, *The History of White People* (New York: W. W. Norton, 2010).

55 Painter, *History of White People*, 39.

56 Painter, *History of White People*, 43.

57 "Circassian Beauty Exhibit," the Lost Museum Archive, https://lostmuseum.cuny.edu/archive/exhibit/star/, accessed January 9, 2021.

58 Victor Halperin, dir., *White Zombie* (U.S.: Victor & Edward Halperin Productions, 1932).

59 Jacques Tourneur, dir., *I Walked with a Zombie* (U.S.: RKO Radio Pictures, 1943).

60 George A. Romero, dir., *Night of the Living Dead* (U.S.: Image Ten, 1968).

61 Loving v. Virginia, 388 U.S. 1 (1967).

62 Cf. the connection between sexual aggression and lynching proposed by Niambi M. Carter, "Intimacy without Consent: Lynching as Sexual Violence." *Politics & Gender* 8, no. 3 (September 2012): 414–421.

63 See Grace Elizabeth Hale, *Making Whiteness: The Culture of Segregation in the South, 1890–1940* (New York: Vintage Books, 1999), esp. chap. 5.

64 Kinitra D. Brooks, "The Importance of Neglected Intersections: Race and Gender in Contemporary Zombie Texts and Theories," *African American Review* 47, no. 4 (Winter 2014): 461.
65 Mati Diop, dir., *Atlantics* (*Atlantique*) (France/Belgium: Ad Vitam Production, Arte France Cinéma, Canal Plus, 2019); Bertrand Bonello, dir., *Zombi Child* (France: My New Pictures, Les Films du Bal, Arte France Cinéma, 2019).
66 Frank B. Wilderson III, *Afropessimism* (London: Liveright Publishing, 2020).
67 "Human Trafficking and Smuggling in Asia," Asian Century Institute, April 24, 2016, https://asiancenturyinstitute.com/society/1120-human-trafficking-and-smuggling-in-asia.
68 For examples of modern slavery, see Owen Pinnell and Jess Kelly, "Slave Markets Found on Instagram and Other Apps," *BBC News*, October 31, 2019, https://www.bbc.com/news/technology-50228549.
69 Sang-ho Yeon, dir., *Seoul Station* (*Seoulyeok*) (South Korea: Studio Dadashow, 2016).
70 U.S. Department of State, *Trafficking in Persons Report*, June 2019, https://www.state.gov/wp-content/uploads/2019/06/2019-Trafficking-in-Persons-Report.pdf.
71 In his essay "The Mental Lives of Zombies," Declan Smithies makes a distinction between consciousness and cognition. Smithies's interpretation favors zombies as having intentional states, but those are not cognitive states because zombies are excluded from the realm of reason. From *Philosophical Perspectives* 26, no. 1 (December 2012): 343–372.
72 Shinsuke Sato, dir., *I Am a Hero* (Japan: Avex Pictures, Dentsu, East Japan Marketing & Communications, 2015).
73 The video production *Milonga Queer* by Susy Schock y la Bandada de Colibríes depicts the transformation to a zombie by introducing color gradually.
74 Hakola, "Zombies, Vampires and Frankenstein's Monster," 96.
75 Matthew Kohnen, dir., *Aaah! Zombies!!* (*Wasting Away*) (U.S.: Shadowpark Pictures, Wasted Pictures, 2007).
76 Ben Howling and Yolanda Ramke, dirs., *Cargo* (Australia: Addictive Pictures, Causeway Films, Head Gear Films, 2018).
77 Mabel Moraña, *The Monster as War Machine*, trans. Andrew Ascherl (Amherst, NY: Cambria Press, 2018), 241.
78 Juan Antonio de la Riva, dir., *Ladronas de almas* (Mexico: Eficine, 2015).
79 Moraña, *Monster as War Machine*, 241.
80 Benjamin Wilkins, dir., *Pretty Dead* (*Human Meat—Mörder. Kannibale. Zombie*) (U.S.: Dangerously Low Productions, ReKon Productions, 2013).
81 Steve Jones, "Pretty, Dead: Sociosexuality, Rationality, and the Transition into Zom-being," in *Zombies and Sexuality: Essays on Desire and the Living Dead*, ed. Shaka McGlotten and Steve Jones (Jefferson, NC: McFarland, 2014), Kindle edition, Location 3375/4017.
82 Hisayasu Satô, dir., *Splatter: Naked Blood* (*Nekeddo Burâddo: Megyaku*) (Japan: Museum, 1996).
83 Julia Kristeva, *Powers of Horror: An Essay on Abjection*, trans. Leon S. Roudiez (New York: Columbia University Press, 1982), 4.
84 Thomas Laqueur, *Making Sex: Body and Gender from the Greek to Freud* (Cambridge, MA: Harvard University Press, 1990).
85 *Carrie* (Bryan De Palma, 1976), based on Stephen King's novel, constructs a moment of horror around Carrie's (Sissy Spacek's) ignorance about female

menstruation. She has her first period in her high school locker room and believes she is dying; her classmates mock her and throw tampons at her. Her mother tells her menstruation is a result of impurity and uses it as an excuse for abusing her. Other examples include *Ginger Snaps* (2000), *A Tale of Two Sisters* (Jee-woon Kim, 2003) and *Excision* (2012).

86 Colin Minihan, dir., *It Stains the Sands Red* (U.S./Canada: Digital Interference Productions, Grasswood Media, 2016).

87 Campbell, *Contours of Ableism.*

88 Rafael Arévalo, dir., *The Year of the Apocalypse* (*El año del apocalipsis*) (Peru: El Topo Producciones, 2016).

89 Alison Kafer, *Feminist, Queer, Crip* (Bloomington: Indiana University Press, 2013), 36, 40–42.

90 Though the numbers of infected children continue to rise. Erika Edwards, "More than 61,000 Children Got Covid-19 Last Week, a Record," NBC News, November 2, 2020, https://www.nbcnews.com/health/health-news/more-61-000-children-got-covid-19-last-week-record-n1245851.

91 Kafer, *Feminist, Queer, Crip*, 32.

92 Hilary Brueck, "CDC: Almost All of the US Kids and Teens Who've Died from COVID-19 Were Hispanic or Black," *Business Insider*, September 15, 2020, https://www.businessinsider.com/cdc-black-and-brown-children-dying-from-the-coronavirus-2020-9.

93 Hall, "No Failure," 206.

94 Rosi Braidotti, "A Theoretical Framework for the Critical Posthumanities," *Theory, Culture & Society* 36, no. 6 (November 2019): 31–61.

95 Hall, "No Failure," 230.

96 In the style of Stacy Alaimo, for whom human corporality is always mixing itself with all that is more than human, making it erroneous to consider nature to be "mere background." Hall, "No Failure," 222.

Chapter 5

1 Eva Horn, *The Future as Catastrophe: Imagining Disaster in the Modern Age*, trans. Valentine Pakis (New York: Columbia University Press, 2018).

2 Revelation, 12.

3 Cf. *The allegory of Vanity* by Juan de Valdés Leal (1660).

4 Cf. Matilde Marcolli, "Still Life as a Model of Spacetime," http://www.its.caltech.edu/~matilde/StillLifeSpacetime.pdf, accessed January 17, 2021.

5 Cf. Joel-Peter Witkin, "Feast of Fools (Mexico City)," Cleveland Museum of Art, https://www.clevelandart.org/art/1995.204.12, accessed October 30, 2018. See also the *Contemporary Vanitas* show at the Soho Gallery in London in 2016, as well as Víctor Conde's *Naturaleza muerta* (2009), in which zombies interact with macabre still lifes studied by David R. Castillo in *Zombie Talk: Culture, History, Politics* (New York: Palgrave Macmillan, 2016), 54–56.

6 Horn, *Future as Catastrophe*, 57.

7 Horn, *Future as Catastrophe*, 8–9.

8 Horn, *Future as Catastrophe*, 10.

9 Horn, *Future as Catastrophe*, 11.

10 Priscilla Wald, *Contagious: Cultures, Carriers, and the Outbreak Narrative* (Durham, NC: Duke University Press, 2008), introduction.

11 Colby Itkowitz, "Trump Again Uses Racially Insensitive Term to Describe Coronavirus," *Washington Post*, June 23, 2020, https://www.washingtonpost.com/politics/trump-again-uses-kung-flu-to-describe-coronavirus/2020/06/23/0ab5a8d8-b5a9-11ea-aca5-ebb63d27e1ff_story.html.

12 For example, see @realDonaldTrump tweet of December 11, 2018, "They want Open Borders for anyone to come in. This brings large-scale crime and disease."

13 For more on Oscar Brown Jr. and further analysis of Trump's favored metaphors, see Karen Pinchkin, "Insects, Floods and 'The Snake': What Trump's Use of Metaphors Reveals," PBS, *Frontline*, October 22, 2019, https://www.pbs.org/wgbh/frontline/article/insects-floods-and-the-snake-what-trumps-use-of-metaphors-reveals/.

14 Where securitization refers to the process by which Western political elites construct immigration as a security threat.

15 Giuseppe Campesi, "Migraciones, seguridad y confines en la teoría social contemporánea," *Crítica penal y poder* no. 3 (September 27, 2012), https://revistes.ub.edu/index.php/CriticaPenalPoder/article/view/3657. Cited by Ariadna Estévez, "Biopolítica y necropolítica: ¿Constitutivos u opuestos?," *Espiral: Estudios sobre estado y sociedad* 25, no. 3 (September–December 2018): 14.

16 Robert Moore, "Six Children Died in Border Patrol Care. Democrats in Congress Want to Know Why," ProPublica, January 13, 2020, https://www.propublica.org/article/six-children-died-in-border-patrol-care-democrats-in-congress-want-to-know-why.

17 Flavio Pedota, dir., *Infection* (*Infección*) (Venezuela/Mexico: Luz Creativa Producciones, Desenlace Films, 2019). *Chavismo* is a political ideology that is based on the ideas associated with the former Venezuelan president Hugo Chávez.

18 See chapters 2 and 3 in this volume.

19 Gloria Anzaldúa, *Borderlands/La frontera: The New Mestiza* (San Francisco: Aunt Lute Books, 1987).

20 See chapter 3.

21 Wald, *Contagious*, introduction.

22 The theory that the matter is made up of tiny indivisible particles called atoms.

23 Lucretius, *The Nature of Things: De rerum natura*, ed. and trans. Anthony M. Esolen (Baltimore: Johns Hopkins University Press, 1995), book I, lines 69–73.

24 See Alexandre Pinheiro Hasegawa, "A Peste no De rerum natura (6.1138-286) de Lucrécio—Parte I," *Estado da arte*, April 23, 2020, https://estadodaarte.estadao.com.br/a-peste-de-rerum-natura-lucrecio/.

25 Cf. Jaime Nogueira Pinto, *Contágios: 2500 anos de pestes* (Alfragide: Publicações Dom Quixote, August 2020), 20–22.

26 Alison Kafer, *Feminist, Queer, Crip* (Bloomington: Indiana University Press, 2013), 130.

27 Colm McCarthy, dir., *The Girl with All the Gifts* (U.K.: BFI Film Fund, Creative England, Altitude Film Entertainment, 2016).

28 Estévez, "Biopolítica y necropolítica," 17; Robert Esposito, *Persons and Things*, trans. Zakiya Hanafi (Cambridge: Polity Press, 2015). See also chapter 2 for the one-drop theory.

29 Paul B. Preciado, "Learning from the Virus," *Artforum*, May/June 2020, 3, https://www.artforum.com/print/202005/paul-b-preciado-82823.

30 Preciado, "Learning from the Virus," 3.

31 David Freyne, dir., *The Cured* (Ireland/France: Bac Films, Savage Productions, Tilted Pictures, 2017).

32 As in the case of Brazil, Mexico, Argentina, Colombia, and Peru. Claudia Vaca, from the Universidad Nacional de Colombia, is concerned about the lack of transparency about agreements reached between government and business regarding the practice of clinical tests. Doctors don't have access to the complete research protocols used by Johnson and Johnson. Sergio Felipe Garcia Hernandez, "Los cuestionamientos éticos a los ensayos clínicos de vacunas COVID-19 en Latinoamérica," Anadolu Agency, November 9, 2020, https://www.aa.com.tr/es/mundo/los-cuestionamientos-éticos-a-los-ensayos-clínicos-de-vacunas-covid-19-en-latinoamérica/1970603. For the exclusive use of the questionable Sputnik vaccine in Argentina, see Jason Beaubien, "Argentina Takes a Shot with Russia's Sputnik Vaccine," NPR, January 15, 2021, https://www.npr.org/sections/goatsandsoda/2021/01/15/957301807/argentina-takes-a-shot-with-russias-sputnik-vaccine.

33 See also the effect of infatuation and pop-cultural makeover on the zombie in *The Odd Family: Zombie on Sale.*

34 Lee Min-jae, dir., *The Odd Family: Zombie on Sale* (aka *Zombie for Sale, Gimyohan Gajok*) (South Korea: Cinezoo, Oscar 10 Studio, 2019).

35 It is a theme that appears in *28 Days Later* (2002), *I Am Legend* (2007), *Resident Zombie* (aka *The Neighbor Zombie*, 2010), and *Dead Trigger* (2017), among others.

36 Juan Carlos Fresnadillo, dir., *28 Weeks Later* (U.K./Spain: Fox Atomic, DNA Films, UK Film Council, 2007); Francis Lawrence, dir., *I Am Legend* (U.S.: Warner Bros., Village Roadshow Pictures, Weed Road Pictures, 2007). Other examples include *Exit Humanity* and *Wyrmwood.*

37 Mikhail Red, dir., *Block Z* (Philippines: Star Cinema, Keep Filming, PelikulaRed, 2020).

38 Stephanie Dalley, ed. and trans., *Myths from Mesopotamia: Creation, the Flood, Gilgamesh, and Others* (Oxford: Oxford University Press, 2008).

39 Dan Diamond, "'We Want Them Infected': Trump Appointee Demanded 'Herd Immunity' Strategy, Emails Reveal," Politico, December 16, 2020, https://www.politico.com/news/2020/12/16/trump-appointee-demanded-herd-immunity-strategy-446408.

40 Also known as *Cannon Fodder*, directed by Eitan Gafny (Israel: White Beach Productions, Israeli Film Fund, 2013).

41 Mike Cuff and Scott Windhauser, dirs., *Dead Trigger* (U.S.: Aldamisa Entertainment, Badhouse Studios Mexico, Distant Shore Films, 2018).

42 Wald, *Contagious*, introduction.

43 In her book *The Extractive Zone: Social Ecologies and Decolonial Perspectives* (Durham, NC: Duke University Press, 2017), Macarena Gómez-Barris defines "*extractivismo* as extractive capitalism as known in the Americas, indicates an economic system that engages in thefts, borrowings, and forced removals, violently reorganizing social life as well as the land by thieving resources from Indigenous and Afro-descendent territories" (Kindle edition, location 192/4818).

44 Eric England, dir., *Contracted* (U.S.: Boulder Light Pictures, Southern Fried Films, 2013).

45 Jonathan King, dir., *Black Sheep* (New Zealand/South Korea: New Zealand Film Commission, New Zealand On Air, The Daesung Group, 2006).

46 Maria Mies and Vandana Shiva, *Ecofeminismo: Teoría, crítica y perspectivas* (Barcelona: Icaria, 2015).

47 Alicia H. Puleo, "Ecofeminismo: La perspectiva de género en la conciencia ecologista," in *Claves del ecologismo social* (Madrid: Ecologistas en acción, 2009), 169–173.

48 Puleo, "Ecofeminismo."
49 Puleo, "Ecofeminismo."
50 Puleo, "Ecofeminismo," 170.
51 Carolina Hellsgård, dir., *Ever After* (*Endzeit*) (Germany: ARTE, Das kleine Fernsehspiel ZDF, Grown Up Films, 2019).
52 A title change from the darker apocalyptic tone in German to one based in fairy-tale language to describe a happy ending.
53 In this sense, the Gardener coincides with Moody's understanding of the zombies as "an allegory for the failings of mankind more than any other movie monster." Greg Moody and Clint Schnekloth, *Zombie Theology: A Developmental View of the Religious Dimensions of Zombie Films* (n.p.: Dust Publishing, 2014), Kindle edition, chap. 1.
54 Janet Biehl and Peter Staudenmaier, *Ecofacism Revisited: Lessons from the German Experience* (Porsgrunn, Norway: New Compass Press, 2011), Kindle edition, location 338/3199, in reference to Richard Walther Darré, *Um Blut und Boden: Reden und Aufsätze* (Munich: Zentralverlag der NSDAP, Franz Eher Nachf., 1940).
55 The manifesto of Brenton Tarrat contains this approach. Noted by Alexandra Mina Stern in "The Revival of Eco-Fascism," *Progressive Charlestown*, August 27, 2019, http://www.progressive-charlestown.com/2019/08/the-revival-of-eco-fascism.html. See also Michael Koziol, "Christchurch Shooter's Manifesto Reveals an Obsession with White Supremacy over Muslims," *Sydney Morning Herald*, March 15, 2019, https://www.smh.com.au/world/oceania/christchurch-shooter-s-manifesto-reveals-an-obsession-with-white-supremacy-over-muslims-20190315-p514ko.html.
56 Darré, *Um Blut und Boden*, 28.
57 Arne Naess, "The Shallow and the Deep, Long-Range Ecology Movement: A Summary," *Inquiry* 16, no. 1–4 (January 1973): 95–100.
58 Stacy Alaimo, *Bodily Natures: Science, Environment, and the Material Self* (Bloomington: Indiana University Press 2010), 2, cited in Kim Q. Hall, "No Failure: Climate Change, Radical Hope, and Queer Crip Feminist Eco-Futures," *Radical Philosophy Review* 17, no. 1 (2014): 222.
59 Hall, "No Failure," 223.
60 C. J. "Fiery" Obasi, dir., *Ojuju* (Nigeria: Fiery Film Company, 2014). The same region in which a protest against SARS (Special Anti-Robbery Squad) ended in a number of shootings by the police.
61 In *Blood Quantum* we do have a character that, like Saturn, devours her own infant.
62 Cary L. Klemmer and A. McNamara, "Deep Ecology and Ecofeminism: Social Work to Address Global Environmental Crisis," *Affilia* 35, no. 4 (November 2020): 503–515.
63 Richard Horton, "Offline: COVID-19 Is Not a Pandemic," *The Lancet* 396, no. 10255 (September 26, 2020): 874, https://www.thelancet.com/pdfs/journals/lancet/PIIS0140-6736(20)32000-6.pdf.
64 Carthage Film Festival, "Interview: C. J. Obasi," November 4, 2019, https://www.youtube.com/watch?v=KHpieMpdceg.
65 The term is a combination of "Nigeria" and "Hollywood." According to CNN, Nollywood occupies second place in global cinematic production with a total of 50 films per week and more that 1,200 per year. It produces a profit of up to $600

million per year. Number one is the Indian film industry known as Bollywood, placing Hollywood as third biggest. Milena Veselinovic, "More than Feuds and Dramas, Nollywood Is a Mighty Economic Machine," CNN, July 10, 2015, https://edition.cnn.com/2015/07/10/africa/nollywood-mighty-economic-machine/index.html.

66 Manfred B. Steger, *Globalization: A Very Short Introduction* (Oxford: Oxford University Press, 2013), 11.

67 Howard James Fyvie, dir., *Last Ones Out* (South Africa: Another World, 2015).

68 For more information, see Marcela Gaviria and Will Cohen, "Firestone and the Warlord," PBS, *Frontline*, November 18, 2014, https://www.pbs.org/wgbh/frontline/film/firestone-and-the-warlord/.

69 "Flint Water Crisis Fast Facts," CNN, January 14, 2021, https://edition.cnn.com/2016/03/04/us/flint-water-crisis-fast-facts/index.html.

70 Breck Eisner, dir., *The Crazies* (U.S./United Arab Emirates: Overture Films, Participant, Imagenation Abu Dhabi FZ, 2010).

71 Alexander Quezada, dir., *Zugar Zombie* (Colombia: Quevil Films, 2013).

72 From the DNA study of thirty skeletal remains in the Oaxaca region of México, the Max Planck Institute has discovered that the conquistadors brought salmonella to the Americas. Angus Chen, "One of History's Worst Epidemics May Have Been Caused by a Common Microbe," *Science*, January 16, 2018, https://www.sciencemag.org/news/2018/01/one-history-s-worst-epidemics-may-have-been-caused-common-microbe.

73 Lucio A. Rojas and Cristian Toledo, dirs., *Zombie Dawn* (Chile: Toledo y Rojas, 2011).

74 The Bolivian *Zombie minero*, which we were not able to view, should also give us an important perspective on mining in the Andean region.

75 Gómez-Barris, *The Extractive Zone*, location 214/4818.

76 Gómez-Barris, *The Extractive Zone*, location 208–220.

77 Steger, *Globalization*, 92.

78 Bill McGuire, *Global Catastrophes: A Very Short Introduction* (Oxford: Oxford University Press, 2014), 19.

79 McGuire, *Global Catastrophes*, 19.

80 Our World in Data, "Coronavirus (COVID-19) Deaths," https://ourworldindata.org/covid-deaths, accessed January 9, 2021.

81 Dipesh Chakrabarty, "The Climate of History: Four Theses," *Critical Inquiry* 35, no. 2 (Winter 2009): 201.

82 Chakrabarty, "Climate of History," 207.

83 Chakrabarty, "Climate of History," 213.

84 Chakrabarty, "Climate of History," 223.

85 U.S. Energy Information Administration, "EIA Expects Total U.S. Fossil Fuel Production to Reach Record Levels in 2018 and 2019," Today in Energy, January 18, 2018, https://www.eia.gov/todayinenergy/detail.php?id=34572.

86 During the transition to the Biden administration in the United States, the Trump government accelerated the distribution of contracts for fracking in the Arctic National Wildlife Refuge in Alaska. Juliet Eilperin, "Trump Officials Rush to Auction off Rights to Arctic National Wildlife Refuge before Biden Can Block It," *Washington Post*, November 16, 2020, https://www.washingtonpost.com/climate-environment/2020/11/16/arctic-refuge-drilling-trump/. Additionally, more public lands are being opened up to mining operations for the extraction of

uranium, helium, lithium, and copper all over the country. See Eric Lipton, "In Last Rush, Trump Grants Mining and Energy Firms Access to Public Lands," *New York Times*, December 19, 2020, https://www.nytimes.com/2020/12/19/us/politics/in-last-rush-trump-grants-mining-and-energy-firms-access-to-public-lands.html.

87 His opinions differ from those of the scientific accords of the Intergovernmental Panel on Climate Change. See Naomi Oreskes, "The Scientific Consensus on Climate Change," *Science* 306, no. 5702 (December 3, 2004).

88 This is very similar to what we hear in the United States: scientists are not believed and the public is given contradictory information. As a result, the United States has one of the worst records of COVID-19 response in the world.

89 Alfred Hitchcock, dir., *Psycho* (U.S.: Shamley Productions, 1960).

90 Germán Gutiérrez, Diana R. Granados, and Natalia Piar, "Interacciones humano-animal: características e implicaciones para el bienestar de los humanos," *Revista colombiana de Psicología* 16 (January 2007): 164.

91 Centers for Disease Control and Prevention, "COVID-19 and Your Health," February 11, 2020, https://www.cdc.gov/coronavirus/2019-ncov/daily-life-coping/animals.html.

92 The forthcoming *Army of the Dead* (Zack Snyder, 2021) will feature a zombie tiger, but it was unavailable to screen at the time of this writing.

93 Jon Henley, "Culled Mink Rise from the Dead to Denmark's Horror," *The Guardian*, November 25, 2020, https://www.theguardian.com/world/2020/nov/25/culled-mink-rise-from-the-dead-denmark-coronavirus.

94 Jordan Rubin, dir., *Zombeavers* (U.S.: Armory Films, BenderSpink, Canal+, 2014).

95 King, *Black Sheep*.

96 Shakti Soundar Rajan, dir., *Zombie* (*Miruthan*) (India: Global Infortainment, Ayngaran International, 2016).

97 Rosi Braidotti, *Posthuman Knowledge* (Medford, MA: Polity Press, 2019), chap. 1.

98 Rosi Braidotti, "A Theoretical Framework for the Critical Posthumanities," *Theory, Culture & Society* 36, no. 6 (2019): 51.

99 Sarah Juliet Lauro, "Afterword: Zombie (R)evolution," in *Better Off Dead: The Evolution of the Zombie as Post-Human*, ed. Deborah Christie and Sarah Juliet Lauro (New York: Fordham University Press, 2011), 233.

100 In the Deleuzian sense. Braidotti, "A Theoretical Framework for the Critical Posthumanities," 52.

101 Fernando Alle, dir., *Mutant Blast* (U.S./Portugal: Alle Films, Troma Entertainment, 2020).

102 Sylvaine Giakoumi, François Guilhaumon, Salit Kark, Antonio Terlizzi, Joachim Claudet, Serena Felline, Carlo Cerrano, et al., "Space Invaders: Biological Invasions in Marine Conservation Planning," ed. Lucy Hawkes, *Diversity and Distributions* 22, no. 12 (December 2016): 1220–1231.

103 Cf. the 2006 BBC documentary *Galápagos: The Islands That Changed the World*, narrated by Tilda Swinton, who plays Zelda in *The Dead Don't Die*. It is said that more than 1,579 alien terrestrial and marine species have been introduced to the Galápagos by humans. M. Verónica Toral-Granda et al., "Alien Species Pathways to the Galapagos Islands, Ecuador," *PLoS One*, September 13, 2017, https://journals.plos.org/plosone/article?id=10.1371/journal.pone.0184379.

104 Fernando Montenegro, dir., *Inner Trip* (*Entonces Ruth*) (Peru: Perromostro Producciones, 2013).

105 Rafael Arévalo, *A Prequel to Chaos* (*La precuela del caos*) (Peru: El Topo Producciones, 2014).

106 A highlight of dispensationalism, a movement that began with John Nelson Darby at the start of the nineteenth century. His thinking was popularized in the United States through Hal Lindsey and Carole Carlson's *The Late Great Planet Earth* (Grand Rapids, MI: Zondervan, 1970). The *Left Behind* series of novels by Tim LaHaye and Jerry Jenkins include dispensionalist elements.

107 Cf. Patricia Saldarriaga, "La iconoclasia trumpista como manifestación de antiamericanismo," in *Resistiendo al imperio: Nuevas aproximaciones al antiamericanismo desde el siglo XX hasta la actualidad*, ed. Misael Arturo López Zapico and Irina Alexandra Feldman (Madrid: Sílex, 2019).

108 Colóquio TERRATERRA (Cúpula dos Povos) Conference on June 15, 2012.

109 Guy D. Middleton even warns us about applying the term "collapse" to radical changes in civilizations. See "Do Civilisations Collapse? The Idea That the Maya or Easter Islanders Experienced an Apocalyptic End Makes for Good Television but Bad Archaeology," *Aeon*, https://aeon.co/essays/what-the-idea-of-civilisational-collapse-says-about-history, accessed January 9, 2021.

110 Jaclyn Peiser, "Twitter Bans Steve Bannon for Video Suggesting Violence against Fauci, FBI Director Wray," *Washington Post*, November 6, 2020, https://www.washingtonpost.com/nation/2020/11/06/twitter-bannon-beheaded-fauci-wray/.

111 Braidotti, "A Theoretical Framework for the Critical Posthumanities,"35.

112 Paul Virilio and Bertrand Richard, *The Administration of Fear*, trans. Ames Hodges (Los Angeles: Semiotext(e), 2012).

Conclusion

1 For the relationship between visuality and ableism, see chapter 4.

2 Not all Christians. Of course, diversity in current Christian thought is real, and it includes areas of Progressive Christianity and Liberation Theology, for example.

3 Steven Shaviro, *The Cinematic Body* (Minneapolis: University of Minnesota Press, 1993), 99.

4 Nicholas Mirzoeff, *The Right to Look: A Counterhistory of Visuality* (Durham, NC: Duke University Press, 2011).

5 Marco Abel, *Violent Affect: Literature, Cinema, and Critique after Representation* (Lincoln: University of Nebraska Press, 2007).

6 Wai-Lun Lo, dir., *Zombiology: Enjoy Yourself Tonight* (*Gam man da song si*) (Hong Kong: Creation Cabin, Entertaining Power, KD Multimedia, 2017).

7 Arme Öhman, "Fear and Anxiety: Evolutionary, Cognitive, and Clinical Perspectives," in *Handbook of Emotions*, ed. Michael Lewis and Jeannette M. Haviland-Jones, 2nd ed. (New York: Guilford Press, 2000), 587; Mathias Clasen, "The Horror! The Horror!," *On Stories*, 112–119, accessed January 17, 2021, https://www.academia.edu/217296/The_Horror_The_Horror_.

8 Spencer Bruttig, Megan Yoder, and Nathan Baca, "Comparing Police Reactions to Capitol Rioters versus Black Lives Matter Demonstrators," WUSA9, January 13, 2021, https://www.wusa9.com/article/news/nation-world/comparing-police-reactions-capitol-riots-black-lives-matter/507-64eed087-6db2-41af-9a65-66be46289774.

9 Rosi Braidotti, "A Theoretical Framework for the Critical Posthumanities," *Theory, Culture & Society* 36, no. 6 (2019): 36.

10 Following Genette's *Palimpsests*. A hypotext is the oldest piece of art from which the hypertext is derived. *Juan of the Dead* (*Juan de los muertos*) (2010), for example, could be considered a hypertext and the horror comedy *Shaun of the Dead* (2004) a hypotext. Gerard Genette, *Palimpsests: Literature in the Second Degree* (Lincoln: University of Nebraska Press, 1997).

11 For more on use of classical literature as source material in pornography, see Patricia Saldarriaga, "Pornifying *Don Quixote*: A Quest for Seminal Adventures," in *Re-Imagining Don Quixote (Film, Image and Mind)*, ed. Antonio Cortijo Ocaña and Eloi Grasset Morell (Newark, DE: Juan de la Cuesta, 2017), 29–49. On z-narratives, see, for example, Hazáel González, *Quijote Z* (Palma de Mallorca, Spain: Dolmen, 2010) and *Pride and Prejudice and Zombies* (2016 film based on the 2009 text by Seth Grahame-Smith). In *Zombies: A Cultural History* (London: Reaktion Books, 2015), Roger Luckhurst points out the way in which *I Walked with a Zombie* rewrites *Jane Eyre*.

12 Shaviro, *The Cinematic Body*, 99.

13 John McPhail, dir., *Anna and the Apocalypse* (Scotland: Blazing Griffin, Parkhouse Pictures, Creative Scotland, 2017).

14 Charles Band, dir., *Corona Zombies* (U.S.: Full Moon Features, 2020).

15 Jim Jarmusch, dir., *The Dead Don't Die* (U.S./Sweden/South Africa: Focus Features, Kill The Head, Longride, 2019).

16 Oh Young-doo, Ryu Hoon, Hong Young-geun, and Jang Youn-jung, dirs., *Resident Zombie* (aka *The Neighbor Zombie, Yieutjib jombi*) (South Korea: Kino Mangosteen, 2010).

17 Bruce LaBruce, dir., *Otto; or, Up with Dead People* (Germany/Canada: Jürgen Brüning Filmproduktion, Existential Crisis Productions, New Real Films, 2008).

18 Following Gerald Genette.

19 Mike Cuff and Scott Windhauser, dirs., *Dead Trigger* (U.S.: Aldamisa Entertainment, Badhouse Studios Mexico, Distant Shore Films, 2018).

20 Daniel Myrick and Eduardo Sánchez, dirs., *The Blair Witch Project* (U.S.: Haxan Films, 1999).

21 Jaume Balagueró and Paco Plaza, dirs., *REC* (Spain: Castelao Producciones, Filmax, Instituto de la Cinematografía y de las Artes Audiovisuales [ICAA)], 2007).

22 Phil Guidry, Simon Herbert, and David Whelan, dirs., *Savageland* (U.S.: Massive Film Company, 2017).

23 Christoph Behl, dir., *What's Left of Us* (*El desierto*) (Argentina: Duermevela, Instituto Nacional de Cine y Artes Audiovisuales [INCAA], Subterránea Films, 2015).

24 Shin'ichirô Ueda, dir., *One Cut of the Dead* (*Kamera Wo Tomeruna!*) (Japan: ENBU Seminar, Panpokopina, 2017).

25 Santiago Fillol, Glòria Salvadó-Corretger, and Núria Bou i Sala, "El imaginario del zombi cinematográfico en la representación de los desamparados: Del esclavo del clasicismo hollywoodense al inmigrante de la contemporaneidad europea," *Comunicacion y sociedad* 29, no. 1 (January 2016): 53–67, https://doi.org/10.15581/003.29.1.sp.53-67.

26 Pedro Costa, dir., *Down to Earth* (*Casa de lava*) (Portugal: Madragora Filmes, Gemini Films, Pandora Filmproduktion, 1995).

27 Pedro Costa, dir., *Horse Money* (*Cavalo dinheiro*) (Portugal: Sociedade Óptica Técnica, 2014).

28 Fillol, Salvadó-Corretger, and Bou i Sala, "El imaginario del zombi cinematográfico."

29 Nicolas Klotz, dir., *Low Life* (France: Agora Films, Centre Images–Région Centre, Les Films du Losange, 2011).

30 Affonso Uchôa, dir., *Seven Years in May* (*Sete Anos Em Maio*) (documentary, short) (Brazil: Affonso Uchôa, Victoria Marotta, Jerónimo Quevedo, Camila Bahia Braga, 2019).

31 The *Allgemeines Handwörterbuch der philosophischen Wissenschaften* from 1827, quoted by Olaf Briese and Timo Günther, "Katastrophe: Terminologische Vergangenheit, Gegenwart und Zukunft," *Archiv für Begriffsgeschichte* 51 (2009): 163–174.

32 Ignacio Padilla, *La industria del fin del mundo* (Mexico D.F.: Taurus, 2012), Kindle; John Gray, *Black Mass: Apocalyptic Religion and the Death of Utopia* (New York: Farrar, Strauss and Giroux, 2008), Kindle.

33 A brief but detailed history of these sectarian beliefs in American evangelist religion, along with a history of the interpretations of the Book of Revelation, can be found in the first chapter of Craig R. Koester's *Revelation and the End of All Things* (Grand Rapids, MI: W. B. Eerdmans, 2001).

34 "En la medida en que desconoce la falibilidad y la miseria de los hombres, la utopía es una ficción . . . la promesa de un inminente reino de felicidad ha venido siempre aparejada con un apartarse del mundo antes de que éste sea modificado por la fuerza." Translation by the authors. Padilla, *La industria del fin del mundo*, Kindle (931/2990).

35 Gray, *Black Mass*, Kindle (2/244).

36 Precolonial time as an epoch of happiness. Cf. Alberto Flores Galindo, *In Search of an Inca: Identity and Utopia in the Andes*, ed. and trans. Carlos Aguirre, Charles F. Walker, and Willie Hiatt (Cambridge: Cambridge University Press, 2010).

Bibliography

Abel, Marco. *Violent Affect: Literature, Cinema, and Critique after Representation.* Lincoln: University of Nebraska Press, 2007.

Adams, Rachel. *Sideshow U.S.A.: Freaks and the American Cultural Imagination.* Chicago: University of Chicago Press, 2001.

Agamben, Giorgio. *State of Exception.* Chicago: University of Chicago Press, 2004.

Alaimo, Stacy. *Bodily Natures: Science, Environment, and the Material Self.* Bloomington: Indiana University Press, 2010.

Alberti, Leon Battista. *On Painting.* London: Penguin, 1991.

Anzaldúa, Gloria. *Borderlands: La Frontera: The New Mestiza.* San Francisco: Aunt Lute Books, 1987.

Baker, Mike, and Sheri Fink. "At the Top of the Covid-19 Curve, How Do Hospitals Decide Who Gets Treatment?" *New York Times,* March 31, 2020. https://www.nytimes.com/2020/03/31/us/coronavirus-covid-triage-rationing-ventilators.html.

Bakhtin, Mikhail. *Rabelais and His World.* Translated by Hélène Iswolsky. Bloomington: Indiana University Press, 1984.

Bartra, Roger. *Historias de salvajes.* Mexico City: Siglo XXI, 2017.

Bataille, Georges. *The Accursed Share: An Essay on General Economy.* New York: Zone Books, 1988.

Bataille, Georges. *Lo que entiendo por soberanía.* Translated by Pilar Sánchez Orozco and Antonio Campillo. Buenos Aires: Paidós, 1996.

Beaubien, Jason. "Argentina Takes a Shot with Russia's Sputnik Vaccine." NPR, January 15, 2021. https://www.npr.org/sections/goatsandsoda/2021/01/15/957301807/argentina-takes-a-shot-with-russias-sputnik-vaccine.

Bebinger, Martha. "Another COVID-19 Medical Mystery: Patients Come Off Ventilator But Linger in a Coma." NPR, August 24, 2020. https://www.npr.org/sections/health-shots/2020/08/24/904347130/another-covid-19-medical-mystery-patients-come-off-ventilator-but-linger-in-a-co.

Benjamin, Walter. *The Arcades Project.* Translated by Howard Eiland and Kevin McLaughlin. Cambridge, MA: Belknap Press of Harvard University Press, 2002.

Benjamin, Walter. *Ursprung des deutschen Trauerspiels.* Frankfurt am Main: Suhrkamp Taschenbuch Wissenschaft, 1996.

Biehl, Janet, and Peter Staudenmaier. *Ecofacism Revisited: Lessons from the German Experience.* Porsgrunn, Norway: New Compass Press, 2011.

Blest, Paul. "Teachers Are Making Their Own Gravestones and Coffins to Protest Going Back to School." Vice, August 4, 2020. https://www.vice.com/en/article/y3zxp5/teachers-are-making-their-own-gravestones-and-coffins-to-protest-going-back-to-school.

Braidotti, Rosi. *Posthuman Knowledge.* Medford, MA: Polity Press, 2019.

Braidotti, Rosi. "A Theoretical Framework for the Critical Posthumanities." *Theory, Culture & Society* 36, no. 6 (November 2019): 31–61.

Briese, Olaf, and Timo Günther. "Katastrophe: Terminologische Vergangenheit, Gegenwart und Zukunft." *Archiv für Begriffsgeschichte* 51 (2009): 155–195.

Brooks, Kinitra D. "The Importance of Neglected Intersections: Race and Gender in Contemporary Zombie Texts and Theories." *African American Review* 47, no. 4 (Winter 2014): 461–475. https://doi.org/10.1353/afa.2014.0062.

Browning, John Edgar. "Survival Horrors, Survival Spaces: Tracing the Modern Zombie (Cine)Myth through to the Post-Millennium." In *Zombie Talk: Culture, History, Politics,* edited by David R. Castillo, David Schmid, David A. Reilly, and John Edgar Browning. New York: Palgrave Macmillan, 2016, 9–38.

Brueck, Hilary. "CDC: Almost All of the US Kids and Teens Who've Died from COVID-19 Were Hispanic or Black." *Business Insider,* September 15, 2020. https://www.businessinsider.com/cdc-black-and-brown-children-dying-from-the-coronavirus-2020-9.

Bruttig, Spencer, Megan Yoder, and Nathan Baca. "Comparing Police Reactions to Capitol Rioters versus Black Lives Matter Demonstrators." WUSA9, January 13, 2021. https://www.wusa9.com/article/news/nation-world/comparing-police-reactions-capitol-riots-black-lives-matter/507-64eed087-6db2-41af-9a65-66be46289774.

Bude, Heinz, and Jessica Spengler. *Society of Fear.* Malden, MA: Polity Press, 2018.

Burns, Sarah. "'Better for Haunts': Victorian Houses and the Modern Imagination." *American Art* 26, no. 3 (Fall 2012): 2–25.

Camara, Mandy, and Ruth Maclean. "Hundreds Die at Sea Off Senegal's Coast on a Perilous Route to Europe." *New York Times,* November 3, 2020. https://www.nytimes.com/2020/11/02/world/africa/senegal-migrants-drown.html.

Campbell, Fiona Kumari. *Contours of Ableism: The Projection of Disability and Abledness.* London: Palgrave Macmillan, 2009.

Campesi, Giuseppe. "Migraciones, seguridad y confines en la teoría social contemporánea." *Crítica penal y poder* no. 3 (September 27, 2012). https://revistes.ub.edu/index.php/CriticaPenalPoder/article/view/3657.

Canadian Broadcasting Corpopration. "Jeff Barnaby Recalls the Incident at Restigouche." *George Stroumboulopoulos Tonight.* Accessed January 7, 2021. https://www.cbc.ca/strombo/videos/web-exclusive/jeff-barnaby-the-incident-at-restigouche.

Cano Esteban, Amparo, and Miguel Ferreira. "Pero . . . ¿Qué es un zombi? ¿Todos somos zombies?" *Nómadas: Critical Journal of Social and Juridical Sciences* 51, no. 2 (2017): 133–155.

Carroll, Noël. *The Philosophy of Horror, or, Paradoxes of the Heart.* New York: Routledge, 1990.

Carter, Niambi M. "Intimacy without Consent: Lynching as Sexual Violence." *Politics & Gender* 8, no. 3 (September 2012): 414–421.

Castillo, David R., David Schmid, David A. Reilly, and John Edgar Browning. *Zombie Talk: Culture, History, Politics.* New York: Palgrave Macmillan, 2016.

Centers for Disease Control and Prevention. "COVID-19 and Your Health." February 11, 2020. https://www.cdc.gov/coronavirus/2019-ncov/daily-life-coping/animals.html.

Centers for Disease Control and Prevention. "Zombie Preparedness." October 1, 2020. https://www.cdc.gov/cpr/zombie/index.htm.

Césaire, Aimé. *Discourse on Colonialism*. Translated by Joan Pinkham. New York: Monthly Review Press, 2000.

Chakrabarty, Dipesh. "The Climate of History: Four Theses." *Critical Inquiry* 35, no. 2 (Winter 2009): 197–222.

Chen, Angus. "One of History's Worst Epidemics May Have Been Caused by a Common Microbe." *Science*, January 16, 2018. https://www.sciencemag.org/news/2018/01/one-history-s-worst-epidemics-may-have-been-caused-common-microbe.

Chen, Mel Y. "Agitation." *Wildness (South Atlantic Quarterly)* 117, no. 3 (July 2018): 551–566.

Chen, Mel Y. "Lurching for the Cure? On Zombies and the Reproduction of Disability." *GLQ: A Journal of Lesbian and Gay Studies* 21, no. 1 (January 2015): 24–31.

Christie, Deborah, and Sarah Juliet Lauro, eds. *Better Off Dead: The Evolution of the Zombie as Post-Human*. New York: Fordham University Press, 2011.

Clasen, Mathias. "The Horror! The Horror!" *On Stories*. Accessed January 17, 2021. https://www.academia.edu/217296/The_Horror_The_Horror_.

Comaroff, Jean, and John Comaroff. "Alien-Nation: Zombies, Immigrants, and Millennial Capitalism." Reproduced in *Zombie Theory: A Reader*, edited by Sarah Juliet Lauro. Minneapolis: University of Minnesota Press, 2017, 137–156.

Dalley, Stephanie, ed. and trans. *Myths from Mesopotamia: Creation, the Flood, Gilgamesh, and Others*. Rev. ed. Oxford: Oxford University Press, 2008.

Darré, Walther Richard. *Um Blut und Boden: Reden und Aufsätze*. Munich: Zentralverlag der NSDAP, Franz Eher Nachf, 1940.

De León, Jason. *The Land of Open Graves: Living and Dying on the Migrant Trail*. Oakland: University of California Press, 2015.

Derrida, Jacques. *Specters of Marx: The State of the Debt, the Work of Mourning and the New International*. Translated by Peggy Kamuf. New York: Routledge, 2006.

Descartes, René. *Meditations on First Philosophy: With Selections from the Objections and Replies*. Translated and edited by John Cottingham. 2nd ed. Cambridge: Cambridge University Press, 2017.

Diamond, Dan. "'We Want Them Infected': Trump Appointee Demanded 'Herd Immunity' Strategy, Emails Reveal." *Politico*, December 16, 2020. https://www.politico.com/news/2020/12/16/trump-appointee-demanded-herd-immunity-strategy-446408.

Díaz, Julio, and Carolina Meloni. "La noche del capitalismo viviente." In *Abecedario zombi: La noche del capitalismo viviente*. Madrid: El salmón contracorriente, 2016, 179–180.

Echeverría, Bolívar, ed. *Modernidad, mestizaje cultural y ethos barroco*. Mexico City: UNAM-El Equilibrista, 1994.

Edelman, Lee. *No Future: Queer Theory and the Death Drive*. Durham, NC: Duke University Press, 2004.

Edwards, Erika. "More than 61,000 Children Got Covid-19 Last Week, a Record." NBC News, November 2, 2020. https://www.nbcnews.com/health/health-news/more-61-000-children-got-covid-19-last-week-record-n1245851.

Edwards, Tyler. *Zombie Church: Breathing Life Back into the Body of Christ*. Grand Rapids, MI: Kregel Publications, 2011.

Eilperin, Juliet. "Trump Officials Rush to Auction off Rights to Arctic National Wildlife Refuge before Biden Can Block It." *Washington Post*, November 16, 2020. https://www.washingtonpost.com/climate-environment/2020/11/16/arctic-refuge-drilling-trump/.

Esposito, Roberto. *Persons and Things*. Translated by Zakiya Hanafi. Cambridge: Polity Press, 2015.

Estévez, Ariadna. "Biopolítica y necropolítica: ¿Constitutivos u opuestos?" *Espiral: Estudios sobre estado y sociedad* 25, no. 3 (September–December 2018): 9–43.

Fanon, Frantz. *The Wretched of the Earth*. Translated by Richard Philcox. New York: Grove Press, 2005.

Fillol, Santiago, Glòria Salvadó-Corretger, and Núria Bou i Sala. "El imaginario del zombi cinematográfico en la representación de los desamparados: Del esclavo del clasicismo hollywoodense al inmigrante de la contemporaneidad europea." *Comunicacion y sociedad* 29, no. 1 (January 2016): 53–67. https://doi.org/10.15581/003.29.1.sp.53-67.

Fisher, Saul. "Pierre Gassendi." In *The Stanford Encyclopedia of Philosophy*, edited by Edward N. Zalta. Spring 2014. https://plato.stanford.edu/archives/spr2014/entries/gassendi/.

"Flint Water Crisis Fast Facts." CNN.com. January 14, 2021. https://edition.cnn.com/2016/03/04/us/flint-water-crisis-fast-facts/index.html.

Florenski, Pável. *La perspectiva invertida*. Edited by Felipe Pereda. Translated by Xenia Egórova. Madrid: Siruela, 2005.

Flores Galindo, Alberto. *In Search of an Inca: Identity and Utopia in the Andes*. Edited and translated by Carlos Aguirre, Charles F. Walker, and Willie Hiatt. New York: Cambridge University Press, 2010.

Foucault, Michel. *The History of Sexuality: An Introduction*. Vol. 1. Translated by Robert Hurley. New York: Pantheon Books, 1978.

Freeman, Elizabeth. *Time Binds: Queer Temporalities, Queer Histories*. Durham, NC: Duke University Press, 2010.

Galt-Miller, Jave, and Wayne A. Brown. *Lesbian Zombies from Outer Space*. Vol. 1. N.p.: Big Things Productions, 2016.

Garland Thomson, Rosemarie, ed. *Freakery: Cultural Spectacles of the Extraordinary Body*. New York: New York University Press, 1996.

Gaviria, Marcela, and Will Cohen. "Firestone and the Warlord." PBS, *Frontline*, November 18, 2014. https://www.pbs.org/wgbh/frontline/film/firestone-and-the-warlord/.

Genette, Gerard. *Palimpsests: Literature in the Second Degree*. Lincoln: University of Nebraska Press, 1997.

Giakoumi, Sylvaine, François Guilhaumon, Salit Kark, Antonio Terlizzi, Joachim Claudet, Serena Felline, Carlo Cerrano, et al. "Space Invaders; Biological Invasions in Marine Conservation Planning." Edited by Lucy Hawkes. *Diversity and Distributions* 22, no. 12 (December 2016): 1220–1231.

Gilloch, Graeme. *Myth and Metropolis: Walter Benjamin and the City*. Cambridge: Polity Press, 1996.

Giorgi, Gabriel, and Fermín Rodríguez, eds. *Ensayos sobre biopolítica: Excesos de vida*. Buenos Aires: Paidós, 2007.

Goldwin, Robert A. "Is There an American Right of Revolution?" American Enterprise Institute, January 1, 1990. https://www.aei.org/articles/is-there-an-american-right-of-revolution/.

Gómez-Barris, Macarena. *The Extractive Zone: Social Ecologies and Decolonial Perspectives*. Durham, NC: Duke University Press, 2017.

Gonyea, Don, and Lorenzo Sierra. "Arizona Lawmaker Reflects on Surviving COVID-19." NPR, December 26, 2020. https://www.npr.org/2020/12/26/950476637/arizona-lawmaker-reflects-on-surviving-covid-19.

González, Hazáel. *Quijote Z*. Palma de Mallorca, Spain: Dolmen, 2010.

Gordon, Avery. *Ghostly Matters: Haunting and the Sociological Imagination*. Minneapolis: University of Minnesota Press, 2008.

Gray, John. *Black Mass: Apocalyptic Religion and the Death of Utopia*. New York: Farrar, Straus and Giroux, 2008.

Grossman Kantor, Wendy. "Witness to Rioters Jumping through Capitol Building Window Says 'It Was Like Out of a Zombie Movie.'" *People*, January 9, 2021. https://people.com/politics/witness-to-rioters-jumping-through-capitol-window-like-out-of-zombie-movie/.

Gutiérrez, Germán, Diana Granados, and Natalia Piar. "Interacciones humano-animal: Características e implicaciones para el bienestar de los humanos." *Revista colombiana de psicología* 16 (January 2007): 163–184.

Hakola, Outi. "Zombies, Vampires and Frankenstein's Monster: Embodied Experiences of Illness in Living Dead Films." *Thanatos* 8, no. 1 (2019): 91–119.

Halberstam, Jack, and Tavia Nyong'o. "Introduction: Theory in the Wild." *South Atlantic Quarterly* 117, no. 3 (July 1, 2018): 453–464.

Hale, Grace Elizabeth. *Making Whiteness: The Culture of Segregation in the South, 1890–1940*. New York: Vintage Books, 1999.

Hall, Kim Q. "No Failure: Climate Change, Radical Hope, and Queer Crip Feminist Eco-Future." *Radical Philosophy Review* 17, no. 1 (2014): 203–225.

Hanbury, Mary. "50 Haunting Photos of Abandoned Shopping Malls across America." *Business Insider*. Updated November 8, 2019. https://www.businessinsider.com/american-retail-apocalypse-in-photos-2018-1.

Hardt, Michael, and Antonio Negri. *Empire*. Cambridge, MA: Harvard University Press, 2000.

Hardt, Michael, and Antonio Negri. "Empire, Twenty Years On." *New Left Review* 120 (November–December 2019). https://newleftreview.org/issues/ii120/articles/empire-twenty-years-on.

Hardt, Michael, and Antonio Negri. *Multitude: War and Democracy in the Age of Empire*. New York: Penguin, 2004.

Harjo, Suzan Shown. "Vampire Policy Is Bleeding Us Dry—Blood Quantums, Be Gone!" In *The Great Vanishing Act: Blood Quantum and the Future of Native Nations*, edited by Kathleen Ratteree and Norbert Hill. Golden, CO: Fulcrum Publishing, 2017, 77–79.

Hasegawa, Alexandre Pinheiro. "A peste no de rerum natura (6.1138-286) de Lucrécio—Parte I." *Estado da arte*, april 23, 2020. https://estadodaarte.estadao.com.br/a-peste-de-rerum-natura-lucrecio/.

Hatfield, Gary. "René Descartes." In *The Stanford Encyclopedia of Philosophy*, edited by Edward N. Zalta. Summer 2018. https://plato.stanford.edu/archives/sum2018/entries/descartes/.

Hatfield, Gary. "The Senses and the Fleshless Eye: The *Meditations* as Cognitive Exercises." In *Essays on Descartes' Meditations*, edited by Amèlie Rorty. Berkeley: University of California Press, 1986, 45–79.

Henley, Jon. "Culled Mink Rise from the Dead to Denmark's Horror." *The Guardian*, November 25, 2020. http://www.theguardian.com/world/2020/nov/25/culled-mink-rise-from-the-dead-denmark-coronavirus.

Hernandez, Bonar Ludwig. "The Las Casas–Sepúlveda Controversy: 1550–1551." *Ex Post Facto* 10 (2001): 95–105. https://history.sfsu.edu/sites/default/files/images/2001_Bonar%20Ludwig%20Hernandez.pdf.

Hernandez, Sergio Felipe Garcia. "Los cuestionamientos éticos a los ensayos clínicos de vacunas COVID-19 en Latinoamérica." Anadolu Agency, November 9, 2020. https://www.aa.com.tr/es/mundo/los-cuestionamientos-éticos-a-los-ensayos-clínicos-de-vacunas-covid-19-en-latinoamérica/1970603.

Holley, Peter. "Police Killed the Black 'Miami Zombie.' So Why Did a Terrifying, Face-Eating White Teen Live?" *Washington Post*, August 24, 2016. https://www.washingtonpost.com/news/post-nation/wp/2016/08/24/police-killed-a-black-face-eater-heres-why-they-say-a-white-guy-turned-zombie-lived/.

Horn, Eva. *The Future as Catastrophe: Imagining Disaster in the Modern Age*. Translated by Valentine Pakis. New York: Columbia University Press, 2018.

Horton, Richard. "Offline: COVID-19 Is Not a Pandemic." *The Lancet* 396, no. 10255 (September 26, 2020): 874. https://www.thelancet.com/pdfs/journals/lancet/PIIS0140-6736(20)32000-6.pdf.

"Human Trafficking and Smuggling in Asia." Asian Century Institute, April 24, 2016. https://asiancenturyinstitute.com/society/1120-human-trafficking-and-smuggling-in-asia.

Itkowitz, Colby. "Trump Again Uses Racially Insensitive Term to Describe Coronavirus." *Washington Post*, June 23, 2020. https://www.washingtonpost.com/politics/trump-again-uses-kung-flu-to-describe-coronavirus/2020/06/23/0ab5a8d8-b5a9-11ea-aca5-ebb63d27e1ff_story.html.

Jáuregui, Carlos. *Canibalia: Canibalismo, calibanismo, antropofagia cultural y consumo en América Latina*. Madrid: Iberoamericana/Vervuert, 2008.

Jones, Steve. "Pretty, Dead: Sociosexuality, Rationality, and the Transition into Zom-being." In *Zombies and Sexuality: Essays on Desire and the Living Dead*, edited by Shaka McGlotten and Steve Jones. Jefferson, NC: McFarland, 2014.

Kafer, Alison. *Feminist, Queer, Crip*. Bloomington: Indiana University Press, 2013.

Keetley, Dawn. "Zombie Republic: Property and the Propertyless Multitude in Romero's Dead Films and Kirkman's *The Walking Dead*." *Journal of the Fantastic in the Arts* 25, no. 2–3 (2014): 295–313.

Kim, Eunjung. "Continuing Presence of Discarded Bodies: Occupational Harm, Necro-Activism, and Living Justice." *Catalyst: Feminism, Theory, Technoscience* 5, no. 1 (April 1, 2019): 1–29. https://doi.org/10.28968/cftt.v5i1.29616.

Kindy, Kimberly. "More than 200 Meat Plant Workers in the U.S. Have Died of Covid-19. Federal Regulators Just Issued Two Modest Fines." *Washington Post*, September 13, 2020. https://www.washingtonpost.com/national/osha-covid-meat-plant-fines/2020/09/13/1dca3e14-f395-11ea-bc45-e5d48ab44b9f_story.html.

Kirsch, Sharon J., and Michael Stancliff. "'How Do You Not Understand a Word?' Language as Contagion and Cure in *Pontypool*." *Journal of Narrative Theory* 48, no. 2 (Summer 2018): 252–278.

Klemmer, Cary L., and Kathleen A. McNamara. "Deep Ecology and Ecofeminism: Social Work to Address Global Environmental Crisis." *Affilia* 35, no. 4 (November 2020): 503–515.

Koester, Craig R. *Revelation and the End of All Things*. Grand Rapids, MI: W. B. Eerdmans, 2001.

Koziol, Michael. "Christchurch Shooter's Manifesto Reveals an Obsession with White Supremacy over Muslims." *Sydney Morning Herald*, March 15, 2019. https://www.smh.com.au/world/oceania/christchurch-shooter-s-manifesto-reveals-an-obsession-with-white-supremacy-over-muslims-20190315-p514ko.html.

Kristeva, Julia. *Powers of Horror: An Essay on Abjection*. Translated by Leon S. Roudiez. New York: Columbia University Press, 1982.

Laqueur, Thomas. *Making Sex: Body and Gender from the Greeks to Freud*. Cambridge, MA: Harvard University Press, 1990.

Lau, Kimberly J. "The Vampire, the Queer, and the Girl: Reflections on the Politics and Ethics of Immortality's Gendering." *Signs: Journal of Women in Culture and Society* 44, no. 1 (August 13, 2018): 3–24.

Lauro, Sarah Juliet. *The Transatlantic Zombie: Slavery, Rebellion, and Living Death*. New Brunswick, NJ: Rutgers University Press, 2015.

Lauro, Sarah Juliet, ed. *Zombie Theory: A Reader*. Minneapolis: University of Minnesota Press, 2017.

Le Goff, Jacques. "Church Time and Merchant Time in the Middle Ages." *Social Science Information* 9, no. 4 (August 1970): 151–167. https://doi.org/10.1177/053901847000900411.

Le Roy, Frederik. "Ragpickers and Leftover Performances: Walter Benjamin's Philosophy of the Historical Leftover." *Performance Research* 22, no. 8 (2017): 127–134. https://doi.org/10.1080/13528165.2017.1433391.

Lindsey, Hal, and Carole C. Carlson. *The Late Great Planet Earth*. Grand Rapids, MI: Zondervan, 1970.

Linnemann, Travis, Tyler Wall, and Edward Green. "The Walking Dead and Killing State: Zombification and the Normalization of Police Violence." *Theoretical Criminology* 18, no. 4 (April 7, 2014): 506–527. https://doi.org/10.1177/1362480614529455.

Lipton, Eric. "In Last Rush, Trump Grants Mining and Energy Firms Access to Public Lands." *New York Times*, December 19, 2020. https://www.nytimes.com/2020/12/19/us/politics/in-last-rush-trump-grants-mining-and-energy-firms-access-to-public-lands.html.

Livingston, Abby. "Texas Lt. Gov. Dan Patrick Says a Failing Economy Is Worse than Coronavirus." *Texas Tribune*, March 24, 2020. https://www.texastribune.org/2020/03/23/texas-lt-gov-dan-patrick-says-bad-economy-worse-coronavirus/.

Livius, Titus. *Ab urbe condita*. Edited by John Briscoe. Oxford: Oxford University Press, 2016.

The Lost Museum Archive. "Circassian Beauty Exhibit." Accessed January 9, 2021. https://lostmuseum.cuny.edu/archive/exhibit/star/.

Lowenstein, Adam. *Shocking Representation: Historical Trauma, National Cinema, and the Modern Horror Film*. New York: Columbia University Press, 2005.

Luckhurst, Roger. *Zombies: A Cultural History*. London: Reaktion Books, 2015.

Lucretius. *The Nature of Things: De rerum natura*. Edited and translated by Anthony M. Esolen. Baltimore: Johns Hopkins University Press, 1995.

Lugones, Maria. "The Coloniality of Gender." *Worlds & Knowledges Otherwise* (Spring 2008): 1–17.

Lugones, María. "Toward a Decolonial Feminism." *Hypatia* 25, no. 4 (Fall 2010): 742–759.

Maldonado-Torres, Nelson. "On the Coloniality of Being: Contributions to the Development of a Concept." *Cultural Studies* 21, no. 2–3 (2007): 240–270.

Manini, Emy, and Patricia Saldarriaga. "Zombis nada más: *Juan de los muertos*, iconoclasta y antiimperialista." In *Nuevas miradas sobre el antiimperialismo y/o el antiamericanismo desde la historia, la literatura y el arte*, edited by Misael Arturo López Zapico, Aida Rodríguez Campesino, and Gonzalo Vitón. Madrid: Instituto de Estudios Internacionales y Europeos Francisco de Vitoria, 2019, 147–161.

Marcolli, Matilde. *Still Life as a Model of Spacetime*. n.d. https://www.its.caltech.edu/~matilde/StillLifeSpacetime.pdf.

Marx, Karl, and Friedrich Engels. *Capital: A Critique of Political Economy*. New York: International Publishers, 1967.

Mbembe, Achille. "Necropolitics." Translated by Libby Meintjes. *Public Culture* 15, no. 1 (2003): 11–40.

McDaniel, Jamie. "'You Can Point a Finger at a Zombie. Sometimes They Fall Off': Contemporary Zombie Films, Embedded Ableism, and Disability as Metaphor." *Midwest Quarterly* 57, no. 4 (Summer 2016): 423–447.

McGlotten, Shaka, and Steve Jones. *Zombies and Sexuality: Essays on Desire and the Living Dead*. Jefferson, NC: McFarland, 2014.

McGuire, Bill. *Global Catastrophes: A Very Short Introduction*. 2nd ed. Oxford: Oxford University Press, 2014.

McNally, David. *Monsters of the Market: Zombies, Vampires and Global Capitalism*. Chicago: Haymarket Books, 2011.

McNeil, W. K., ed. *Encyclopedia of American Gospel Music*. New York: Routledge, 2005.

McRuer, Robert. *Crip Theory: Cultural Signs of Queerness and Disability*. New York: New York University Press, 2006.

Membe, Achille. "Necropolitics." Translated by Libby Meintjes. *Public Culture* 15, no. 1 (2003): 11–40.

Mencimer, Stephanie. "Evangelicals Love Donald Trump for Many Reasons, but One of Them Is Especially Terrifying: End Times." *Mother Jones* (blog), January 23, 2020. https://www.motherjones.com/politics/2020/01/evangelicals-are-anticipating-the-end-of-the-world-and-trump-is-listening/.

Mendoza, Breny. "Coloniality of Gender and Power: From Postcoloniality to Decoloniality." In *The Oxford Handbook of Feminist Theory*, edited Lisa Disch and Mary Hawkesworth. Oxford: Oxford Handbooks Online, 2015. https://www.escuelaformacionpolitica.com/uploads/6/6/7/0/66702859/003_breny_coloniality-gender-power.pdf .

Mendoza, Breny. "Decolonial Theories in Comparison." *Journal of World Philosophies* 5, no. 1 (2020): 43–60. https://scholarworks.iu.edu/iupjournals/index.php/jwp/article/view/3600.

Middleton, Guy D. "Do Civilisations Collapse? The Idea That the Maya or Easter Islanders Experienced an Apocalyptic End Makes for Good Television but Bad Archaeology." *Aeon*. Accessed January 9, 2021. https://aeon.co/essays/what-the-idea-of-civilisational-collapse-says-about-history.

Mies, Maria, and Vandana Shiva. *Ecofeminismo: Teoría, crítica y perspectivas*. Barcelona: Icaria, 2015.

Mignolo, Walter D. "I Am Where I Think: Epistemology and the Colonial Difference." *Journal of Latin American Cultural Studies* 8, no. 2 (1999): 235–245.
Mirzoeff, Nicholas. *The Right to Look: A Counterhistory of Visuality*. Durham, NC: Duke University Press, 2011.
Moody, Greg, and Clint Schnekloth. *Zombie Theology: A Developmental View of the Religious Dimensions of Zombie Films*. N.p.: Dust Publishing, 2014.
Moore, Robert. "Six Children Died in Border Patrol Care. Democrats in Congress Want to Know Why." ProPublica, January 13, 2020. https://www.propublica.org/article/six-children-died-in-border-patrol-care-democrats-in-congress-want-to-know-why?token=UvH6WeRiCc8nAyV7r_TRsmoANqWk2uRM.
Moraña, Mabel. *The Monster as War Machine*. Translated by Andrew Ascherl. Amherst, NY: Cambria Press, 2018.
Motlagh, Jason. "Border Crisis: Arizona Desert Crossing Has Claimed Thousands of Lives." *Rolling Stone*, September 30, 2019. https://www.rollingstone.com/politics/politics-features/border-crisis-arizona-sonoran-desert-882613/.
Nadler, Steven. "Eternity and Immortality in Spinoza's Ethics." *Midwest Studies in Philosophy* 26 (2002): 224–244.
Naess, Arne. "The Shallow and the Deep, Long-Range Ecology Movement: A Summary." *Inquiry* 16, no. 1–4 (January 1973): 95–100.
Negri, Antonio. "El monstruo político: Vida desnuda y potencia." In *Ensayos sobre biopolítica: Excesos de vida*, compiled by Gabriel Giorgi and Fermín Rodríguez. Buenos Aires: Paidós, 2007, 93–140.
Office of the Chairman of the Joint Chiefs of Staff. *DOD Dictionary of Military and Associated Terms*. Washington, DC: The Joint Staff, August 2021. https://www.jcs.mil/Portals/36/Documents/Doctrine/pubs/dictionary.pdf.
Öhman, Arme. "Fear and Anxiety: Evolutionary, Cognitive, and Clinical Perspectives." In *Handbook of Emotions*, edited by Michael Lewis and Jeannette M. Haviland-Jones. 2nd ed. New York: Guilford Press, 2000, 573–593.
Oreskes, Naomi. "The Scientific Consensus on Climate Change." *Science* 306, no. 5702 (December 3, 2004): 1686. https://doi.org/10.1126/science.1103618.
Orsi, Peter. "In Mexican Capital, Red Shoes to Protest Killings of Women." AP News, January 11, 2020. https://apnews.com/article/bbd6e02268849ee6d34cdd110865c041.
Orwell, George. *1984*. New York: Penguin Books, 1949.
Osmond, Chris. "Time to Die: Zombie as Educational Evolution in *The Girl with All the Gifts*." *Journal of Curriculum Theorizing* 34, no. 5 (October 31, 2019). https://journal.jctonline.org/index.php/jct/article/view/873.
Our World in Data. "Coronavirus (COVID-19) Deaths." Accessed January 9, 2021. https://ourworldindata.org/covid-deaths.
Padilla, Ignacio. *La industria del fin del mundo*. México, D.F.: Taurus, 2012.
Painter, Nell Irvin. *The History of White People*. New York: W. W. Norton, 2011.
Painter, Nell Irvin. "What Whiteness Means in the Trump Era." *New York Times*, November 12, 2016. https://www.nytimes.com/2016/11/13/opinion/what-whiteness-means-in-the-trump-era.html.
Peiser, Jaclyn. "Twitter Bans Steve Bannon for Video Suggesting Violence against Fauci, FBI Director Wray." *Washington Post*, November 6, 2020. https://www.washingtonpost.com/nation/2020/11/06/twitter-bannon-beheaded-fauci-wray/.
Perera, Suvendrini, and Joseph Pugliese. "Introduction: Combat Breathing: State Violence and the Body in Question." *Somatechnics* 1, no. 1 (March 2011): 1–14. https://doi.org/10.3366/soma.2011.0002.

Petersen, Amanda. "Breaking Silences and Revealing Ghosts: Spectral Moments of Gendered Violence in Mexico." *Interdisciplianry Mexico (iMex)* 16, no. 2 (2019): 22–40.

Pinchin, Karen. "Insects, Floods and 'The Snake': What Trump's Use of Metaphors Reveals." PBS, *Frontline*, October 22, 2019. https://www.pbs.org/wgbh/frontline/article/insects-floods-and-the-snake-what-trumps-use-of-metaphors-reveals/.

Pinnell, Owen, and Jess Kelly. "Slave Markets Found on Instagram and Other Apps." *BBC News*, October 31, 2019. https://www.bbc.com/news/technology-50228549.

Pinto, Jaime Nogueira. *Contágios: 2500 anos de pestes*. Alfragide: Dom Quixote, 2020.

Polidori, John William. *The Vampyre and Other Tales of the Macabre*. Edited by Robert Morrison and Chris Baldick. Oxford: Oxford University Press, 2008.

Powell, Anna. *Deleuze and Horror Film*. Edinburgh: Edinburgh University Press, 2005.

Preciado, Paul B. "Learning from the Virus." *Artforum*, May/June 2020. https://www.artforum.com/print/202005/paul-b-preciado-82823.

Puleo, Alicia H. "Ecofeminismo: La perspectiva de género en la conciencia ecologista." In *Claves del ecologismo social.* Madrid: Ecologistas en acción, 2009, 169–173.

Quijano, Anibal. "Coloniality of Power, Eurocentrism, and Latin America." Edited by Michael Ennis. *Nepantla: Views from South* 1, no. 3 (2000): 533–580.

Rutherford, Jennifer. *Zombies*. New York: Routledge, 2013.

Saldarriaga, Patricia. "La iconoclasia trumpista como manifestación de antiamericanismo." In *Resistiendo al Imperio: Nuevas aproximaciones al antiamericanismo desde el siglo XX hasta la actualidad*, edited by Misael Arturo López Zapico and Irina Alexandra Feldman. Madrid: Sílex, 2019, 235–257. https://dialnet.unirioja.es/servlet/articulo?codigo=7119884.

Saldarriaga, Patricia. "Pornifying *Don Quixote*: A Quest for Seminal Adventures." In *Re-Imagining Don Quixote (Film, Image and Mind)*, edited by Antonio Cortijo Ocaña and Eloi Grasset Morell. Newark, DE: Juan de la Cuesta, 2017, 29–49.

Sánchez Prado, Ignacio M. "La utopía apocalíptica del México neoliberal." *AlterTexto* 5, no. 10 (2007): 9–15.

Schwartz, Matthew. "In Selma, a 'Final Crossing' for John Lewis across the Edmund Pettus Bridge." NPR, July 26, 2020. https://www.npr.org/2020/07/26/895149942/in-selma-a-final-crossing-for-john-lewis-across-the-edmund-pettus-bridge.

Schwarzschild, Edward L. "Death-Defying/Defining Spectacles: Charles Willson Peale as Early American Freak Showman." In *Freakery: Cultural Spectacles of the Extraordinary Body*, edited by Rosemarie Garland Thomson. New York: New York University Press, 1996, 82–96.

Schweitzer, Dahlia. *Going Viral: Zombies, Viruses, and the End of the World.* New Brunswick, NJ: Rutgers University Press, 2018.

Schwenger, Peter. *The Tears of Things: Melancholy and Physical Objects*. Minneapolis: University of Minnesota Press, 2006.

Scrivner, Coltan, John Anthony Johnson, Jens Kjeldgaard-Christiansen, and Mathias Clasen. "Pandemic Practice: Horror Fans and Morbidly Curious Individuals Are More Psychologically Resilient during the COVID-19 Pandemic." Preprint. PsyArXiv, June 30, 2020. https://doi.org/10.31234/osf.io/4c7af.

Seabrook, William. *The Magic Island.* Illustrations by Alexander King. New York: Harcourt, Brace, 1929.

Serés, Guillermo. *La historia del alma: Antigüedad, Edad Media, Siglo de Oro*. Barcelona: Galaxia Gutenberg SL, 2019.

Serrano, Aarón Rodríguez. "Spaces of Contemporary Horror: Poverty and Social

Exclusion as 21st Century Spectres." *Home Cultures* 16, no. 3 (2019): 191–211. https://doi.org/10.1080/17406315.2020.1757380.
Shapiro, Joseph. "As Hospitals Fear Being Overwhelmed by COVID-19, Do the Disabled Get the Same Access?" NPR, December 14, 2020. https://www.npr.org/2020/12/14/945056176/as-hospitals-fear-being-overwhelmed-by-covid-19-do-the-disabled-get-the-same-acc.
Shaviro, Steven. "Capitalist Monsters." *Historical Materialism* 10, no. 4 (2002): 281–290.
Shaviro, Steven. *The Cinematic Body*. Minneapolis: University of Minnesota Press, 1993.
Shaviro, Steven. "Contagious Allegories: George Romero." In *Zombie Theory: A Reader*, edited by Sarah Juliet Lauro. Minneapolis: University of Minnesota Press, 2017, 7–19.
Shin, Hisup. "Monstrous National Allegory: The Making of Monstrous Otherness in Na Hong-Jin's *The Wailing*." *Journal of Film and Video* 72, no. 3–4 (2020): 90–101. https://doi.org/10.5406/jfilmvideo.72.3-4.0090.
Smithies, Declan. "The Mental Lives of Zombies." *Philosophical Perspectives* 26, no. 1 (December 2012): 343–372.
Solana, Mariela. "Asincronía y crononormatividad: Apuntes sobre la idea de temporalidad queer." *El banquete de los Dioses: Revista de filosofía y teoría política contemporánea* 5, no. 7 (November 2016): 37–65.
Spinoza, Benedictus de. *Ethics*. Cambridge: Cambridge University Press, 1996.
Stark, Cortlynn, and Bryan Lowry. "Robocalls Sent by GOP Attorneys General Group Pushed March to Capitol, NBC Reports." *Kansas City Star*, January 9, 2021. https://www.kansascity.com/news/local/article248392700.html.
Steger, Manfred B. *Globalization: A Very Short Introduction*. Oxford: Oxford University Press, 2013.
Stern, Alexandra Minna. "The Revival of Eco-Fascism." *Progresssive Charlestown*, August 27, 2019. http://www.progressive-charlestown.com/2019/08/the-revival-of-eco-fascism.html.
Stoddard, Lothrop. *The Rising Tide of Color against White World-Supremacy*. New York: Charles Scribner's Sons, 1920.
Stoker, Bram. *Dracula*. 1897. Reprint, New York: Oxford University Press, 1990.
Taggart, John, and Kevin Granville. "From 'Zombie Malls' to Bonobos: What America's Retail Transformation Looks Like." *New York Times*, April 15, 2017. https://www.nytimes.com/2017/04/15/business/from-zombie-malls-to-bonobos-americas-retail-transformation.html.
Thucydides. *History of the Peloponnesian War*. Book II, chapter 47. Perseus Digital Library. Accessed January 9, 2021. https://www.perseus.tufts.edu/hopper/text?doc=Perseus%3Atext%3A1999.04.0105%3Abook%3D2%3Achapter%3D47.
Toral-Granda, M. Verónica, et al. "Alien Species Pathways to the Galapagos Islands, Ecuador." *PLoS One*, September 13, 2017. https://journals.plos.org/plosone/article?id=10.1371/journal.pone.0184379.
Tyner, James. *Dead Labor: Toward a Political Economy of Premature Death*. Minneapolis: University of Minnesota Press, 2019.
"US Capitol Riot: 'It Was Like a Zombie Movie.'" *BBC News*, January 8, 2021. https://www.bbc.com/news/av/world-us-canada-55581269.
U.S. Energy Information Administration. "EIA Expects Total U.S. Fossil Fuel Production to Reach Record Levels in 2018 and 2019." Today in Energy, January 18, 2018. https://www.eia.gov/todayinenergy/detail.php?id=34572.

Valencia, Sayak. *Gore Capitalism*. Translated by John Pluecker. South Pasadena, CA: Semiotext(e), 2018.

Veselinovic, Milena. "More than Feuds and Dramas, Nollywood Is a Mighty Economic Machine." CNN, July 10, 2015. https://www.cnn.com/2015/07/10/africa/nollywood-mighty-economic-machine/index.html.

Virilio, Paul, and Bertrand Richard. *The Administration of Fear*. Translated by Ames Hodges. Los Angeles: Semiotext(e), 2012.

Wald, Priscilla. *Contagious: Cultures, Carriers, and the Outbreak Narrative*. Durham, NC: Duke University Press, 2008.

Waltenburg, Michelle A., et al. "Update: COVID-19 among Workers in Meat and Poultry Processing Facilities—United States, April–May 2020." Centers for Disease Control and Prevention, *MMWR: Morbidity and Mortality Weekly Report* 69(27) (2020): 887–892. https://doi.org/10.15585/mmwr.mm6927e2.

Warren, James. "Removing Fear." In *The Cambridge Companion to Epicureanism*, edited by James Warren. Cambridge: Cambridge University Press, 2009, 234–248.

Weber, Max. *Die protestantische Ethik, und der Geist des Kapitalismus*. 1905. Reprint, Tübingen: Mohr, 1934.

Wilderson, Frank B., III. *Afropessimism*. London: Liveright, 2020.

Wong, Edward. "The Rapture and the Real World: Mike Pompeo Blends Beliefs and Policy (Published 2019)." *New York Times*, March 30, 2019. https://www.nytimes.com/2019/03/30/us/politics/pompeo-christian-policy.html.

Žižek, Slavoj. "Coronavirus Is 'Kill Bill'–esque Blow to Capitalism and Could Lead to Reinvention of Communism." Íkaro, March 19, 2020. http://www.revistaikaro.com/slavoj-zizek-coronavirus-is-kill-bill-esque-blow-to-capitalism-and-could-lead-to-reinvention-of-communism/.

Zondervan Bibles. *NIV Study Bible*. Grand Rapids, MI: Zondervan, 2011.

Filmography

Africa

Atlantics (*Atlantique*). France/Senegal/Belgium: Mati Diop, 2019.
Last Ones Out. South Africa: Howard James Fyvie, 2015.
Ojuju. Nigeria: C. J. "Fiery" Obasi, 2014.

Asia

Attack of the Soviet Zombies (*Ataka Sovetskikh Zombi*). Russia/Italy: Andreas Marfori, 2016.
Bio-Zombie (*Sang Faa Sau See*). Hong Kong: Wilson Yip, 1998.
Block Z. Philippines: Mikhail Red, 2020.
I Am a Hero. Japan: Shinsuke Sato, 2015.
Miss Zombie. Japan: SABU, 2013.
The Odd Family: Zombie on Sale (aka *Zombie for Sale, Gimyohan Gajok*). South Korea: Lee Min-jae, 2019.
One Cut of the Dead (*Kamera wo tomeruna!*). Japan: Shin'ichirô Ueda, 2017.
Resident Zombie (aka *The Neighbor Zombie, Yieutjib jombi*). South Korea: Oh Young-doo, Ryu Hoon, Hong Young-geun, and Jang Youn-jung, 2010.
Seoul Station (*Seoulyeok*). South Korea: Sang-ho Yeon, 2016.
Splatter: Naked Blood (*Nekeddo Burâddo: Megyaku*). Japan: Hisayasu Satô, 1996.
Tokyo Ghoul (*Tôkyô Gûru*). Japan: Kentarô Hagiwara, 2017.
Train to Busan (*Busanhaeng*). South Korea: Sang-ho Yeon, 2016.
Train to Busan Presents: Peninsula. South Korea: Sang-ho Yeon, 2020.
Versus. Japan: Ryûhei Kitamura, 2000.
The Wailing (*Gokseong*). South Korea/U.S.: Hong-jin Na, 2016.
Zombie (*Miruthan*). India: Shakti Soundar Rajan, 2016.
Zombiology: Enjoy Yourself Tonight (*Gam man da song si*). Hong Kong/China: Wai-Lun Lo, 2017.

Europe and United Kingdom

Anna and the Apocalypse. Scotland: John McPhail, 2017.
The Cured. Ireland/France: David Freyne, 2017.
Down to Earth (*Casa de lava*). Portugal: Pedro Costa, 1995.
Ever After (*Endzeit*). Germany: Carolina Hellsgård, 2019.
Extinction. Spain/U.S./Hungary/France: Miguel Ángel Vivas, 2015.
Fist of Jesus (short). Spain: Adrián Cardona and David Muñoz, 2012.
Galápagos (documentary miniseries). U.K.: 2006.
The Girl with All the Gifts. U.K.: Colm McCarthy, 2016.
Horse Money (*Cavalho Dinheiro*). Portugal: Pedro Costa, 2014.
I'll See You in My Dreams (short). Portugal: Miguel Ángel Vivas, 2003.
Low Life. France: Nicolas Klotz, 2011.
Mutant Blast. U.S./Portugal: Fernando Alle, 2020.
The Night Eats the World (*La nuit a dévoré le monde*). France: Dominique Rocher, 2018.
The Plague of the Zombies. U.K.: John Gilling, 1966.
Qu'ils reposent en révolte (*Des figures de guerre*). France: Sylvain George, 2010.
REC. Spain: Jaume Balagueró and Paco Plaza, 2007.
Shaun of the Dead. U.K./France/U.S.: Edgar Wright, 2004.
Sint (*Saint Nick*). Netherlands: Dick Maas, 2010.
28 Days Later. U.K.: Danny Boyle, 2002.
28 Weeks Later. U.K./Spain: Juan Carlos Fresnadillo, 2007.
The Unliving (*Återfödelsen*). Sweden: Hugo Lilja, 2010.
Zombi Child. France: Bertrand Bonello, 2019.
Zombi 2 (*Zombie*). Italy: Lucio Fulci, 1979.
Zombie World. Spain: Juan José Patón, 2013.

Latin America and Caribbean

Descendents (*Solos*). Chile/Spain/Venezuela: Jorge Olguín, 2007.
Halley. Mexico: Sebastián Hofmann, 2013.
Infection (*Infección*). Venezuela/Mexico: Flavio Pedota, 2019.
Inner Trip (*Entonces Ruth*). Peru: Fernando Montenegro, 2013.
Juan of the Dead (*Juan de los muertos*). Spain/Cuba: Alejandro Brugués, 2012.
Ladronas de almas. Mexico: Juan Antonio de la Riva, 2015.
Phase 7 (*Fase 7*). Argentina: Nicolás Goldbart, 2011.
A Prequel to Chaos (*La precuela del caos*). Peru: Rafael Arévalo, 2014.
Seven Years in May (*Sete anos em maio*) (short, documentary). Brazil: Affonso Uchoa, 2019.
Tigers Are Not Afraid (*Vuelven*). Mexico: Issa López, 2017.
What's Left of Us (*El desierto*). Argentina: Christoph Behl, 2015.
The Year of the Apocalypse (*El año del apocalipsis*). Peru: Rafael Arévalo, 2016.
Zombie Dawn (*Muerte ciega*). Chile: Lucio A. Rojas and Cristian Toledo, 2011.
Zugar Zombie (short). Colombia: Alexander Quezada, 2013.

Middle East

Altered Skin. Canada/Pakistan: Adnan Ahmed, 2018.
Battle of the Undead (*Cannon Fodder*). Israel: Eitan Gafny, 2014.

North America (United States and Canada)

Aaah! Zombies!! (*Wasting Away*). U.S.: Matthew Kohnen, 2007.
Avatar. U.S.: James Cameron, 2009.
Black Summer (series). Canada/U.S.: John Hyams and Abram Cox, 2019–.
The Blair Witch Project. U.S.: Daniel Myrick and Eduardo Sánchez, 1999.
Blood Quantum. Canada: Jeff Barnaby, 2019.
Carrie. U.S.: Brian De Palma, 1976.
Contracted. U.S.: Eric England, 2013.
Corona Zombies. U.S.: Charles Band, 2020.
The Crazies. U.S./United Arab Emirates: Breck Eisner, 2010.
Dawn of the Dead. U.S./Italy: George A. Romero, 1978.
Day of the Dead. U.S.: George A. Romero, 1985.
The Dead Don't Die. U.S./Sweden/South Africa: Jim Jarmusch, 2019.
Deadgirl. U.S.: Marcel Sarmiento and Gadi Harel, 2013.
Dead Trigger. U.S.: Mike Cuff and Scott Windhauser, 2018.
Exit Humanity. Canada: John Geddes, 2011.
Fido. Canada: Andrew Currie, 2006.
I Am Legend. U.S.: Francis Lawrence, 2007.
It Stains the Sands Red. U.S./Canada: Colin Minihan, 2016.
I Walked with a Zombie. U.S.: Jacques Touneur, 1943.
iZombie (series). U.S.: 2015–2019.
Land of the Dead. U.S./Canada/France: George A. Romero, 2005.
L.A. Zombie. U.S./Germany: Bruce LaBruce, 2010.
The Matrix. U.S.: Lana Wachowski and Lilly Wachowski, 1999.
Mayhem. U.S.: Joe Lynch, 2017.
Night of the Living Dead. U.S.: George A. Romero, 1968.
Otto; or, Up with Dead People. Germany/Canada: Bruce LaBruce, 2008.
Planet Terror. U.S./Mexico: Robert Rodriguez, 2007.
Pontypool. Canada: Bruce McDonald, 2008.
Pretty Dead (*Human Meat—Mörder. Kannibale. Zombie*). U.S.: Benjamin Wilkins, 2013.
Ravenous (*Les affamés*). Canada: Robin Aubert, 2018.
Savageland. U.S.: Phil Guidry, Simon Herbert, and David Whelan, 2017.
The Walking Dead (series). U.S.: 2010–2022.
Warm Bodies. U.S./Canada: Jonathan Levine, 2013.
White Zombie. U.S.: Victor Halperin, 1932.
World War Z. U.S./U.K./Malta: Marc Forster, 2013.
Zombeavers. U.S.: Jordan Rubin, 2014.
Zombied (short). U.S.: Matthew Van Vorst, 2019.
Z-O-M-B-I-E-S. U.S.: Paul Hoen, 2018.

Oceania

Black Sheep. New Zealand/South Korea: Jonathan King, 2006.
Cargo. Australia: Ben Howling and Yolanda Ramke, 2018.
Wyrmwood (*Wyrmwood: Road of the Dead*). Australia: Kiah Roache-Turner, 2014.

Index

Note: Page numbers in *italics* indicate figures.

About the Authors

PATRICIA SALDARRIAGA is a professor of Luso-Hispanic studies at Middlebury College in Vermont. She is the author of *Los espacios del "Primero Sueño" de Sor Juana Inés de la Cruz* and coeditor (with M. Júdice, I. Araújo-Branco, and R. Marques) of *Sor Juana e Portugal.*

EMY MANINI is an independent scholar writing in Seattle, Washington.

Printed in the United States
by Baker & Taylor Publisher Services